Driving Lessons

Driving Lessons

A Road Trip through American Travel Literature

Christopher B. Strain

The University of Alabama Press
Tuscaloosa

The University of Alabama Press
Tuscaloosa, Alabama 35487-0380
uapress.ua.edu

Copyright © 2025 by the University of Alabama Press
All rights reserved.

Inquiries about reproducing material from this work should
be addressed to the University of Alabama Press.

Typeface: Miller

Cover images: Bus, topshots/stock.adobe.com;
map, Nataly-Nete/stock.adobe.com
Cover design: Lori Lynch

Cataloging-in-Publication data is available from the Library of Congress.
ISBN: 978-0-8173-2227-4 (cloth)
ISBN: 978-0-8173-6199-0 (paper)
E-ISBN: 978-0-8173-9549-0

FOR MELANIE

Contents

List of Illustrations   ix

Introduction: Road to Nowhere   xi

1. The Trip   1

2. Into the Wild   12

3. The Legend of Lawnchair Larry, American Hero   25

4. The M-Factor   47

5. The Ghosts of Montana   67

6. On the Road in Yellowstone   85

7. Land Bad   100

8. Crossing Over   118

9. Homeward Bound   132

10. The Last Road Trip   149

Acknowledgments   169

Appendix   173

Notes   175

Works Cited   187

Index   193

Illustrations

Figure 1.
The Bus   5

Figure 2.
Into the Cascades   17

Figure 3.
Larry Walters   37

Figure 4.
Motel   48

Figure 5.
Teepee frames   81

Figure 6.
Yellowstone   89

Figure 7.
Little Big Horn   106

Figure 8.
Jean and Tom   130

Figure 9.
See Rock City barn   148

Figure 10.
Old elixirs   164

Introduction

Road to Nowhere

In Appalachia, there is a road in the woods. The road stops at a tunnel. There is nothing on the other side. The tunnel sits next to a town, and the town sits at the bottom of a lake. There's a story there.

In the 1930s and 1940s, the people of western North Carolina gave up a large chunk of Swain County to the federal government for the creation of Fontana Lake and the Great Smoky Mountains National Park. Fontana Lake is actually a reservoir for Fontana Dam, built by the Tennessee Valley Authority (TVA) during World War II to produce electricity for the Aluminum Company of America (ALCOA) plants in Tennessee and for Oak Ridge National Laboratory's Manhattan Project. It was a devil's bargain, of sorts, but a logical arrangement: the government needed aluminum for aircraft, ships, and munitions, and ALCOA needed hydroelectric power to give the US War Department its metal.

The plan involved damming the Little Tennessee River with a massive concrete wall—as tall as a skyscraper, still the tallest dam in the eastern United States—and flooding the surrounding valley to create the lake. Six hundred people living in Judson were forced to abandon their cabins and homesteads, leaving the little mountain town that had been their home for generations. Left behind were the sawmill, the general store, the postal depot, the barbershop, and the school. Their houses disappeared beneath the deep, dark waters of Fontana Lake, as did the road to those houses, Highway 288.

Uncle Sam promised to replace the submerged highway with a new road. Lakeview Drive would stretch along the lake's northern shore, winding its way between Bryson City and Fontana, thirty miles to the west. Importantly, it would provide access to the old family cemeteries where generations of ancestors remained, tucked deep in the hollows and glens of Appalachia.

Construction began with great hopes, but the road was never completed. As they cut into the newly created Great Smoky Mountains National Park, workers noticed that snowflakes melted quickly—too quickly—on the newly exposed rock; the workers also smelled large amounts of sulfur. The devil had come not to avenge those moved off their land but rather to add a final cruel twist: the uncovered rock had the potential to acidify runoff, poison nearby streams, and endanger wildlife. Too expensive to change, with no remedy or solution, the roadwork stopped cold amid environmental concerns. The would-be motorway ended at a large tunnel some distance into the national park: a $52 million dead end. Swain County residents gave the unfinished road its new name, "The Road to Nowhere," and there it remains. During the summer, on certain weekends, the National Park Service still ferries Swain County residents across Fontana Lake for "Reunion Days" to visit old family gravesites.

In August 2020—amid a global pandemic, at the beginning of a contentious election cycle, and at the start of hurricane season—I found myself standing at the tunnel at the end of the Road to Nowhere. My wife and daughter and I had driven along the scenic six-mile stretch from Bryson City to its abrupt end in the middle of, well, nowhere. Like many other American families that summer, we had opted to take advantage of the only real leisure option available to us during the pandemic: a road trip. We had planned to escape virus-ridden South Florida to the mountains of western North Carolina to enjoy some hiking and tubing and clean mountain air. We rented a cabin up a mountainside on the edge of the Great Smoky Mountains National Park, as "socially distanced" as we could be. A tropical storm threatened to derail our family vacation, but we stuck to our plans, chased up the Florida Turnpike and I-75 by Hurricane Isaias. We hoped we weren't bringing the coronavirus with us.

The enormous archway was impressive, covered in rainbows of fresh graffiti. Much of the graffiti was garden-variety—So-and-So wuz here, a few curse words, etcetera—but some of it was inspired. "Do Not Seek the Treasure" read one tag, echoing a bit of dialogue from the Coen Brothers'

2000 film *O Brother, Where Art Thou?*, about a southern community flooded to make a lake. "I Don't Feel At All What I Thought I Would," one introspective painter admitted. "In A World Of Chickens, Be A Bear," counseled another. Given the very white and rural demographic of the surrounding area, there was a surprising amount of support for #BLM.

Past the entrance, the graffiti became increasingly difficult to make out. The tunnel dimmed a few yards in, where daylight faded to murk. We plunged into the darkness, pausing now and then to cast a flashlight beam on the graffiti, hurrying through the quarter-mile-long gloom toward the horseshoe of light at the far end. Emerging from the tunnel was anticlimactic. The path stopped, the end of the road. On the other side was forest, gold-washed and sunny, stretching in all directions. Should I have been surprised that the Road to Nowhere led nowhere? I felt as if I'd been here before, and perhaps I had. Little did I know then that it would be the last road trip for a while.

Both curse and blessing, the pandemic-induced lockdown gifted us time and an opportunity to assess priorities. My wife, who had always wanted to learn how to play an instrument, got a ukelele and was soon strumming chords. I began to type, determined to write down a story that had been rattling around in my head for a long time: the story of a journey in the fall of 1998, a side trip I took when I was very much on a road to somewhere. This unintentional odyssey came to define my life in profound ways, a definitive experience in my education and personal development. At the time I was a graduate student in California, where I studied US history, African American history, and ethnic studies. Compelled by something I didn't quite understand, I left town for a while and drove—a lot. In the process I learned a few lessons that I recount here.

While I couldn't fully realize it or appreciate it then, traveling across the United States by car may be the best way to learn about this sprawling, audacious country. There are over four million miles of road in the United States, according to the Federal Highway Administration. They are the veins and arteries of the nation, wide asphalt corridors of freight traffic, but they are also the capillaries of the American body, smaller and shorter routes for not only commerce and commuting but also rest and ease. Seventy-two percent are rural, and while most are paved, almost 35 percent of US roads are gravel and dirt roads that require grading and frequent maintenance. Streets, roads, avenues, ways, paths, lanes, boulevards,

INTRODUCTION · xiii

thoroughfares, highways, byways . . . they go most everywhere, these roads, and exploring them is an American rite of passage for tight-knit families and lonesome voyagers alike.

The road trip has been lauded and lampooned in Hollywood, from the pre–Hays Code rom-com *It Happened One Night* (1934) to countercultural icon *Easy Rider* (1969), from the family mishaps of *National Lampoon's Vacation* (1983) to the raunchy teen comedies *Road Trip* (2000) and *Sex Drive* (2008). While it's easy to parody the backseat whining and elbow slinging, missed bathroom breaks, and questionable destinations of family excursions (like Clark W. Griswold's much anticipated "Second-Largest Ball of Twine" on Earth), the road trip comes in many flavors, from quiet reflection to wide-open debauchery. It is not only a path of discovery but also a classroom, proving ground, and asylum. It is a break from the norm, a flirtation with adventure and, oddly, a place of healing for those who cannot heal at home. And it is undeniably, quintessentially, 100 percent American. But why? What makes this custom a prototypically *American* one?

To answer this question we must, as historian John Hope Franklin suggested, "go beyond textbooks, go out into the bypaths and untrodden depths of the wilderness and travel and explore and tell the world the glories of our journey." Whether you're a globetrotter or homebody, a road warrior or armchair traveler, a nature lover or urbanite, a camper or daytripper, a national park aficionado or history buff, a van lifer or tiny houser, a westerner or easterner (or a somewhere in-betweener), there's hopefully something here for you. At a time when Americans recently found themselves homebound, imprisoned by an uncaring and indiscriminate virus; at a time of political rancor, when we find ourselves as divided as ever in recent memory; and at a time of long-awaited racial reckoning, I am hoping that this book offers readers more than an escapist, vicarious road trip. I hope that in the wake of the COVID-19 pandemic, the Trump era, and the George Floyd protests it speaks to meanings of Americanness and stirs our imaginations as we think about how to reconnect on the other side of all three.

Driving Lessons

Driving Test

1

The Trip

May 1998: The electric clock on the classroom wall hummed, a low buzz like a late-summer hornet nest. *Dzzzzzzz*. The midcentury relic had three hands: an hour hand that moved imperceptibly, a minute hand that slowly crept, and a second hand that spun smoothly around the dial, lapping the other two. I watched, waiting, squirming in the ill-fitting suit I had bought for the occasion. In due course one of my professors meandered in, then another, and another. They chatted amiably, pulling desks into a rough semicircle around my own single seat in the center of the room. They sipped coffee, talked about the news and departmental politics. My mind wandered. *"See how high the hornet's nest / 'twill tell how high the snow will rest."* Eventually someone suggested we get started with my PhD oral qualifying exams.

I was ready, maybe even "born ready." Everything in my twenty-seven-year-long existence had been grooming me for this moment. Born and raised in Dalton, Georgia—a small city tucked in the foothills of Appalachia—I was privileged and loved and supported in everything I did. I was happy. The only son of doting parents, I had a great home life with parents who forked over cash for piano and tennis and swim lessons, paid for youth-group and choir trips, and sent me to summer camp. I read everything I could find, and I excelled. Straight As in school, near the top of my class, good athlete, Eagle Scout, president of the student council, voted Most Likely to Succeed. I was well poised to become a doctor or banker or businessman, especially well poised to become an attorney like my father. My grandma told me I'd be president of the United States one day, and I believed her. I was the golden boy and I knew it.

An infinite well of confidence, I launched off for the University of Virginia, where I lost myself even further in books. I loved school, loved learning, wanted more. After undergrad, I went to the University of Georgia and then the University of California at Berkeley, where I evolved from student to scholar of US history. Master's degree, PhD, then become a history professor. That was the plan, and these exams were a key part.

I was cocky and relaxed, even though the people sitting across from me were larger-than-life, high-powered academics: greater deities in the world of historians. Ron Takaki, my outside committee member, was a giant in the field of ethnic studies who had in fact helped to *create* that very field. The descendant of Japanese immigrants who worked sugarcane plantations in Hawaii, he had in 1966 taught the first Black history course at UCLA. The son of working-class Jewish immigrants, Leon Litwack had become president of the Organization of American Historians after winning a National Book Award and Pulitzer Prize. When he wasn't being brilliant at Berkeley, Waldo Martin was leading National Endowment for the Humanities (NEH) Summer Institutes at Harvard University with Henry Louis Gates and Patricia Sullivan; these recurring workshops at the W. E. B. Du Bois Research Institute introduced cutting-edge research methodologies and teaching pedagogies to civil rights scholars. Between the three of them were eighteen published books—and they were far from finished. Titans all.

The first question caught my completely off guard. "Chris," Professor Takaki asked, "what is capitalism?" *Dzzzzzzz.*

The question was intended as a softball to set me at ease, but I felt instead like Ralphie who, when asked on Santa's lap what he wants for Christmas in the holiday classic *A Christmas Story*, can only dumbly agree to something else. Capitalism? Um, sure, I thought—but aren't we going to talk about all the books on my reading lists? I fumbled through a lukewarm reply about ownership and means of production and blah-blah-blah, suddenly growing uncomfortable. It was my moment to shine—my golden opportunity to request an Official Red Ryder Carbine-Action 200-Shot Range Model Air Rifle—and all I could do was mumble something about a football.

I'd been prepping for months and months—years, really—learning all of the historiographical debates and arguments among historians over the past two centuries. I was ready to discuss Bernard Bailyn and Richard Hofstadter and Charles Beard and John Hope Franklin and the Dunning School. I knew the names and dates and places and all the obscure factoids that historians and only historians are expected to know. It was a necessary rite of passage, this verbal interrogation required of every graduate student on his or her way to a PhD, and I thought I had been ready. I knew the historiography. But it occurred to me at that moment that anything was on the table during this examination. No questions were off-limits. They were not only going to test my knowledge of US history: they were going to poke around in my head and see how smart I was, to see if I was clever enough to join the club. *Dzzzzzzz*. I began to sweat uncontrollably, tugging at my collar and looking around the room, wondering if the thermostat were broken. It was so hot, but no one else seemed to notice. In their crew-neck sweaters with their steaming mugs of coffee, my professors looked back comfortably and coolly. It was me and me alone. I was in the hot seat, and I was coming undone.

It was then that I wished that I'd postponed my comps, or "orals," as they're often called. My confidence ebbed. Maybe I shouldn't be at Berkeley. Maybe I wasn't smart enough. Maybe everyone who'd encouraged me along this academic path was wrong. Doubt and Panic pulled up chairs to join us in the semicircle.

The questioning continued for the next three hours or so, and we eventually settled into a discussion about history and historians, which I adequately managed, but the harm had already been done. Instead of marching out triumphantly, I limped out, hobbling on a bruised psyche and sprained ego. I had survived but only barely. I had always done well in school, always fancied myself clever, but I now faced up to my own intellectual insignificance in the company of bigger brains.

That summer I advanced to candidacy, formed a dissertation committee, got approval for my dissertation prospectus. I got a prestigious fellowship. I figured out what libraries and archives I needed to visit to complete my dissertation. Everything was falling into place as it should. But the memory of my choking lingered. Like a tiger at the zoo, I was wearing a worry track around the perimeter of my mind. I wondered if I had blown a fuse.

It was then that the nanites of a plan began to self-assemble in the recesses of my brain. I had just been awarded a generous fellowship. Intended to sustain me for a year as I researched my dissertation, the award from the Andrew W. Mellon Foundation came with a refreshing amount of trust and a fortunate lack of oversight. The foundation sent me a $10,000 check. No budget proposal required in advance, no receipts submitted afterward, no strings attached whatsoever. It was understood that I would use the check to write my dissertation—and I intended to use every penny toward that end. But there were no stipulations on *how* I should spend the money and do my research. And it was here that I allowed myself a little creativity.

The plan became clearer, a plan involving much driving. I needed to visit archives across the country, and, like any reasonable person, I could've flown to visit the necessary research spots in Palo Alto and Ann Arbor and Boston and Atlanta. Palo Alto was close enough for day trips, but with my temperamental '65 Mercury Comet, even those were dicey. Its straight-six engine was reliable enough, but the steering was super loose and the old drum brakes practically required me to stand on the pedal to get the car to stop. It was not fun to drive around town in traffic, let alone on an extended trip. So I began to scour the classified ads for a suitable vehicle for what I had in mind. I would kill two birds with one stone. I would get my research done, and in the process I would actually *see* the places I'd been studying in my undergraduate and graduate courses: the cities and landmarks and national parks and monuments that constituted US history. No one would care, so long as I was being productive. And frankly I had no other choice. I was fried. I had to get out of town, regroup, get myself together.

Having arranged a meetup with a seller, I snaked my way up into the Oakland Hills. We met on the roadside in front of her house. She was a single mother of two and needed something different. She was the second owner, she thought, possibly the third. It was a camper van conversion, with a pop top, fold-down bench-seat bed, sink, icebox, and stove. There was a second bed up top, even a hammock for a kid or extra gear. A full spare tire was mounted on the front, right underneath the expansive windscreen. The engine had been replaced with the 1600-cc, air-cooled engine standard in VW Beetles. It was otherwise original, except for the replacement curtains that she had sewn and installed with snaps and an elastic

Fig. 1: The Bus, 1998. Photo by author.

cord, and it was in excellent shape for its age. Had I driven one before, she asked. No, I confessed. "But I think I can manage." After a jerky test drive, I gave her $2,200 and drove away in a twenty-five-year-old, technically antique, new-to-me, alabaster-white, '72 Volkswagen Westfalia Bus.

The ridiculousness of my new purchase morphed into fresh regret as I veered and swerved back down into the flatlands, the steering loose, the brakes chiding me for all the squats and leg presses I'd skipped at the gym. What exactly had I upgraded, trading a crappy old Mercury for a crappy old Volkswagen, a notoriously finicky ride that left its drivers stranded with stereotypical regularity? And forget safety considerations. Crumple zones? Airbags? Shoulder harnesses? Nope, nope, and nope. It didn't even have a hood; there was nothing between me and a front-end collision except a thin sheet of metal. But the worst thing was the silly predictability of it all: a long-haired Berkeley student acquiring a VW Bus, a hippie time machine. I had become a caricature, living another generation's dream, a Gen-X anachronism actualizing a Baby Boomer fantasy.

A couple of hundred dollars scrimped and I had a laptop computer to bring along. I explained the idea to friends and family, including my undoubtedly confused but inexplicably supportive girlfriend, Jen, who instructed me to call when I could, graciously reassuring me she'd be here when I got back. She must have intuited that I was a bit scrambled, that I was speaking the truth when I said the decision to leave had nothing to do with our relationship or my happiness in it. It was, I heard myself saying, just something I had to do. I sold the Comet to my buddy Frank, ended my lease, got a stack of AAA TripTik travel planners and a big road atlas, tied up loose ends, and prepared to hit the highway.

I began my research with a few day-long sojourns to the south in Palo Alto, where I delved into the Martin Luther King Jr. Papers Project at Stanford University under the watchful eye of historian Clayborne Carson. While productive, these day trips were still "local," in my Bay Area backyard. The Trip proper would not begin in earnest until I turned northward. The plan, roughly speaking, was to drive up the coast of California into Oregon and Washington, then drive eastward across the top of the nation until I got to the Great Lakes, then turn south toward Georgia, where I hoped to spend Thanksgiving and Christmas with my parents. Mine would be a reverse American migration, west to east, against the grain.

Being southern, I suspected that those people who argued that the different parts of the United States were now all alike—a monocultural nation of identical franchises and fry-lines—were dead wrong, but I didn't know for sure. I wanted to see where and how things differed, and I wanted to see what didn't. No real timeline, no fixed waypoints between the libraries and archives I needed to visit. I would go until I ran out of gas or money or volition. And so it came to pass that on an otherwise unremarkable day in late August 1998 I left my schooling at a prestigious Public Ivy to drift, living out of an old van.

American writers have found inspiration in hitting the road and traveling the United States, and their scribblings have served as instruction, motivation, and vicarious adventure for the vast majority of us who cannot drop what we're doing and do the same. Many have ventured forth in search of America, convinced that the authentic America—the *real* America, not the one represented by their current environs—is out there somewhere: just ahead in the next town, just around the next bend, just over the next rise. The road trip as a means of understanding the nation is a time-honored tradition and a very American concept.

Mark Twain did it twice, first in 1872 with *Roughing It* and again in 1883 with *Life on the Mississippi*, two separate accounts of traveling throughout the United States. In *Roughing It*, the American Shakespeare recounts going west to visit his brother, recently appointed secretary of the Nevada Territory. Here Twain details his exploits as a frontier newspaper reporter and as a prospector, searching for the mother lode. His second memoir describes his career as a steamboat captain on the Mississippi River in the years before the Civil War.

Two years after Twain's *Life on the Mississippi*, Charles Siringo published *A Texas Cowboy, or Fifteen Years on the Hurricane Deck of a Spanish Pony* (1885), one of the first accounts of life in the Old West penned by an actual, honest-to-goodness cowboy. Siringo's autobiographical gallop across the dust and sagebrush helped to mythologize the Wild West and secure the place of the cowboy in this myth. It is decidedly odd that cowboys—whose job it was to move livestock cross-country and whose idea of excitement was a hot bath, a warm shave, and a cool shot of whiskey in some hellhole like Abilene or Dodge City—would become the stuff of American legend, but Siringo's boisterous, first-person account of cowboy life captured the romance of the trail and moved young men to take up lassos and lariats.

In 1920, F. Scott and Zelda Fitzgerald decided on a whim to drive from Connecticut to Zelda's hometown—Montgomery, Alabama—for a breakfast of biscuits and peaches. Eight days and 1,200 miles later, the two had covered enough ground for *The Cruise of the Rolling Junk* (1924), so named for the 1918 Marmon automobile that carried them. A story of car trouble interrupted by stays at grand old hotels, *Rolling Junk* isn't Fitzgerald's best, but it did portend a coming trend in American letters. It was during the mid-twentieth century that books about road trips became a uniquely American form of literary expression, with *On the Road* (1957) charting the course. It was the grandaddy of American road trip stories, a whiplash tale of speed and hedonism that left a broken 1950s orthodoxy in its wake. If Helen of Troy was the face that launched a thousand ships, then Jack Kerouac was the yarn spinner who launched a million Fords across the American West.

Five years after Kerouac, John Steinbeck launched off to rediscover the nation that he had so expertly chronicled, a nation with which he, after a long and illustrious writing career, had lost touch. Traveling the world, Steinbeck returned to the United States to learn that he no longer knew his own country:

> I, an American writer, was working from memory, and the memory at best is a faulty, warpy reservoir. I had not heard the speech of America, smelled the grass and trees and sewage, seen its hills and water, its color and quality of light. I knew the changes only from books and newspapers. But more than this, I had not felt the country for twenty-five years. In short, I was writing about something I did not know about, and it seems to me that in a so-called writer this is criminal. . . . So I was determined to look again, to try to rediscover this monster land.

He loaded a three-quarter-ton pickup with an Alaskan camper, the kind that nestles into the bed of the truck; named it *Rocinante*, after Don Quixote's horse; and rumbled off with his traveling companion, a French poodle named Charley. The result was *Travels with Charley* (1962), a masterwork in American travel lit and one of the finest pieces of American writing, period.

In the mid- to late 1960s, things started to get a little weird. On a 1963 trip to New York, a group of friends pledged to return the following year to see the 1964 World's Fair in Queens "to experience the American landscape, the heartscape," according to Ken Kesey, the group's ringleader. Gathering at Kesey's ranch in La Honda, the group of Merry Pranksters, as they called themselves, sallied forth in a kind of reverse migration across the American West in a 1939 International Harvester school bus they deemed *Further*. The psychedelic road trip, fueled by LSD, became the stuff of 1960s counterculture legend. In the same way that *On the Road* immortalized the Beats, *The Electric Kool-Aid Acid Test* (1968) by Tom Wolfe documents the trippy trips of the Merry Pranksters.

The 1970s brought a trio of classic road trip books: *Fear and Loathing in Las Vegas: A Savage Journey to the Heart of the American Dream* (1971) by Hunter S. Thompson, *Zen and the Art of Motorcycle Maintenance* (1974) by Robert Pirsig, and *A Walk across America* (1979) by Peter Jenkins. "We were somewhere around Barstow on the edge of the desert when the drugs began to take hold." So begins Thompson's manic journey from Los Angeles to Las Vegas to cover the Mint 400, a motorcycle race. Commissioned by *Sports Illustrated* to cover the race, the author speeds across the desert with his lawyer in the *Great Red Shark*, a convertible 1973 Chevrolet Caprice with a trunkful of marijuana, mescaline, pills, cocaine, opiates, LSD, ether (!), and other drugs. The race itself soon becomes secondary to the debauchery of the trip, but Thompson manages to wring some level of poignancy out of his first real foray into gonzo journalism. In the more contemplative *Zen and the Art*, Pirsig delivers a simple father-son motorcycle trip; contrasting two different philosophical approaches, one deliberate and the other more intuitive, the book turns an explanation of motorcycle repair into a guide to life. Finally, when Peter Jenkins shouldered a backpack and walked southward from New York into Appalachia, *National Geographic* twice published articles about his journey, which he later describes in *A Walk across America*; the book ends, "I started out searching for myself and my country, and found both."

When William Least Heat-Moon lost not only his job as an English professor but also his wife, the distraught writer took to the road in a 1975 Ford Econoline van, in which he logged thirteen thousand miles over three months. "A man who couldn't make things go right could at least go," he opines. Avoiding large cities and interstates, he opted to travel along "blue" highways, so called for their color in the Rand McNally Road Atlas. His travels were published as *Blue Highways* (1982), a classic in American travel lit. For him, abandoning routine and living "the real jeopardy of circumstance" was a question of dignity as much as a question of uncertainty. "With a nearly desperate sense of isolation and a growing suspicion that I lived in an alien land," he writes, "I took to the open road in search of places where change did not mean ruin and where time and men and deeds connected." And so he rolled, into "the sticks, the boondocks, the burgs, the backwaters, jerkwaters, the wide-spots-in-the-road, the don't-blink-or-you'll-miss-it-towns," into "those places where you say, 'My god! What if you lived here!' The Middle of Nowhere."

With the exception of Least Heat-Moon, who had changed his surname in the late 1970s to reflect his Native American heritage, these travel narratives offered a fairly homogenous and monochromatic perspective on the American road. While reporter John Howard Griffin had artificially darkened his skin with large doses of methoxsalen in order to experience racism (or at least approximate the kind of bigotry a person of color might encounter) while traveling through the Jim Crow South for *Black Like Me* (1961), it wasn't until 1988 that an African American travel writer deliberately explored race and racism in *Mississippi Solo*. Eddy L. Harris recounts his story of paddling alone down the Mississippi River from Minnesota ("where there ain't no black folks") to New Orleans ("where they still don't like us much"). Following a lifelong dream but propelled by a midlife crisis, Harris canoed through many dangers, from barge waves and wild dogs to shotgun-toting bigots, whose menace was counterbalanced by the scores of people who aided him along the way.

A year after Harris, an American journalist living in England published his account of refamiliarizing himself with his native land. In *The Lost Continent: Travels in Small-Town America* (1989), Bill Bryson describes borrowing his mother's busted Chevy Chevette to explore the heartland as an expatriate: an outsider looking in, attempting to understand from the inside out. Bryson, a Des Moines native, goes in search of the quintessential American small town, a place like the perfectly quaint and familiar hamlets depicted in *The Andy Griffith Show* and other television shows of the 1950s and 1960s. In search of Mayberry, he instead finds an indistinguishable assemblage of look-alike nonplaces, a sea of strip malls and fast-food joints and chain motels and gas stations, which he somehow renders with both melancholy and insightful humor.

Since then, other writers have followed, each with his or her own version of the great American road book. Cheryl Strayed, Shainee Gabel and Kristin Hahn, Donald Miller, the planetwalker John Francis . . . the list goes on and on, all excellent, all worth reading. The story arcs of these travel narratives are oddly similar, following comparable paths. Almost to a fault, these writers travel not only to understand the United States but also to fix something wrong inside them. They are questing, searching, trying to patch broken memories, broken hearts, or broken spirits. In aiming to find America, they hope to find themselves along the way. It is a strange and noteworthy union, this assumption of personal redemption via national discovery. What is it about America as it exists "out there" that promises to redeem and heal? Why these journeys of country and self?

Of course, I knew next to nothing of this literary tradition when I began my trip. I wasn't trying to emulate these others and didn't undertake this trip self-consciously as a writer. I didn't even consider myself to *be* a writer. I had no intention of recording my journey. Instead, I was simply multitasking, traveling not only to do research but also to see with my own eyes the places I had read about in books. Somewhere in the back of my mind, of course, I knew I was out of sorts. I couldn't place exactly what was wrong, but I knew I needed to go. So, I drove, eager to find the horizon.

2

Into the Wild

August 1998: Arriving in San Francisco by sea is a major event. One can imagine the 325 hopeful men from Guangdong who arrived in 1849 to try their hand at prospecting along the American River in the Sierra Nevada Mountains. Following tales of fabulous riches, they left their impoverished province on China's south coast in search of Gam Saan—Gold Mountain—joining seventy thousand other hopeful '49ers in the quest for quick fortune. Emerging from below decks after a perilous and sickening Pacific crossing, these Celestials (as white Californians called them, after the old name for the Celestial Empire) wrapped in woolen blankets to supplement their loose-fitting cotton shirts and trousers, wooden shoes, and *kasa*, or conical straw hats. They sailed silently into the dense fog, through the treacherous strait between the San Francisco headlands and the Marin Peninsula, as yet to be spanned by the iconic bridge whose warm vermilion color contrasts the cool grays, greens, and blues of the mist, the coastal range, and the bay itself, respectively.

Having made the trek in 1995, I knew firsthand that arriving overland from the east is also a near magical experience. Traversing the middle part of the state, the great Central Valley, can be monotonous, particularly after crossing the breathtaking Sierra Nevadas. There is plenty of agriculture and a staggering array of crops in the field—what's that? and that?—but after a while the tomatoes and grapes and apricots and asparagus all begin to blend like ingredients in a smoothie. Entering the East

Bay Area after this blur of veggies and fruits, seeing the thrum of activity—the crunch of cars and traffic and houses, spilling away to the bay with the San Francisco skyline, Alcatraz, the Bay Bridge, and the postcard-ready Golden Gate Bridge—is exhilarating. It's where the interstate stops, the end of the road, and it's well worth the effort to get there. As John Steinbeck wrote, San Francisco puts on a show for you, "rising on her hills like a noble city in a happy dream":

> This gold and white acropolis rising wave on wave against the blue of the Pacific sky was a stunning thing, a painted thing like a picture of a medieval Italian city which can never have existed. . . . She leaves a mark.

Coming here is a thrill by land or by sea—and by air too, flying into San Francisco Airport with a bird's-eye view of the finest natural harbor on the continent.

Leaving San Francisco, on the other hand, is much less dramatic than getting there. Driving out of the city, eastward over the golden hills of Berkeley and Oakland, is to put that splendor and mystery behind you. To the east lies Sacramento, where my uncle lives—in Roseville, to be precise, a one-hundred-thousand-resident suburb northeast of Sacto's city center. When the Central Pacific Railroad constructed its tracks through this stagecoach stop in 1864, the junction became a bustling rail town. Today Interstate 80 runs through Roseville, and it was along I-80 I bounced in my vintage hippy mover. My uncle's house would be my first stop, a short hour and a half away, and on the way, I ran through my checklist of essentials.

The van was well stocked, ready to go. I did a lot of camping, so I had the necessary gear, including clothes, cookware, lanterns, flashlights, and so forth. I had a sleeping bag instead of sheets and an extra blanket. There was a decent heater but no air conditioner. There was a sink and a water reservoir, which I kept dry, preferring instead to lug a couple of gallons in jugs for drinking, cooking, and washing; the jugs rode comfortably in the sink. While the van did not have a refrigerator, it did have a built-in icebox that would keep food cold, which I supplemented with a small cooler. I carried simple foods, mainly canned goods that I could easily reheat. There was a built-in gas cook stove; I had a backup Sterno stove as well

INTO THE WILD • 13

that I could use outside. I had a small solar shower, a plastic bag whose clear side would allow in sunlight and whose black side would heat water to scalding temperatures on a bright day; I could hang it up on the outside of the van for a quick rinse or to wash pots and pans. I had tools and a spiral-bound copy of John Muir's essential *How to Keep Your Volkswagen Alive: A Manual of Step-by-Step Procedures for the Compleat Idiot* (1969), which came with the van, for repairs. I had a small library of paperbacks, several of which were deliberately chosen to read on the road. I even had a tiny bar, stocked with airplane bottles of booze. Best to be prepared: *I* didn't need a drink, but at some point, someone deep inside of me might.

Before dinner Uncle Ed peppered me with questions, which I answered as best I could. Where are you headed? North into Oregon's Cascade Mountains, then northwest up the coast to Seattle. From there I'd head eastward across Washington, the Idaho panhandle, Montana, the Dakotas, Wisconsin, Michigan, then southward to Ohio, Kentucky, Tennessee, and Georgia, where I would spend the holidays before turning westward again, back to California through the Southwest. Where will you stop along the way? Wherever—that's the beauty of a camper van. The van had a pop top that would allow standing room in camping mode, but I could simply pull over and sleep on the side of the road when tired without needing to pop the top. "Stealth mode," I called it. What's your timetable? I don't really have one, but I do want to turn southward before winter. Got what you need? I think so. Palm on the kitchen table, he dropped his fingers in a rolling tap, like the felt-covered hammers in a piano. *Ta-da-dump, ta-da-dump, ta-da-dump.* Ring, middle, index, repeat. He finally asked: What are you doing again? I knew what he meant, but I simply replied: Writing a dissertation, Unc, taking a trip. *Ta-da-dump, ta-da-dump.* Alright, man, I hope you have a great trip, he offered reassuringly, smiling.

After a delicious pasta meal, I stared sleeplessly at the guest room ceiling. What *was* I doing? Fumbling an opportunity? Running away? Perhaps it seemed that way to others, and maybe they were right. As I pulled out of Ed's driveway early the next morning and headed up Highway 65, I imagined my uncle's next phone conversation, his report to my mother. *Hello, Jean? It's your brother . . . Well, I saw Christopher . . . Mmm-hmm . . . He just left . . . Yeah, I think he's lost his marbles.* But now that I was rolling the worries quickly faded. Uncle Ed had been supportive, as had my parents, and as I motored out of Sacramento, I felt like I was doing the right thing, on the right path, however undefined and undiscovered it remained.

I cruised through Yuba City and Chico, picking up I-5 at Red Bluff. The weather was California perfect: warm, sunny, clear, the sky a ludicrous shade of blue. Wearing frayed cargo shorts, Teva sandals, and a ratty old once-black Aerosmith T-shirt (from the 1986 Done With Mirrors Tour), I settled in behind the wheel. I was excited to leave.

Passing through Redding, I entered the Shasta-Trinity National Forest, past Mount Shasta, which juts abruptly and heavily, towering ten thousand feet above its surroundings. Shasta is massive, one of California's twelve "fourteeners," with an elevation of at least fourteen thousand feet. I thought of the Native Americans who had lived within view of this mountain—the Shasta, Modoc, and Klamath, among others—who listened to the mountain's occasional rumblings. Klamath legend tells of the Spirit Above-the-World who fought the Spirit Below-the-World by hurling rocks and lava from the mountain's slopes toward Mount Mazama, sixty miles away in the southern Cascades. Non-Indian legends abound here too. In 1877, John Muir (the famed nineteenth-century Scottish-American naturalist, not the twentieth-century VW expert) described surviving an overnight blizzard on Mount Shasta by lying in the hot sulfur springs near the summit. A focus of New Age spirituality, Shasta supposedly conceals a hidden city of advanced beings from the lost continent of Lemuria, according to modern Rosicrucians, a group of mystics claiming to possess esoteric wisdom passed down from the ancients.

I scooted up the highway past little towns with names like Wyntoon and Black Butte and Weed. Anxious to get to the border, I cruised through Yreka (pronounced why-REEK-uh) and crossed into Oregon. At Ashland—as scenic a city as I've seen, the historic 1925-built Ashland Springs Hotel anchoring downtown in the foreground of Mount Ashland like a giant chunk of scrimshaw, at one time the tallest building between Portland and San Francisco—I veered northeast, winding my way into the Cascade Mountains, past the town of Climax and into Crater Lake National Park. My goal was the lake itself. In a great rush—or as great a rush as one can manage in a twenty-five-year-old VW Bus, winding into the mountains—I puttered on, gaining altitude. The temperature plummeted and I closed the vents. My purpose in taking this trip was to visit points of interest, to see sights, and Crater Lake was high on my list of places to see. The road ahead snaked through a ridgeline snapped into rusty points like the teeth of a broken saw.

I wound up, up, the road ribboning through switchbacks and armpit-drenching drop-offs. At times the microbus hung suspended as if on the wire arm of a mobile, jutting over sky and space, wobbling briefly before swinging back toward the road, clinging precariously to the mountainside's inner hug. At the base of one cliff ahead I glimpsed the mangled remains of what had once been an automobile, now a crumpled twist of metal. Trees flitted past, the black cottonwoods and dogwoods and maples of the foothills giving way to bigger, older evergreens, a shadowscape of moss and mist and ferns. Higher I climbed. The van groaned.

Finally, after a five-thousand-foot gain in altitude, I curved into the parking lot of the old lodge and visitor center on the lake's rim. Plunking the door handle, I stepped out of the van and gasped: the temperature here was a good forty degrees lower than it had been in Sacramento. In a day's drive, I had gone from the sunny side of eighty degrees to somewhere in the mid- to low forties—*in August*. I stood there, teeth chattering, gazing out across the water. No one else was around, with only a few cars dotting the parking lot. I learned that the park is open year-round, twenty-four hours a day, but many of the park's roads, trails, and facilities are closed seasonally due to snow. Each winter deep snow forces closure of the park's Rim Drive and North Entrance to cars. In fact, Rim Drive becomes a trail for skiing and snowshoeing, and the North Entrance road becomes a snowmobile trail. These roads close for the season with the first big snowstorm in October, or on November 1, whichever comes first. I later learned that Crater Lake is one of the snowiest inhabited places in the United States.

The lake itself was magnificent, the deepest water in the country—1,949 feet deep, filling a sleeping volcano. Because it is almost entirely snowmelt, it is one of the clearest lakes in the world. Pictures and words do not do it justice. It needs to be seen and relished, this sapphire on a mountaintop. But I was freezing and it was getting late, the sun sagging toward the rim. I snagged a sweatshirt, clambered into the van, and headed down off the rim toward warmer air, having learned the first of many road lessons (which were in fact life lessons). *Lesson # 1: Think about where you're headed.*

As I descended from Crater Lake, I searched for a spot to bed down and spend the night. I was concerned about security, about running afoul

Fig. 2: Into the Cascade Mountains. Photo by author.

of ne'er-do-wells. I knew that the edges of national forests were meeting grounds for skulking teenagers and thirsty rednecks. I knew that trail-heads were prime hunting grounds for break-ins and smash-and-grabs, and I knew that I didn't want any late-night visitors. Somewhere, deep in the recesses of my brain, I also heard banjos and bow twangs, and I wanted to disappear deep into the woods, far from anything and anyone. So I turned off the main road—first, onto smaller county roads, and then forking onto graveled logging roads that snaked further into the forest. Again, the van climbed. I kept turning and turning, driving until I finally came to a cul-de-sac at the end of an unnamed, unmarked logging road. Killing the engine, I looked around, enjoying the silence—then prayed that I'd be able to find my way back to civilization in the morning. *Lesson # 2: Leave a trail of breadcrumbs.* Darkness came quickly, not so much falling or descending as welling up from the ground itself like oil. One lightly warmed can of ranch beans and a couple of tortillas later, I curled into my sleeping bag in the back of the van, ready for sleep.

Something interrupted my shut-eye, a noise outside. It was loud, the sound of wood fracturing, but it didn't sound like a bough falling from a tree. When a dead limb breaks away, one hears the initial snap, a whoosh, and then the crash of the limb hitting the ground. This noise was different, a loud crack alone, as if a large animal stepped on a downed branch. No thud, no reverberations. This noise originated at ground level, coming from an indeterminate distance back in the woods: the sound of a large piece of wood being forcefully broken *by someone or something.* But who? Or what? It was the dead of night, and I was miles and miles from anywhere in the middle of nowhere, presumably alone.

The woods were black. Not ink black with no light whatsoever, but a filmy deep-woods dark, illuminated just enough to suggest shapes—hulking ominous shapes, bulbous outlines, malevolent doppelgangers, Lovecraftian forms. I recalled the Scottish prayer cross-stitched and framed on the wall of my room as a boy: "From ghoulies and ghosties / And long-legged beasties / And things that go bump in the night / Good Lord deliver us." My nerves properly jangled, I drew the curtains tight, burrowed into my mummy bag, and listened to every night noise—every insect, every puff of wind, every whispering leaf—until daybreak.

The morning dawned bright and fair, the light clear and pale in a rain-rinsed sky of thin blue. Gossamer nets gleamed wetly on every shrub and bush beneath the tall trees. I wound my way back to pavement and double yellow lines while groggily processing my sleepless night. My mind had clearly played tricks on me. It was natural that I had been on edge. It was my first night on the road. I was stressed out—that, after all, was the reason I was out here. I was excited about the trip, kinda nervous, admittedly jumpy, probably just hearing things.

And there was another factor too. I loved the outdoors, loved camping and hiking and backpacking. I went whenever I could, exploring the woods and mountains. I loved being in nature. But I don't think I'd ever spent the night outside—not once slept under canvas or nylon or starlight—when I didn't feel something akin to what Algernon Blackwood describes in his 1907 short story "The Willows" as a "curious feeling of disquietude" in the untamed dark. As Blackwood's nameless narrator puts it:

> The psychology of places, for some imaginations at least, is very vivid; for the wanderer, especially, camps have their "note" either of welcome or rejection. At first it may not always be apparent, because the busy preparations of tent and cooking prevent, but with the first pause—after supper usually—it comes and announces itself. And the note of this willow-camps now became unmistakably plain to me: we were interlopers, trespassers; we were not welcome.

So perhaps I had a fervid imagination, or perhaps my camp had sounded a note of rejection. At least I'd picked a classic terror: a primal, Jungian dread. Fear of the dark is a common childhood anxiety, one that creeps into adulthood. So it's normal enough. And maybe it was okay. Maybe I kinda liked it, the tingle. It's a test of sorts, seeing what you can handle and what you can't. If you're never afraid, you never have a chance to be courageous. Maybe that's one of the reasons we go into the woods or onto the road—to stare down our fears, to see what makes us blink. Still, too many tingles are unnerving, and fear of the dark isn't really about the darkness. It's a dread of possible and imagined dangers concealed in the shadows. Deep down I realized there were other factors at play, other fears I had yet to drag into the light.

I pulled over to check my map to make sure I was on the right track. I was carrying an oversized Rand McNally Road Atlas, the kind where each state, alphabetically listed, has at least two entire pages devoted to

INTO THE WILD • 19

it, with some of the larger states having even more, with insets for major cities. Flipping through the pages I found Oregon, sandwiched between Oklahoma and Pennsylvania, and as I scanned the lower part of the state, there I saw it. I rubbed my eyes, refocusing, but it was definitely there: in the southern Cascades, in the middle of the vast wilderness where I currently sat, was a tiny, shaggy, man-shaped silhouette with oversized feet. I blinked, scanning the legend in the corner, an unremarkable key with the usual symbols for roads and bridges and peaks and campgrounds. Nothing unusual there. I rubbed the little figure with my finger. Had someone drawn in my atlas? Nope. It was printed in black on the map. No accompanying text, no explanation, no nothing—just a tiny, shaggy, man-shaped silhouette with oversized feet. I couldn't believe it. I guess even cartographers have a sense of humor.

Maybe it was for these reasons—the unexplained crashing in the woods that first night, the unexpected map symbol—that a particular book caught my eye a week later when visiting one of Portland's most famous landmarks, Powell's Books. On the edge of downtown, Powell's is the largest independent bookstore in the world, and it is not to be missed, a department store of approximately one million books that occupies an entire city block, a bibliophile's dream. There, in a pile of books comprising a display of regional authors, I chanced upon a copy of Dr. Robert Michael Pyle's *Where Bigfoot Walks: Crossing the Dark Divide* (1995), which became the newest addition to my mobile library.

Pure luck—and a newly reawakened fascination with cryptozoology—led me to Pyle, who, unbeknownst to me, had already become one of the nation's finest natural history writers. His latest book was a foray into the mysteries of the Dark Divide: the rugged, roadless region in western Washington State, a vast diamond-shaped wilderness roughly delineated by Mount Rainier, Mount Adams, Mount St. Helens, and Mount Hood. Ostensibly a book about the author's search for Bigfoot, the book is simultaneously a meditation on the meanings of wildness in modern American life, a wildness under threat as nature is gobbled up by sprawl, poor management, and human intrusion.

The author's search for Bigfoot was the occasion for the book, not the cause. While there's some Sasquatch lore in this book—sightings and stories and legends and chills—those looking for new proof to confirm their beliefs might be disappointed, though they stand to gain much more than mere evidence of a missing link. Answering the question of the creature's existence is not the purpose of this book, the author confesses:

> How our hearts are carried off by hairy monsters that live only in our minds, how we behave when we suspect that stunning discovery and great reward might lie on our own overgrown doorsteps, and how much wildness will survive our rough handling of the land—these are some of the questions I explored in the territory of the Dark Divide.

The book is less *about* Bigfoot than it is *around* Bigfoot. One realizes that Pyle could take or leave "the Big Galoot," as he calls him. He is neither a dyed-in-the-wool believer nor a confirmed skeptic, instead possessing the mindset of a curious tourist, passing through the known haunts and supposed habitats of North America's ape-man. "I wanted to get inside the head of Grendel, to watch the fleeing forest from within," he writes. "Most of all, I wanted a perspective only the mountains would give." Wide-eyed, clear-headed, and open-minded, he is the consummate scientist: realistic about the chance of an undiscovered hominid living in our midst, rigorous in his demand for evidence, yet flexible about the possibility of new discovery. "Just as true believers sometimes 'find' things that aren't there," he observes, "rock-solid skeptics often miss what is." Knowing better than to say yes, he refuses to say no. "No one can prove that Bigfoot isn't there," he reminds the reader. "Extinction, or absolute absence, is difficult to demonstrate." Man or monster? Hominid or hominoid? *Gigantopithecus* or *Homo nocturnis*? Something or nothing?

Pyle ponders the future of what's left of the continent's old-growth forest, the part that "still resembles the condition of the whole before the arrival of ferrous metal saws." A veteran of the environmental wars of the mid-1990s, when the fate of the spotted owl turned America's remaining temperate rain forest into a battleground between loggers and environmentalists, Pyle bemoans the locals who don't know or don't care about the breadth of life forms at risk—yet also befriends these same locals and respects their viewpoints. Admiring the resilience of pikas, or conies, the little rock-dwelling rabbits who make their homes on the talus slopes and scree, he notes their "broader ecological amplitude," their many ways to live, and suggests that we discover a few more of our own. As the "naked ape," humankind has lost its adaptability, lost its connection to the earth,

INTO THE WILD · 21

its ability to be both human and animal at once. Sasquatch, if he exists, is "the better beast," having retained its perfect suitability to its environment; no atavistic throwback, he instead represents "the advanced condition, that of the superior ape."

Whether Bigfoot strides the forest primeval or not, the author acknowledges that he already exists in sensationalized accounts and blurry "blobsquatch" photos. If the creature *were* discovered roaming the wilds of North America, it would be the greatest scientific discovery of our time; instead, he galumphs through sleazy supermarket tabloids, cheap paperbacks, and low-budget horror flicks. Silliness abounds, along with an indiscriminate tendency to lump cryptohominids with UFOs and astral projections and paranormal activity. Calling this grimy exploitation "the Bigfoot rodeo," Pyle suggests this development is less a scientific failure than a spiritual one:

> We live in an age when control—the grid, the boot, the gun, the nozzle, the law—has the upper hand. We have lost the wild repositories of power beyond the campfire, the mythic figures in which we might invest our fears, whom we might supplicate in pursuit of hope.

This argument for paganism laments the loss of reverence for the unknown and mysterious in nature. In this view it is not the discovery that is important but rather the search.

The last section of the book takes the US Forest Service (USFS) to task, lambasting poor forest management as bad barbering, or timbering with extreme prejudice. The strains on the ancient forests of this region are legion, with many constituents desirous of many different functions and outcomes: where Pyle, like John Muir, sees a temple, off-roaders see virgin land to carve with their Enduros and ATVs. But it is the major logging operations that raise the most questions about "right use" of these forests. The last chapters are exposés of USFS policy and politics, often mired in the same muck where Bigfoot leaves his clearest tracks. Pyle's clarion call for enlightened timber management is, in many ways, the book's biggest take-home message. *Lesson # 3: Hug a tree. Protect your mother.*

The Bigfoot hunters are a sad bunch, I concluded, spending time and fortune on a quixotic endeavor. Then again, how different were they from those searching for the American Dream on the open road? Even Jack

Kerouac had had his Bigfoot encounters, once startling awake at Desolation Peak in the North Cascades, an episode he describes in *The Dharma Bums* (1958):

> In the middle of the night while half asleep I had opened my eyes a bit, and then suddenly I woke up with my hair standing on end, I had just seen a huge black monster standing in my window, and I looked, and it had a star over it, and it was Mount Hozomeen miles away by Canada leaning over my backyard and staring in my window. . . . As darkness enveloped my mountain and soon it would be night again and stars and Abominable Snowman stalking on Hozomeen, I started a crackling fire in the stove and baked delicious rye muffins and mixed up a good beef stew.

The wilderness holds beauty and dread, the latter beaten back with blades and fire and rye muffins and beef stew until the wild becomes the tamer and friendlier place we call nature; but, as Pyle reminds us, we need the fierceness of wilderness too. When we invite a cat or dog to share space with us, we acknowledge the need for a little wildness in our lives; when we walk in the woods, we step away from comfort and convenience and allow ourselves to reconnect with the planet we inhabit and the living things with which we share it. There is a terrible sublimity in the wild places, and it is important to keep them wild, for us as much as for them. "No man should go through life without once experiencing healthy, even bored solitude in the wilderness," Kerouac insists, "finding himself depending solely on himself and thereby learning his true and hidden strength."

Reading Pyle helped me to realize why I was putting myself "out there." Many have taken to the road to find space to ruminate, but it occurred to me that I wasn't driving in order to ponder and think. Introspection was clearly not my problem: I was already self-reflective, overly so. It's a double-edged sword, this introspection—not only a handy mirror but also a destructive force when internal chatter becomes a deafening din. I didn't need to zoom in. I needed to zoom *out*, to step back. It was the ritual of the road and the green spaces and the awe that pulled me.

Toward the end of *Where Bigfoot Walks*, Pyle quotes outdoor writer David Quammen, who notes in *Outside* magazine that "the essence of travel is relinquishing full control over the texture and path of your own life—and one aspect of that relinquishment is a chronic shortage of decent reading." I guess I suspected as much when I began my journey, because I had tossed a number of paperbacks and a hardcover or two into the van to keep me company. Books had always been my best teachers, and I saw no need to give up what Longfellow called "the love of learning, the sequestered nook, and all the sweet serenity of books." Mine would be a trip of miles logged, books read, sights seen, and lessons learned. And the Bus would be my nook.

3

The Legend of Lawnchair Larry, American Hero

After Crater Lake, I wound my way over to the Oregon Coast Highway and lazed up the edge of the world. California's coast is better known, but the Oregon Coast is every bit as rugged, remote, and beautiful. The towns of Seal Rock, Otter Rock, and Beaver tell something of the wildlife here. A hunk of fresh cheese made a satisfying lunch one day in Tillamook. Cannon Beach is particularly scenic, a gargantuan rock plunked into the ocean, as if casually tossed there by a passing giant. I spent many days exploring this area. I was settling in, calming down, and learning: learning the picadilloes of the Bus, learning how to relax at night while camping, learning how to see what's out there. I drove. I saw the sights. I parked. I gathered firewood. I built a small campfire. I cooked and ate. I read. I bathed. I breathed. I slept. The next day I would drink some coffee, drive some more, and repeat the process. The Bus would dutifully crank and carry me further along.

Somewhere along this stretch I also got a quick look at my enemy. He'd been stalking me from the start, following since San Francisco, shadowing my movements, mechanistically persistent and unshakable. He was with me in the woods that first night. I finally caught a glimpse of my nemesis somewhere on that twisted path between Medford and Portland. There he was, furtively glancing at me in the rearview mirror. He wouldn't leave me alone—but at least now I recognized him. Phaedrus. Me. Before, he'd been hidden, often in plain sight, blurred on the periphery like Bigfoot. Now I was learning his patterns, the haunts he frequented, his likes and dislikes. Soon I'd be able to drag him out and stare him down if he gave me any trouble.

In classical Jungian analysis, one does not fight devils so much as listen to what they have to say; they are, after all, disowned parts of oneself. To fight one's demons—whether doubts or fears or impurities or something else—is to become them. "Battle not with monsters, lest ye become a monster," Nietzsche cautions, warning that when you stare into the abyss, the abyss stares back into you. Yet he also recognized that in this void a person may glimpse core truths about the cosmos, about the world, about the self—not through the seeing, conscious ego but rather through the clear nothingness of the empty unconscious. If it was inadvisable for me and me to have a knock-down-drag-out fight, then perhaps at least we could have a come-to-Jesus moment: a stern talking-to, rather than a good thrashing.

I wondered what it was that had compelled me to take to the highway. Was I losing my mind? My mojo? I had certainly lost my self-assuredness. While I couldn't properly articulate it, I suspected that I'd experienced a crisis of confidence, born of the suspicion that I didn't really belong at Berkeley, that my colleagues were leagues ahead of me in brainpower and IQ points. I was smart enough, but I wasn't blindingly brilliant and I never had been—not at Berkeley or UGA or UVA or even growing up in Dalton— and I was trying to crack into one of the professions where raw smarts really counted. Shouldn't professors be geniuses? I ought to have done as my parents expected and gone to law school.

I didn't make it to Cape Disappointment and the mouth of the Columbia River, where in November 1805 Meriwether Lewis's partner, William Clark, celebrated the conclusion of their epic journey across the American West. "Great joy in camp," Clark had written in his journal, "we are in view of the ocean, this great Pacific Ocean which we been so long anxious to see." Instead, I turned east to delve again into the forests and mountains, driving through tunnels of trees and camping this fogscape upholstered in lichen and moss, all the while pulled northward, inescapably caught in Seattle's gravitation pull. The pinnacles in this area contrast markedly with one another, the sharp-peaked cone of Mt. Hood differing from the blunted blob of post-eruption Mt. St. Helens, and the colossal Mt. Rainier, a scoop of bubble-gum ice cream on Seattle's horizon at sunset.

There was an uptick in traffic outside Seattle, and I was soon swept up in a surge of cars. My hands tightened on the wheel, the tension traveling up my arms into my trapezius muscles. I watched the morning commuters humming past in their sedans and coupes. Many had steaming cups of coffee—the thin, bright kind that I and many other Americans prefer—in fists and laps and cupholders. I spied a couple of breakfast sandwiches, and some sort of burrito contraption spilling its contents liberally down the driver's shirt front. A few primpings and preenings in visor mirrors, but mostly eyes forward, concentrating on the road ahead—all except for one gent, calmly reading a paperback novel as he hurtled down the interstate. He held it pinned to the steering wheel, his hands at 12 o'clock. Busy, buzzy Americans on their way to work.

Hard work is a central tenet of the American Dream: the idea that one can get ahead and prosper in American society through sweat equity. It was this idea that has drawn immigrants from around the world to the United States, a true meritocracy where one can strive and succeed through those efforts, where one can work freely to make a better life for oneself and one's children. No class restrictions holding people back, no glass ceilings keeping people down. At least that's the idea. It hasn't always worked out that way, especially for women and minorities—racism and sexism have soiled this paradigm—but that's the idea at least.

In its most general sense, the American Dream is (def. 1) *a varying constellation of ideas by which we as Americans orient our lives.* It is an ethos, a shared set of sometimes ill-defined assumptions clustered around the exceptionalist sense that life in the United States is much different from, and much better than, life in other nations. Most Americans share a sense that the brightest star in this constellation is the idea that one can get ahead here. Indeed, this idea holds such powerful allure over native-born citizens, naturalized citizens, and foreigners alike that it might be said to be a primary definition of the Dream itself. That is, the American Dream is (def. 2) *the notion that anyone, through hard work and perseverance, can succeed in American society.*

How one defines this success provides its own set of challenges. While most Americans seem to define success in terms of financial gain, it is a highly subjective concept that need not be explained solely in terms of material acquisition. People are free to name their own dreams above and beyond naked wealth: a fulfilling or remunerative job, for example, or freedom to worship without interference or self-sufficiency or safety. Success may be measured absolutely (I have), relatively (I have more), or competitively (I have more than you). When expressed absolutely, it can be an opening or prospect or break; when expressed relatively, it can be defined as progress or improvement. Accordingly, the American Dream at its simplest is (def. 3) *opportunity* or (def. 4) *betterment.*

This notion began to crystalize during the Jacksonian Era, when white men began to enjoy broader participation in politics and reform movements emerged to address some of the inequalities in American society. By the 1830s, the disappearance of inherited social ranks and clearly defined aristocracies or privileged groups struck European visitors like Alexis de Tocqueville as the most radical feature of democracy in America. Tocqueville, a French nobleman, spent nine months in America in 1831–32 and wrote *Democracy in America*, a two-volume book of profound insight into the American character. Tocqueville writes that the "general equality of condition among the people" was the fundamental fact from which all other characteristics of American society flowed; in this way, the United States was becoming much different from her parent nations in Europe. "What most astonishes me," he writes, "is not so much the marvelous grandeur of some undertakings, as the innumerable magnitude of small ones." The individual efforts of tens of thousands of artisans and inventors, working without consciousness of class as they struggled to get ahead in society, propelled the nation forward. Tocqueville popularized a new word, *individualisme*, to describe the conditions and values of native-born white Americans who lived a more solitary existence than their European brethren, "no longer attached to each other by any tie of caste, class, association, or family."

There was of course not only an economic component to American individualism but also a political one. Beginning in the late 1810s, one state after another had revised their constitutions to remove property qualifications for voting, which gave many ordinary farmers and wage earners the right to vote and laid the foundation for the rise of mass politics. All states admitted to the Union after 1815 adopted universal white male suffrage, and between 1807 and 1821, others abolished the property and tax qualifications for voting. These developments had a dramatic effect on national elections. White men of lowly origins could rise more readily to positions of power and influence. Exclusiveness and aristocratic pretensions were increasingly scorned.

This dramatic loosening of suffrage restrictions caused some to herald the Era of the Common Man; but, by modern standards, the United States was far from democratic. Women could not vote or hold office in any state and were legally under the control of their husbands; "free blacks" as they were called were, if not completely disfranchised, still considered second-class citizens at best; and slavery was strengthening in the southern states. Moreover, the same period witnessed the resettlement of Native Americans west of the Mississippi River and the concentration of wealth in fewer and fewer hands. The trick then as now was to ensure that freedoms were extended equitably to all Americans, to make the nation live up to the ideals expressed in its founding documents, the Declaration and Constitution.

Many peoples around the world have taken those documents at face value and flocked to the place where they can live out their own American dreams. It's fascinating to learn that the phrase "American Dream" is not included somewhere in those same documents, penned by James Madison or Alexander Hamilton or one of the other Founding Fathers. It seems like such a fundamental and enduring concept—baked into the American cake since the beginning—but the term itself is more a product of twentieth-century pluralism than eighteenth-century republicanism. It first appeared in print one hundred years *after* the heyday of Andrew Jackson, who was himself a boy during the Revolutionary War. James Truslow Adams, a historian, coined the phrase in 1931 in his monumental work *The Epic of America*. Writing at the advent of the Great Depression, Adams aimed to trace the beginnings "of such American concepts as 'bigger and better,'" of attitudes toward business, of typically "American" traits, and particularly "of that American dream of a better, richer, and happier life for all our citizens of every rank," which he recognized as this nation's greatest contribution to the world. Adams named a complex of ideals, beliefs, and standards that had been in existence for a long time, but he was the first to use the words "American" and "dream" together. His phraseology, so familiar and ubiquitous, entered the American lexicon with such ease in the 1930s that it is difficult to imagine the Founding Fathers not having used the words themselves in the eighteenth century.

There were indeed parallels. James Truslow Adams was very much like Thomas Jefferson in his efforts to nudge his countrymen away from materialist concerns and define something more idealistic in our national aspirations than cash alone. "It is not a dream of motor cars and high wages merely," Adams writes, "but a dream of social order in which each man and each woman shall be able to attain to the fullest stature of which they are innately capable, and be recognized by others for what they are, regardless of the fortuitous circumstances of birth or position." His was a communalist vision of the Dream, emphasizing notions of community and public interest over individual achievement; he seemed to view the Dream as a communitarian ideal, not as a license for consumption. When drafting the Declaration, Thomas Jefferson had similarly tried to define something loftier, changing John Locke's phrasing about "life, liberty, and the pursuit of property" to the now famous "life, liberty, and the pursuit of happiness."

But while his interpretation was quite literally the definitive one, Adams's understanding has typically been lost in "what's-in-it-for-me" Americanism. We have traditionally assumed that power and wealth represent the success intoned in the American Dream. Because there are no governmentally imposed limits to acquisition in this country, and because there is seemingly no limit to what one can acquire, American success can be a fabulous kind of wealth, born of sweat equity and desire. This kind of wealth is celebrated in the Hamptons and in Malibu and in Palm Beach, where mansions and expensive cars abound, and where greed sometimes passes for wanting a lion's share of the finer things in life. The irony is that this kind of wealth is sometimes—perhaps often—generated not through hard work but through privilege or birthright or sometimes even chance. In accumulated wealth, inheritance, and even lotteries, we've somehow managed to replicate the very things that Jacksonians reviled.

The Dream lives in a mélange of American obsessions—hard work, success, individualism, freedom, economic self-determination, mobility (physical, social, and economic), property ownership, egalitarianism—but the economic aspects have often taken precedent in popular imagination. Indeed, as far as the Internet is concerned, the American Dream seems to equal consumerism. The two are often equivalent in the virtual world of the World Wide Web, where it quickly became a marketing catchphrase used to advertise comfort and security, to lure the unwary into get-rich-quick schemes, and to fleece the gullible. It often symbolizes the world of real estate, but it can refer to anything so long as it involves buying and selling.

Shameless advertising aside, it's clear that the American Dream is a kind of national religion, something to which we reverently cling. It is the one creed that US citizens of differing races, ethnicities, and religious backgrounds all seem to embrace—indeed, the one to which we collectively, if unconsciously, encourage all to adhere. In the absence of a state-sanctioned church, it is the closest thing Americans have to a nationwide, faith-based system of belief, though it's not just Americans who accept its sacraments. Conviction that a better life lies just ahead not only sustains our economic, social, and political systems but also pulls in peoples around the world like a tractor beam. Even before its inception, this nation offered a promise: come here, work hard, and you've got a shot. And frankly, we've always needed the help.

Again, that's the idea—a meritocracy based on effort rather than inherited wealth or social class—but in practice, it hasn't always worked out that way. For every example of American success, there are ten examples of people busting their asses and never making it through no fault of their own. The passageway to the Dream has historically been restricted and exclusive, a narrow corridor for white men only—and really for those white men who already had some sort of preexisting advantage. Women and people of color and immigrants needed not apply—unless, of course, there was an immediate and pressing labor need (which there almost always was). An old proverb that expresses the disillusionment one "second-wave" immigrant from Italy found upon arriving in the United States goes something like this:

I came to America because I heard the streets were paved with gold. When I got here, I found out three things. First, the streets weren't paved with gold; second, they weren't paved at all; and third, I was expected to pave them.

The path has widened but it could be wider. It's still pretty rocky. And there's still work to be done. These thoughts turned as morning commuters, all pursuing their respective dreams, sped past my lumbering van.

After a few days in Seattle with my friend Sheila—an undergrad dormmate, one of the first people I met in college—and her husband,

Doug, I bent east and headed across Washington, down Highway 2 toward Spokane and Coeur d'Alene, into parts of the state less traveled by tourists. Someone—I can't remember who—once noted that on every trip there occurs an uncoupling, a letting go. The point of origin recedes, the traveler thinks less about home and what's been left behind, and the gaze fixes ahead. It's a kind of trust fall, not into the arms of a reliable friend but into the trip itself, whose dependability is unknown and now carries the traveler to be either safely delivered at the other end or unceremoniously dumped somewhere along the way. For me it happened somewhere past Seattle after that first major directional shift from north to east. The terrain morphed into river valleys and coulees created by glacial floods that cut, gouged, and shaped the byways through this strange land, leading toward what many Washingtonians consider the state's best-kept secret: its northeast corner, dotted with mountain lakes and old mining towns.

I puttered along, looking at oncoming cars as they approached and passed. Scrutinizing a mercurial blob on the horizon—an amorphous shape emerging from the road's vanishing point—reminded me of my favorite line from *Their Eyes Were Watching God*. "Ships at a distance have every man's wish on board," wrote Zora Neale Hurston in 1937:

> For some they come in with the tide. For others they sail forever on the same horizon, never out of sight, never landing until the Watcher turns his eyes away in resignation, his dreams mocked to death by Time. That is the life of men.

Wheelless at first, a familiar visage materialized, a windshield wriggling out of the road's wet mirage, emerging in the shimmering distance of the opposite lane with a chromed, wide-eyed look, its bay window unmistakable. The lower chassis followed, wheels churning up from the shimmering lake of asphalt. It was a VW Bus, and seeing it was like seeing an old friend. As I passed the pea-green T2 Transporter, the driver—a long-haired guy with Ray Bans—grinned and flashed a peace sign. I felt like I'd been initiated, given the secret handshake to an exclusive club—the Esteemed Order of the Vee Dub Microbus—and in a way I had been. Everywhere I went my breadloaf-shaped van served as a kind of icebreaker. In campgrounds someone would inevitably amble over, always sidling casually. "Nice VW," they'd say, and then tell me about the '73 High Top Safari they used to own, or the '74 Super Beetle their cousin drove, or their girl-friend's old Karmann Ghia, or the Volkswagen Bus they always wanted but never got around to getting. "Underpowered and overflowered," one guy joked. "No oomph." Everyone, it seemed, had positive associations with old VWs and especially VW Buses, even those owners whose vehicles had left them stranded, coughing to a halt in the middle of some congested inter-section or slowly drifting to the shoulder along a stretch of lonely highway or mutely failing to crank atop an oil-stained driveway.

The VW Bus was an iconic ride with hippy implications: a vehicu-lar symbol of 1960s counterculture. There it was—at Haight-Ashbury, at Woodstock, at Altamont, at countless communes dotted across the nation, slowly but happily transporting college kids, activists, New Lefties, flower children, stoners, acid freaks, and bona fide bums to wherever they needed to be, as long as they didn't need to be there quickly. And with my long hair and scruffy appearance, I was playing the part, a carefree dude in a Kombi rumbling to destinations unknown.

However I may have looked, though, there were three facts that belied appearances. First, I wasn't carefree. Despite my relaxed pace, I had a job to do, driving with a purpose, and I was in fact quite full of cares, most of which I hoped would slough off on this trip like an old retread tire. Sec-ond, I wasn't really a hippy. I was a Gen Xer, not a baby boomer, more grungy than groovy, and while some people my age clung to the counter-cultural trappings of our parent's generation, few of my Berkeley friends would have confused me with a dyed-in-the-wool, unshorn communard, of which there were genuine examples in the Bay Area. While my politics leaned leftward, I was pretty middle-of-the-road, socially and otherwise. Political allegiances are subjective, relative, and contextual, of course: in Northwest Georgia I undoubtedly seemed pretty liberal, but in Berkeley I must have seemed quite moderate, even conservative on certain issues. If being an empathetic person troubled about feeding the hungry and nurs-ing the sick made me progressive or "radical" to some then so be it, but those seemed to me ordinary concerns, stuff I had learned about in Sun-day school at First Presbyterian Church in Dalton. Third and finally, I chose the VW in spite of, not because of, its hippy connotations. I needed an affordable camper van and the Westfalia fit the bill. I had also closely eyed a 1976 Toyota Chinook mini-RV, as well as a crimson '74 Datsun 620 pickup with camper top, but ultimately opted for what I hoped would be

Fahrvergnügen: an early '90s VW ad slogan and neologism from the German *fahren*, "to drive," and *vergnügen*, "enjoyment."

I stopped for gas at an express mart above Yakima, a Conoco or Chevron or something, where I shot the breeze with a guy fueling up his candy-apple-red IROC-Z/28. For those who came of age in North Georgia in the 1980s, it was the car to beat, a souped-up version of an already souped-up Camaro. Sixteen-inch aluminum wheels, body cladding, special graphics, growly exhaust, and a Corvette engine: a tuned-port, 350-cubic-inch, 5.7-liter, small-block V8 with enough horsepower to attempt a moon launch. As they say in East Tennessee, it'll getcha there quicker than good corn liquor. But that speed came at a price: it took more fuel to top it off (premium, no less!) than it took to fill up my entire V-Dub tank. If you can picture the car, then you can picture the guy driving it. He lit a cigarette, breathing deep and exhaling at the NO SMOKING sign posted above the pump.

"Nice ride," he said.
"Yours too," I replied. "Wanna race?"

He laughed and countered with an offer to trade vehicles for forty-eight hours. I'll admit I was tempted, imagining myself ripping around upper Washington for a couple of days. I just couldn't figure out where I'd sleep. We made idle small talk, but the smallest talk is often the best: real, honest, not really small at all. He eventually roared off in a cloud of exhaust and cologne.

West of Spokane, something new caught my eye, an object in the sky just above a mountain range to the north. A plane, I assumed—but over the next five or six minutes, it stayed more or less fixed, a silvery orb above the horizon. A blimp? The shape was wrong and it wasn't moving. Definitely well above the mountain, not visibly attached, nothing I could easily identify. Having just left the shadowy Cascade Mountains and their mysterious midnight crashings, I was enjoying the bright sun, uneager to reenter what Carl Sagan criticized as the "demon-haunted world" of the paranormal. I briefly wondered if I had lifted the veil on what Fredrick William Holiday called the "goblin universe," allowing unexplained phenomena to sneak through the dimension overlaid on our own and manifest as shades and resonances on the edges of our sensual periphery, but I quickly flushed the thought. I was done with specters and apparitions. What I was looking at had a logical explanation, and it must be a weather balloon, I deduced, perhaps on a long tether.

Smugly satisfied with my powers of reason, I pondered weather balloons and thought of a man named Larry Walters, a test pilot of sorts. I'd never read about him in any history books and I wasn't quite sure where I'd first heard his story, but part of me figured he might have deserved more than the inchoate asterisk he'd fleetingly earned in American pop culture as an amateur aviator.

On the morning of July 2, 1982, Walters was nearing completion of a long-planned experiment. He scurried to make final preparations for a balloon-borne test flight in his girlfriend's mother's backyard in Long Beach, California. If anything worried him, it was the prospect of getting dumped if the contraption he had dubbed *Inspiration I* tipped forward. He hadn't bothered to install a seatbelt, instead relying on a slightly rearward pitched seat, whose angle he now double-checked. Weighted with water bottles for ballast, the seat was reclined like a dentist's chair, and like a dentist's chair it held the suggestion of potential pain. The attached balloons strained to go higher, bobbing angrily at the ends of their lines. After going inside to pee, he gathered his essentials: a pellet gun, a CB radio, a compass, an altimeter, some sandwiches and something to drink, a camera—even a life jacket in case he drifted out over the ocean. Overkill, of course, for a tethered backyard pleasure cruise, but the array of gear belied his true intentions. He was going to cut the cord and see what happened. He was going to go up.

His adventure that day entered a kitschy corner of American folklore, closer to Annie Edson Taylor—a schoolteacher who in 1901 became the first person to survive a plunge over Niagara Falls in a barrel—than Daniel Boone or Davy Crockett. Rather than a celebrated exploit, Walters's story became a cautionary tale, a knee-slapper for the sports bar and fraternity house and other places men gather to marvel at the dumb things they've done. In 1982, Walters as an "At-Risk Survivor" received an Honorable Mention of the Darwin Award, which is reserved for those individuals who remove themselves from the human gene pool in dramatic fashion. If his special Darwin Award is any indicator, then it may be that he was nothing more than a hapless fool, a no-account dreamer who, as Andy Warhol predicted, enjoyed his fifteen minutes of fame.

Then again, there may be something more to Walters's story, something lasting. There is something there, sandwiched in other layers of meaning, something quite *American*. His ingenuity, his reckless bravery, and his aspiration signify characteristics that Americans have traditionally found laudable. His ordinariness—his everyman anonymity—seemed to prove democratically that anyone in the United States can succeed, an egalitarian testament to the American Dream. Part Thomas Edison, part Charles Lindbergh, part Admiral Farragut, he was in many ways a classic sort of hero, an American Icarus whose wings didn't melt.

Walters had always wanted to fly. He sought to join the air force and become a pilot but was disqualified due to poor eyesight. He joined the army and served in Vietnam. Afterward, he became a truck driver for a company that makes television commercials. When he met his girlfriend Carol Van Deusen in 1972, he told her of his dream of flight. Ten years later, as she watched him tracing balloons on the placemat as they munched hamburgers at a Holiday Inn in Victorville, she knew his dream was still alive.

The scheme took shape. At Carol's insistence, he agreed to wear a parachute and visited the Elsinore Flight School in Perris, California, where after a single jump, he bought his own chute for $900. He procured fifty-five helium cylinders to inflate each balloon to seven feet in diameter, to get a lift of about twelve pounds apiece. Together, the forty-two balloons would have lifted about a quarter ton.

What he intended seemed to differ from what he told others. Carol's mother, Margaret Van Deusen, may have envisioned a tethered kiddie ride, a cursory bounce or two in the backyard. Carol herself may have been promised a quick joyride, though she knew of her boyfriend's ambitions and he had always tried to be honest with her. When sheriff's deputies arrived the night before, poking their heads over the fence to inquire about the 150-foot-high tiers of balloons, grouped vertically in four bunches, they were told that it was for a commercial shoot the next morning. Walters's friends who had gathered at the launch site understood that Larry would rise approximately a hundred feet above the Van Deusen house and hold there, secured by a length of rope wrapped around a friend's 1962 Chevrolet Bonneville on the lawn, to get his bearings, check the apparatus, and hover over the neighborhood for a while.

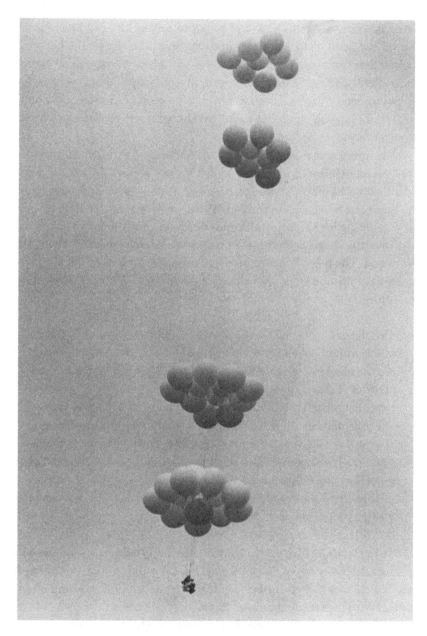

Fig. 3: "Lawnchair Larry" Walters.
AP Photo/Randy Mudrick/San Pedro *News-Pilot*.

All of these plans crumbled when he clambered aboard his makeshift flying machine at 10:30 a.m. and began to release the guy lines that anchored the lawn chair to the ground. He shot into the sky. Whether his main tether broke or he cut it is unclear, but when it snapped he was jostled violently, pitching forward, losing his eyeglasses along with some of his equipment. Carol watched in horror. She called him frantically on the two-way radio, begging him to abort. Walters soared, rocketing upward at one thousand feet per minute.

His intent was to level off and drift northeast in the prevailing winds over the San Gabriel Mountains to the Mojave Desert. In a conversation with George Plimpton, who interviewed Walters twice and wrote about the infamous balloonist in the *New Yorker* in May 1998, Walters said that he was aiming for a cruising altitude of eight or nine thousand feet, to take him over the Angeles National Forest, past Mt. Wilson, and out toward the desert. The pièce de résistance was the pellet gun, which he would use to regulate altitude by popping balloons as needed. Walters's experience is something best conveyed in his own words:

> The higher I went, the more I could see, and it was awesome. Sitting in this little chair, and, you know, Look! Wow! Man! Unreal! I could see the orange funnels of the Queen Mary. I could see that big seaplane of Howard Hughes's, the Spruce Goose, with two commercial tugs alongside. Then, higher up, the oil tanks of the naval station, like little dots. Catalina Island in the distance. The sea was blue and opaque. I could look up the coast, like, forever. At one point, I caught sight of a little private plane below me. I could hear the "bzzz" of its propeller—the only sound. I had this camera, but I didn't take any pictures. This was something personal. I wanted only the memory of it—that was vivid enough.

Still rising, with no directional control, he simply drifted, riding the wind. Exhilarated but worried, Walters used his CB radio to transmit a mayday call, which was picked up by operators on the ground who maintained contact with him throughout the flight.

After a while, Larry worked up the courage to shoot a few of the balloons. He was nervous about doing so, fearful that popping a balloon would jerk everything out of balance, yanking the lines and dumping him out of the chair. Timorously, he took out his pellet gun, carefully aimed upward, and squeezed. Pop! Pop, pop! Pop, pop, pop, pop! Seven of the balloons collapsed, dangling below the chair. Then, the unthinkable: as Walters fished out his altimeter, the pellet gun slipped from his lap. He watched it getting smaller and smaller, tumbling toward the houses below until it disappeared from view. Higher still he went, topping out at 16,500 feet, where the air was thin and dangerously cold. He breathed deeply, trying to catch his breath, shivering uncontrollably in temperatures between five and ten degrees Fahrenheit. He was over three miles high.

Just as it seemed his fate was clinched, the craft peaked and began to drift downward, perhaps as the air within the balloons contracted in the cold or as they began to slowly leak. He floated easily, drifting across the primary approach corridor for Long Beach Municipal Airport. A TWA captain radioed that he was passing a man in a lawn chair at sixteen thousand feet; Delta and United pilots may also have seen the strange sight. Alarmed, the tower located him on radar and began to track him. At around thirteen thousand feet he got into a conversation with air traffic controllers, who repeatedly asked his airport of origin. He in turn repeatedly gave Margaret's street address.

As he descended, he could hear "dogs barking, automobiles, horns— even voices, you know, in calm, casual conversation." But at about two thousand feet, he started dropping fast, too quickly. He cut his ballast, slashing the water-filled, plastic bottles with a pocketknife, sending thirty-five gallons cascading downward. Rooftops and powerlines rushed up to meet him. His feet scraped a house rooftop and he sailed underneath a net of powerlines, which snared the balloons, suspending him a few feet above the ground. Witnesses rescued him with a stepladder, dropping him into the expectant arms of the police, who after detaining him briefly on site, turned him loose, telling him they couldn't determine that he'd done anything wrong. Having returned unscathed, he signed a few autographs, gave the chair to a neighborhood kid, and went home.

Little did he expect the hubbub that followed. Six years before British ski-jumper Eddie the Eagle captured hearts, not by jumping well or far but simply by jumping, Larry Walters garnered international fame for doing something wacky, dangerous, and unexpected. His flight of fancy fired imaginations and drew fiery criticism. Newspapers carried his story;

LAWNCHAIR LARRY • 39

television shows raced to book him. "It was something I had to do," he told the *Los Angeles Times*. He appeared on *The Tonight Show* and was flown to New York to be on *Late Night with David Letterman*, which he later described as "the most fun I've ever had."

In the hours, days, and weeks following his voyage, Walters's story was told and retold, and in the retelling he was transformed from an amateur aviation enthusiast into a reckless yokel, a crank who needlessly endangered himself and others. A reporter on the scene who asked Walters why he'd done it reported that, "as he was led away in handcuffs," he nonchalantly replied, "A man can't just sit around." The facts changed and skewed. The Darwin Awards reported that he had been aloft for fourteen hours, while Walters himself estimated an hour and a half. Somewhere in the retelling of his story, his soda turned into beer: whereas Plimpton reported that he carried two liters of Coca-Cola, subsequent reports mentioned varying quantities of Miller Lite. This seemingly minor detail is rather crucial in fixing Walters's legacy. The beer-instead-of-Coke variation transforms the protagonist from a careful planner and visionary into an impulsive good-times seeker, flying by the seat of his pants in search of a thrill. Other changes followed too. In the retelling, Long Beach Airport became the much bigger Los Angeles International Airport (LAX); the smaller airplanes became massive jetliners; and the Long Beach Police who met Walters upon return morphed into the stone-faced LAPD. The Darwin Awards, who reported that Walters had sailed out over the ocean, were partially to blame for his slide from fame to infamy. Walters's image as shiftless daredevil who dodged death in spite of himself was becoming fixed in the public mind. Lawnchair Larry was born.

This reading of Walters is uncharitable and inaccurate, belying his penchants as both tinkerer and visionary. In his conversation with Plimpton, Walters described visiting Disneyland at age "eight or nine" and seeing a woman "holding what seemed like a zillion Mickey Mouse balloons," a sight that sparked his idea. "I mean, you get enough of those and they're going to lift you up!" Walters told Plimpton. At age thirteen, he spied some surplus weather balloons at an Army-Navy store and "realized that was the way to go—that I had to get some of those big suckers." He began "experimenting with hydrogen gas, making my own hydrogen generators," he said, inflating little balloons and sending them aloft with notes attached, never getting a reply. His Hollywood High School science project, "Hydrogen

40 • CHAPTER 3

and Balloons," received a D. He dabbled in rocketry and "making rocket fuel," which was "always blowing up on me or catching fire." His mother worried—but Larry's obsession with balloon flight was clearly more than a momentary impulse.

Imagining a life as a motivational speaker after his flight, Larry quit his job as a truck driver. He had a few speaking gigs. The police had told him he'd be hearing from the Federal Aviation Administration, and he did. He had violated controlled airspace. The FAA slapped him with a $4,000 fine for violating US Federal Aviation Regulations, including operating an aircraft within an airport traffic area "without establishing and maintaining two-way communications with the control tower." He appealed and the fine was reduced to $1,500.

Postflight, things didn't unfold as Walters anticipated. The attention dried up, as did the speaking gigs; the endorsements and follow-up flights never materialized. Off and on he worked as a security guard. Volunteering for the US Forest Service, he became a forest ranger in the San Gabriel Mountains, the same range over which he had sailed in his lawn chair. He loved camping there. It was one of the few things that made him happy, one of the few places that brought solace. After fifteen years, he and Carol broke up. He never married and had no children. It was not until ten years after the flight that Walters broke even on his expenses and his FAA fines: in 1992 he was featured—mustachioed and greying, looking like a fighter pilot—in a Timex advertisement, part of a print-ad campaign based on "adventurous individuals." The ad offset his expenditures a decade earlier. In October 1993 he went for a hike in the mountains with a pistol in his knapsack and never came back. Search-and-rescue personnel found his body in his sleeping bag in his tent. He had shot himself through the heart. He died at the age of forty-four.

Walters's name might have been remembered alongside celebrated first flyers Orville and Wilbur Wright or test pilot Chuck Yeager, who broke the sound barrier in 1947. Instead he's largely forgotten, having faded into obscurity. Why? There are several reasons. He was uncredentialed, accidental. The way his story was reported and the way his legend corporealized both worked against fame and fortune. There's the matter of the achievement itself, and there's the matter in which it was executed. What exactly had Walters accomplished? And was he deserving of accolades for it? If hurtling skyward in a lawn chair can be considered an accomplishment, then many folks seemed to perceive that he fell into that accomplishment undeservedly and inadvertently.

But was he any less deserving of recognition than, say, Benjamin Franklin? Contrary to popular opinion, the bespectacled inventor and Founding Father did *not* discover electricity: he merely demonstrated that lightning *is* electricity. Nor was his kite struck by lightning, according to the Franklin Institute; instead, his kite picked up an ambient electrical charge from the storm in which he flew it. His idea was simple: he attached a small wire to the top of a simple kite to act as a lightning rod. To the bottom he attached a length of hemp string, followed by a length of silk string; when wet by rain, the hemp would collect a charge, but the silk, kept dry as Franklin stood in the doorway of a shed, would not. A metal key thread on the hemp would also act as a conductor, one toward which Franklin moved his finger during his experiment. As the negative charges in the key were attracted to the positive charges in his hand, he felt a spark; he then used a Leyden jar to collect this "electric fire" to discharge at a later time. Franklin's description of the event appeared in the October 19, 1752, edition of the *Pennsylvania Gazette*, in which he provided instructions for re-creating the experiment. A year later, Baltic German physicist Georg Wilhelm Richmann attempted a similar trial but was killed when he was, predictably, struck by lightning.

If Richmann's fate is any indicator, then apparently the only thing separating Benjamin Franklin from a colonial-era Darwin Award was the good fortune of not being electrocuted. The line between greatness and idiocy is a fine one, and Americans have a knack for finding both. Underscoring the inherent danger of playing with electricity, Richmann's fate changes how we must view Franklin. Both were revered scientists, both respected the medium with which they worked, and both took safety precautions, but Franklin was lucky while Richmann was not. Walters was similarly lucky, but whereas Franklin continued his work with electricity, went on to perfect his lightning rod invention, and in 1753 received the prestigious Copley Medal from the Royal Society in recognition of his "curious experiments and observations on electricity," Walters—whose bravado and feckless naivety enabled him to punch through the mundane into something extraordinary—came crashing back to Earth, figuratively if not actually. In addition to his Honorable Mention Darwin Award, Walters was awarded the top prize from the Bonehead Club of Dallas.

Had he lived today, Walters's story might have ended differently. The Internet would have undoubtedly changed his circumstance. He would have had an online presence: a website and a Facebook page of his own, perhaps some fan pages (both genuine and ironic) to redirect traffic to his official webpage. Such buzz was harder to generate in Walters's time, unlike today's world where false-positive celebrities thrive through little effort of their own. Here was a man who accomplished something, however fleeting and ephemeral. Two decades later, Kim Kardashian and Paris Hilton would parlay image into fame, having done nothing on their own (unless one counts the sex tapes that pushed their bubble-gum *Teen-Beat* popularity in the early 2000s into notoriety, revealing something about the indiscriminate nature of infamy supplanting celebrity in our own time—perhaps in the cyber age it is lascivious men who truly drive fame). In contrast, Walters actually *did* something—something illegal and dangerous, yes, but something. His derring-do predated the corporate slogan, "Just Do It," which originated in 1988, but his chutzpah in sending a lawn chair airborne would have fit perfectly with Nike's ethos of doing without overthinking.

Like the Wright Brothers and Lindbergh and Yeager, there is a certain absurdity to Walters's achievement, another element in American heroism. Americans like their heroes to overcome great odds to achieve the impossible. First it was flying itself, loosing humanity's earthbound shackles, then doing it further and faster. Like these others, Walters's accomplishment was made possible by American ingenuity and know-how, in particular this nation's historic technological innovation. Lindbergh was celebrated in the 1920s in a time of mechanization, when individual accomplishment was becoming less possible in the face of complicated systems and bureaucracies, where people were becoming cogs themselves; but, "Lucky Lindy" was always quick to credit his plane, the *Spirit of St. Louis,* as an equal partner in whatever stardom he garnered. It was the airplane and its state-of-the-art engine, he noted, that enabled his famed transatlantic voyage, a marriage of man and machine that symbiotically powered one another. But it's the element of danger, the hairline between success and catastrophic failure that especially attracts Americans. Being clever is not enough. It is the Icarian plunge into the sea, as Lindbergh threatened and Amelia Earhart performed, that thrills us.

Oddly and relatedly, failure *is* an option in the celebration of American greatness. Earhart herself sits squarely in the pantheon, somewhere between the valiant defenders of the Alamo and Mighty Casey at Bat. We allow our heroes to fall short, so long as they fail spectacularly, going down swinging. In this sense, American heroes are often fallibly human, with feet of clay. It's not simply that heroes are an endangered species (which they are). From John Henry to Captain Marvel, American heroes are allowed latitude, running the gamut from martyrs to infallible superheroes, with plenty of room in between for redeemed failures like Walt Disney, fired from the *Kansas City Star* because his editor felt that he "lacked imagination and had no good ideas."

Icarus's sin was not that he flew; it was rather that he flew too high, ignoring his father's warning. But how high is too high? Unlike that ill-fated flight of feathers and wax, Walters's technology never failed him. If anything, it worked too well, with *Inspiration I* showing no signs of returning to Earth until its pilot began sniping balloons. Unlike the son of Daedalus, the gods seemed to smile upon Walters, guiding him back to Earth safely, if a bit roughly; after all, becoming ensnared in powerlines and walking away unharmed is the very definition of good fortune. If the gods punished him, it happened only later, when depression, disappointment, and self-doubt eroded his will to live.

No, Walters did not crash, failing due to hubris. He did not crash or fail at all. Instead, he hit all the notes of American greatness: as inventor, as pioneer, as explorer, as maverick, as rebel, and as achiever. He had imagination. He had clarity of vision. He had daring and audacity. He was smart enough and strong enough to survive an act that would have killed most people. He was a self-made man, sculpting himself as he carved a social space for an unprecedented exploit. Most importantly, he aspired and lived his dream. As World War II pilot John Gillespie Magee put it in his 1941 poem "High Flight" (and as Pres. Ronald Reagan repeated in 1986, in the wake of the space shuttle *Challenger* disaster), Walters "slipped the surly bonds of Earth" and "touched the face of God."

Had he been born in the early Middle Ages, skaldic bards might have sung about his deeds in Old Norse. Instead, his exploits would percolate into American popular culture, which capitalized on the myth, often posthumously. Plotlines of the television shows *The A-Team* and *Hill Street Blues* in the 1980s featured amateur aviators buoyed by balloons, as did *SpongeBob SquarePants* and *King of the Hill* in the 1990s. The 2003 Australian film *Danny Deckchair* preceded Pixar's animated *Up*, which opened the 2009 Cannes Film Festival before grossing over $735 million as the studio's first film in Disney Digital 3-D; by tying hundreds of balloons to his house, *Up*'s Carl Frederickson (voiced by Ed Asner) is able to see the world and fulfil a promise to his late wife, Ellie. Real-life imitators eventually followed too. Today "cluster ballooning" has been featured on the Science Channel, the History Channel, TechTV, TLC, and MTV, as ballooners chase Guinness World Records for airtime, height, and distance. That Walters—one of the unsung heroes questing "out there" for his version of the American Dream—did not enjoy proper recognition in his lifetime or live to see the creative feats that he inspired is a somber coda to a classic American folktale.

Or so I figured. I couldn't really explain my interest in Walters. There was something about him—Larry the Mundane, Larry the Magnificent—that resonated. I think that, in my moments of cowardice as I pondered the road ahead with trepidation, I found something appealing in his bravery, something empowering in his damn-the-torpedoes-full-speed-ahead commitment to following his aspirations. Perhaps I saw something familiar regarding my own quixotic strivings. In California I was triangulating my American Dream. I was working hard toward my goal of becoming a professor, of learning not only all I could about US history but also the ins and outs of the profession. I was learning how to become a historian. Walters might have been a cautionary tale for some, but for me, he was a muse. Here was a regular guy who went for it: an Average Joe who surprised himself and everyone else around him by reaching out and grasping his dream. Perhaps I, against all odds and against whatever deficits I might have, could do the same. If Walters was a hero of sorts, then perhaps I could become the hero in my own story too.

My daydreams about Lawnchair Larry stopped hard as I was struck by a momentary dizziness—a gaping sensation that made the whole world ephemeral, quivering like a mirage—and then my attention snapped back to the road. A touch of sun blindness, perhaps? A touch of existential crisis? When I glanced up again the weather balloon was no longer visible. I rubbed my eyes. Nothing. A few miles ahead I pulled over for gas and a needed rest.

As the pump handle glugged, I slopped unsoapy water on the bay window, dragging a squeegee across a bloody mosaic of smooshed bugs.

Sometimes while driving you have full pano-vision, a kind of optical omniscience, and the view through the bay window of a VW Bus is particularly commanding and cycloramic in this respect. From its high driver's seat, through its wide expanse of glass, one can see everything ahead and to either side. Magnifying and clarifying, the windshield acts as a telescope, bringing the world to you. At other times, particularly at night, things flit past on the periphery, flickering on the side of the road as you go by, phantoms and apparitions on the shoulder. There is a fine line between the real and the imagined, particularly at sixty-five miles per hour in the dark, but that line exists in full daylight too. Maybe there hadn't been a weather balloon at all. Maybe it was a just a glob of crud, a chip in the glass. Regardless, I was reminded in eastern Washington that, day or night, you can't see much through a dirty windshield. *Lesson #4: Keep your eyes on the road and your windscreen clean.* Scrubbing as best I could, leaving a dull smear on the glass, I clambered back into the Bus and pressed on.

4

The M-Factor

September 1998: The toilet bowl yawned up at me. I yawned back. It was 6:28 a.m. according to my wristwatch—a cheap digital Casio, not nearly as snazzy as Larry Walters's Timex chronograph—at a no-name motel somewhere off I-90. It had been two weeks into the trip before I had taken off the watch and another week before I put it back on, realizing that a watch helps to structure the day even if a person has nowhere to be. Releasing the urban tempos of the Bay Area and the intense pace of graduate school, I was relaxing into the rhythms of the road. Rather than taking the trip, I let the trip take me.

After a few weeks on the road, I was settling into a kind of routine, or as much of a routine as one can have on an unplanned, rather aimless, open-ended road trip. The day-to-day travel became familiar, comforting in its regularity. I'd drive for a while—sometimes only an hour or two, sometimes up to eight hours, but usually around five or six hours—sightsee along the way, then find a place to bed down. The beauty of the camper van was that I could be indiscriminate about the latter.

Sleeping in the Bus was an adventure; but, parked in a good spot with the curtains drawn, it was quite pleasant and comfortable, a cozy cave. The interior was carefully and thoughtfully appointed, like the cabin of a yacht, and while it wasn't luxurious, everything was located within arm's reach, with nooks and shelves to squirrel away small items. The floor was carpeted underfoot, and with the top popped, there was plenty of headroom.

Fig. 4: The occasional motel offered a shower and soft bed. Photo by author.

I'd drop the tan-colored, vinyl backseat into its bed configuration and stretch out, head in the center of the vehicle and feet pointed toward the rear hatch. A sleeping bag and pillow offered a comfy nest. A battery-powered lantern and flashlight provided light by which to read.

I preferred to get off the beaten path and car camp in a natural area—a park or patch of woods—but I'd also pullover and sleep on the side of the road or in a parking lot if I were tired and couldn't find a camping spot. If I liked that place, I'd stay a while and explore. If I didn't, I'd keep rolling. Most nights found me discreetly tucked off the road, secreted away in a quiet pocket away from traffic and passersby. When I started to ripen, and needed more than a quick, splashy birdbath at a rest-stop sink, then I'd pull over at a motel for a proper shower and civilized sleep in a real bed, as I'd enjoyed last night.

A few slugs of coffee and I was on my way into Idaho, whose crisp air awakened me more than the motel-lobby Maxwell House did. I had already gotten into the habit of driving with the driver's- and passenger's-side windows open; if that got too loud or too cold, then I would at least crack the valances to get some ventilation. Like other cars of their vintage, VW Buses have a small-paneled window called a quarter panel, quarter light, quarter glass, or vent glass: a movable, triangular valance in front of the standard, roll-down, side windows. A little push-knob pivots the glass outward, ramming fresh air directly into the vehicle. In autumn it was cooler than the coldest A/C vent, and the constant breeze kept me alert while driving. Plus, more windows meant more visibility all around, and there was so much to see.

It was Thoreau who suggested (somewhat disparagingly) that most of the people he met in Boston were not really awake, shambling through life half asleep, unattuned to their surroundings. His transcendentalist writings all screamed the same basic message: *Wake up!* I supposed that was one of the reasons I was traveling: to wake up and experience America and not discover later as a classroom instructor that I was teaching others about places I'd never seen and known firsthand. It was a peculiarly American kind of worry, born in mid-nineteenth-century transcendentalism and Romanticism when intuition offered a compelling counterpoint to reason. Emerson and Thoreau and the other transcendentalists were learned, educated, well-read scholars who also sensed that life itself was a great teacher. It would be a disservice to the transcendentalists to see them as jettisoning erudition and scholarship for experience alone, but their writings did signal a shift in American thought toward experiential education and firsthand knowledge. Some of the great thinkers of the Romantic Age touted unlocking the mind not through reading and meditation but through hands-on education, as in Walt Whitman's 1865 poem "When I Heard the Learn'd Astronomer":

> When I heard the learn'd astronomer,
> When the proofs, the figures, were ranged in columns
>   before me,
> When I was shown the charts and diagrams, to add, divide,
>   and measure them,
> When I sitting heard the astronomer where he lectured
>   with much applause in the lecture-room,
> How soon unaccountable I became tired and sick,
> Till rising and gliding out I wander'd off by myself,
> In the mystical moist night-air, and from time to time,
> Look'd up in perfect silence at the stars.

Whitman's emphasis on experiential learning is still felt in the way we privilege eyewitness testimony—*I was there! I saw it with my own eyes!* Since his time, Americans have readily adopted the view that thinking and imagining are no substitutes for going and being and seeing. For many, "book learning" is no stand-in for experience, and while I, too, felt I could teach better if I could say that I'd been there, to Yellowstone and Gettysburg and the Edmund Pettus Bridge and all the other theres out there, I was mostly just restless and curious.

The few hours I spent in Idaho—the Gem State—left me clamoring for more but also wary. I crossed the Idaho Panhandle on I-90 from the Washington State line through Coeur d'Alene toward Montana, along one of the prettiest stretches of interstate anywhere in the nation. Softwoods like western white pine, red cedar, and firs edged the highway; beyond them lay fields of wheat, lentils, peas, and rapeseed, which is used to make canola oil. Coeur d'Alene is surrounded by dozens of lakes, none grander than Lake Coeur d'Alene itself, which sparkles brightly in the cool sunlight. It feels more like the Pacific Northwest than the Upper Rockies, this land of the Kootenai and Nez Perce Indians.

All is not as it seems, however, in this corner of the world. I knew something about the region's fraught relationship with white supremacy. Aryan Nations leader Richard Butler had established a stronghold here in Hayden Lake, on the outskirts of Coeur d'Alene, where he bought a forty-acre farmstead in the early 1970s. Butler—who shared the antitax, antigovernment views of the Posse Commitatus—was a proponent of the Northwest Territorial Imperative, the idea that white folks deserve their own homeland and that the rural expanse of northern Idaho, northeastern Washington, and western Montana—where land was cheap, sparsely populated, and already majority white—was the right spot for it. Surrounding himself with muscle—young skinheads and neo-Nazis—he built out his compound, complete with a church he used to spread Christian Identity teachings, less theology than racist ideology. In 1982 he began hosting an annual summer festival, the Aryan World Congress, where white supremacists from across the nation gathered, not only Christian Identity believers but also Ku Klux Klansmen, neo-Nazis, Odinists, militiamen, pro-gun zealots, and antigovernment activists who disavowed the authority of the US federal government. Via newsletter, he reached out to inmates and former inmates and to struggling local farmers with families who were offered a free place to stay in exchange for participation in his movement. Seclusion offered freedom from outside interference, as did Butler's registration of the property as a 501(c)(3) nonprofit, the Church of Jesus Christ-Christian. Only when they began to disseminate racist flyers and pamphlets indiscriminately did they clash with locals who did not share such views.

The group maligned minorities and inspired violent splinter cells. David Lane, who organized for the Aryan Nations in Colorado, met Robert Jay Matthews at the Aryan World Congress at Hayden Lake in 1983. Matthews invited Lane to join him in the Order, which during its brief but destructive lifespan in 1983–84 counterfeited money, hijacked armored cars, and murdered Alan Berg, an outspoken Jewish radio show host in Denver. Butler was able to disavow these violent actions and disassociate himself, though he secretly reveled in the mayhem and used it to continue to recruit and strengthen his base. In the mid-1980s, the Aryan Nations began hosting skinhead music festivals. In 1989, the group hosted a one hundredth birthday party for Adolph Hitler. By the mid-1990s the Aryan Nations was at the height of its power, marching openly in the streets of Coeur d'Alene.

THE M-FACTOR • 51

Seventy miles north, in the Selkirk Mountain range near Naples, Idaho, lies Ruby Ridge, where a deadly showdown occurred at Randy Weaver's cabin in 1992. The standoff between Weaver, accused of federal firearms violations (namely sawing off a shotgun barrel to an illegal length), and the US Bureau of Alcohol, Tobacco, and Firearms (ATF) and Federal Bureau of Investigation (FBI), who sought to use the firearms charges to coerce Weaver to inform on the Militia of Montana and other extremists in the area, occurred after Weaver, who had attended some of Butler's rallies in Hayden Lake, failed to show up for a court appearance. A federal judge issued a bench warrant for his arrest; a grand jury indicted him for failure to appear in court; and US marshals were ordered to pick him up. The situation grew progressively more dangerous, moving from standoff to gun battle to a siege of the Weavers' cabin by federal agents. The Weavers' fourteen-year-old son, Sammy (who became an active participant in the gun battle after agents shot and killed the family dog) was killed by gunfire, as was US marshal William F. Degan. Weaver's wife, Vicki, was shot to death by an FBI sniper while standing in the cabin door with her ten-month-old daughter in her arms. Weaver and his friend Kevin Harris, who fired the shot that killed Degan, were wounded, finally surrendering more than a week later. Weaver was sentenced to eighteen months behind bars and fined $10,000 for missing his original court date and violating his bail conditions. To some, what happened at Ruby Ridge represented the overreach of a federal government that liberally applied force in dealing with its own citizens. The incident inspired a generation of antigovernment attitudes and organizations. To others, Ruby Ridge symbolized the growing danger of militias, extremists, and white supremacists: mistrustful in equal parts of their government and their fellow citizens, amassing firearms, and training in paramilitary tactics.

A few months before I drove through, an incident occurred in Hayden Lake that resulted in the demise of the Aryan Nations. In July 1998, guards at the compound mistook a car backfire for gunfire, chased down two passing motorists, terrorized them, and beat them. In 1999, the Southern Poverty Law Center filed a lawsuit on behalf of the motorists, Victoria and Jason Keenan. In 2001, a jury ruled that Butler and the Aryan Nations had been "grossly negligent" in failing to supervise and control the activities of its guards. The jury awarded $6.3 million in damages to the Keenans. The judgment crippled the group and resulted in seizure of the compound; its leadership in shambles, the organization fell apart. The compound was donated to North Idaho College, which planned to turn the twenty-acre compound into a peace park, and local firefighters burned and doused the eleven Aryan Nation buildings for practice; but, memories of Hayden Lake and Ruby Ridge lingered. Many of the same players are still here, the ideas and the history too, blowing in the winds across Lake Coeur d'Alene, repeated in tiny millenarian churches in the Idaho backwoods, where a few scared and scary white folks arm up and await the apocalypse.

Three things crossed my mind as I drove across this foreboding sliver of Idaho. First, I knew that if I were Black or Latino or Native American or Asian or Jewish or Catholic or pretty much anything other than white, Anglo-Saxon, and Protestant, then I would have been pretty damn uncomfortable here. Even so I did not feel wholly at ease. If I were anyone else I wouldn't be sightseeing in these environs, and if I *did* have to be here, my foot would have found the floorboard as I hurried to somewhere else. Second, it occurred to me that the Idaho Panhandle is not unique with regard to white supremacist sentiment findable here. Racist thoughts and attitudes exist everywhere across the United States: in the South, in the North, in the Midwest, and in the Southwest. They were only a bit more concentrated in places like Hayden Lake, where they found solace and company, at least until the decent majority rose up, spoke out, and made them unwelcome. Third and finally, I realized that (*Lesson #5*) a trip like this one was a white man's prerogative. Women and people of color knew better than to travel alone. As a white man, I was fortunate even to be able to contemplate a trip like this one, let alone take it. I was not immune to getting hassled on the road (as I would learn), but I was better inoculated than many. If you happen to be a white man, then the world is your oyster, the automobile your shucking knife.

For me, the road trip was an exercise in self-discovery, as it was for Kerouac and Steinbeck and Pirsig and others who'd chronicled their journeys. To read their narratives is to view the open road as a therapist's couch, of sorts, capable of unlocking the self. But what of the Nez Perce Indians, forcibly removed from ancestral homelands in the Pacific Northwest and relocated to a smaller reservation here in the Idaho Territory, who resisted and fled Gen. O. O. Howard and the US Army, which cornered them in Montana? Or Brigham Young and the early Mormons, chased by bigots from Illinois to the sterile Great Salt Lake of Utah? What of their journeys? A tale of two Josephs—Chief Joseph and Joseph Smith—reveals a different kind of American road trip. For some like me it was a pleasure cruise, for others a long, tortuous path. There is clearly a danger in romanticizing the American road, in presenting a distorted view of the highway and its freedoms. As Rafia Zakaria notes, pretending that road travel is ennobling may foment "a new genre of virtue signaling that is smugly uncritical of the injustices of who gets to travel and why." Travel stories are often told by white men who sentimentalize the road. It's not that others aren't traveling too, but white male stories dominate this subgenre of travel lit because the adventure is safer: "danger" without true menace.

On the edge of the Coeur d'Alene city limits I pulled over, stopping for lunch at a diner, the old kind that looks like a cross between an Airstream travel trailer and a tuna can. There are places in the United States where one can find only fast-food franchises and there are places—little rural towns in the South and urban neighborhoods in the Northeast and long, long stretches of road in the American West—without a single chain restaurant, not a McDonald's or Shoney's in sight, only family-owned and -operated eateries. I was entering one of those stretches. When traveling, I prefer local flavor anyway and can't understand why someone, given the choice, would opt for the uniformity and blandness of a chain. I winced, stretched, and ambled in, finding a place at the counter. The scrubbers were shot, the air infused with an appealing combination of grilled cheese, Denver omelets, and burnt hamburgers.

Before I had left the Bay Area, a friend had suggested picking a particular food and sampling it across the country in a quest to find the best. My first thought was barbecue, but there were so many different varieties: oak-smoked brisket in Central Texas, mesquite-smoked baby-back ribs in South Texas, hickory-smoked burnt ends in Kansas City, chopped pork sandwiches with vinegar sauce in North Carolina, whole hog with mustard sauce in South Carolina, dry-rub spareribs in Memphis. BBQ was too divergent. I needed something simpler—diner fare that could be found everywhere, something uncomplicated that could be compared across different regions, something that I wouldn't get tired of. I landed on pie in my quest for the nation's best, and for whatever reason, I chose coconut cream pie in particular.

A youngish waitress filling coffee cups along the counter paused long enough to slide a menu in my general direction. She looked at me. "Where you headed?" she inquired.

"Driving cross-country," I replied, nodding in the direction of the van, visible through the diner's front window.

"In that?" She looked at me anew, harder. Then, almost giddily, she blurted, "Take me with you."

I glanced up and realized that, for a fraction of a fraction of a second, she was absolutely serious, ready to rip off her apron and wad it into a ball and throw it in the face of the manager and flip him the bird as she slammed open the front door with both hands and burst into the parking lot with a whoop, free of concern and obligation and accountability, pulling the ripcord as she flung herself out the plane door, and the look in her eye compelled me for a split-second to consider the same, her climbing into the passenger seat and roaring off with me toward Anything-but-the-Tedium-of-the-Diner.

And then it was gone, the bubble popped. As quickly as it appeared, the twinkle in her eye extinguished, all nonsense aside, and everything was safe again, just two people exchanging pleasantries. "Sure," I grinned. "Climb aboard." She smiled good-naturedly, mouthing something about not having enough sick days, and went back to pouring coffee down the line.

I wasn't vain enough to think that she wanted to go with me specifically, and I knew that she didn't really want to drop what she was doing and leave her life behind. But I realized that something about hitting the road without any real destination or plan was deeply appealing to a lot of people; the fact that this scene repeated itself on at least two other occasions during the course of this same trip told me as much. People were ready—or at least pretended to be ready—to stop what they were doing on the spot and climb into a rust bucket on wheels with a random stranger who had never offered to take them anywhere. Maybe it was the prospect of sloughing off the humdrum of the daily grind, or maybe it was the romance of spontaneity. But I liked to imagine that it was something more ingrained: the manifestation of a deeply American need to be out there, the siren song of the open road. *Lesson #6: Like Huckleberry Finn, many Americans appreciate the option to "light out."*

In a 1962 *American Quarterly* article titled "The M-Factor in American History," George Wilson Pierson isolates three components—movement, migration, and mobility—that allow Americans the ability to reposition geographically to realize their desires and ambitions. For Pierson, this "M-Factor" is a crucial part of the American character, a defining element of the American Dream. Americans can always go. No papers, no border crossings—just open roads and fresh starts. It's a large part of what it means to be American, this ability to move. Lewis and Clark explored. Crockett roamed. Douglass fled. Earhart flew. King marched. Dean careened. Gump ran. Citizens of this republic have never needed to make do where they are: they could pick up and leave, going to where opportunity could be found. The frontier held this promise, with its bonanzas, its booms, and its busts. Even after the closing of the frontier, however, which Frederick Jackson Turner prophesied in 1893, westward movement—into the hinterlands, away from population centers—promised what Richard Slotkin recognized as regeneration.

It may be that the American people are migratory and restless, hard to pin down, and easily lured from place to place. It may also be that working-class Americans have been historically buffeted by economic forces wresting them from comfort and security, and that what initially seems to be romantic wanderlust is in fact a mobility born of harsh necessity. Some scholars trace these migrations to the nineteenth century, some earlier, but the trend certainly continued into the twentieth century: by the 1976 bicentennial, one in four or five Americans were moving each year. "It might be argued that most fundamentally the historical geography of North America is a study of the forces that cause men to move," wrote John C. Hudson that same year, "starting with the transatlantic migration itself and carrying on through the wanderings over the continent the migrants reached."

Whether migration is a way of life or merely a response to external stimuli may prompt arguments among historians and geographers, but the answer is crucial to understanding *why* Americans move. The US Census Bureau has been collecting and tabulating data on residential mobility for more than 150 years. The Census Bureau began with questions about state of birth in the 1850 census. The 1940 census introduced a fixed-period migration question (where a person lived five years ago) and queried information on origin and destination too, yielding a wealth of knowledge about Americans as rootless individuals and their accompanying social and economic characteristics. As a result, the existing database on geographical mobility is fairly rich in terms of both historical perspective and the characteristics of migrants.

Traditional sources of geographical mobility data, namely cross-sectional surveys, indicate that slightly less than 20 percent of Americans change their place of residence each year, but these surveys do little to contextualize movement, conveying little about the circumstance surrounding a person's move. In the late 1980s, Donald C. Dahmann and Edith K. McArthur at the Census Bureau figured out how to apply the Survey of Income and Program Participation (SIPP)—which provides longitudinal or time-series data, designed to account for a variety of life-course transitions over time—to this conundrum. Using SIPP data, they found a correlation between various forms of geographic mobility and joint-incidence of life events such as marriage, job change (or loss), and retirement. We now recognize these events as major stressors, in part because they result in displacement and dislocation, both psychological and physical. SIPP data indicates that Americans tend to move in August, rather than the winter months; that renters move more often than homeowners; and that people move for a variety of reasons, some voluntary and some not. This information mostly confirms what we already know, jibing with commonsense.

The migrations of college students are likewise fairly predictable, though my own journey defied logic. Or did it? Leaving Berkeley might seem crazy, but if one can justify it in terms of self-care and mental health, then it made all the sense in the world. I closed my eyes and breathed deeply, feeling the inhalation behind my eyelids, exhaling slowly to the soft din of the diner: the clink of silverware on plates; the mumble of voices, conversations jumbled and decipherable only in snippets; footfalls; low tones and murmurings, the cadence of servers; occasional shouts from deep in the kitchen. I breathed in and out, meditatively munching the burger brought by my coconspirator/waitress. It was terrible. I finished it and ordered another (also terrible), chasing it with Coca-Cola and dessert. The coconut cream pie was pretty good, tasting like coconut cream pie. I was starting to uncoil, to enjoy the voyage, even though I had sped through certain places. While I had lingered in the Cascades, along the Oregon Coast, and in Seattle, I had blasted through Northern California, eastern Washington, and the Idaho panhandle. I felt like I had especially shortchanged Idaho, and frankly I had. Suffice it to say, I was in a hurry to get to Montana.

Perhaps it is the natural features, or the population density, or the name itself, but Montana had always held a special allure for this hiker. Carved out of the Idaho Territory in 1864, Montana seemed like an outdoorsman's paradise. Officially known as the Treasure State, Montana has abundant geological riches: from precious metals such as copper, gold, and silver to gemstones such as sapphires and garnets. But it has another nickname too, one popularized by the Montana Highway Department in the early 1960s. Adapted from the A. B. Guthrie novel *The Big Sky* (1947), which takes place primarily in preterritorial Montana, the Highway Department's moniker—Big Sky Country—had beckoned for as long as I could remember.

The largest landlocked state and the fourth largest in area behind Alaska, Texas, and California, Montana has a fraction of the people, as the eighth least populous and the third least densely populated. The Continental Divide splits the state into eastern and western halves. Most of the state's mountain ranges are in the west, extensions of the Northern Rocky Mountains, with the Absaroka and Beartooth ranges in the south-central part of the state extending up from the Central Rocky Mountains. The Bitterroot Mountains, one of the longest ranges between Alaska and Mexico, separates Montana from Idaho. Interestingly, 60 percent of the state is prairie, the northernmost section of the Great Plains. Smaller ranges, foothills, tableland prairies, buttes, and badlands—comprised of canyons, ravines, gullies, mesas, and hoodoos—can also be found here between the rich river valleys formed by the Clark Fork of the Columbia, Blackfoot, Bitterroot, Flathead, Missouri, and Yellowstone Rivers, among others. Montana has the largest grizzly bear population in the lower forty-eight states.

I had been warned before I got to Montana that my usual calling card—my accent, a mostly tempered Appalachian intonation—would not be as problematic as my California license plate. My accent, what little of it I had, was my distinguishing characteristic, an instantly recognizable signifier that pegged me as southern. Growing up, I had always been able to hear it in myself and in others, which is probably why I was able to modulate it and control it a bit. I was proud of my hometown, my region, and my heritage (much of it, at least), and I never consciously tried to downplay my accent, but as I ventured out of the South, I found that southerners were sometimes treated prejudicially by those who equated slow speech with slow thought. So I preferred to reveal my accent rather than have it reveal me. It was always there—hiding behind a drink or two, ready to come yawling out of my mouth when on the phone with family and friends back home—and it was not a particularly pretty inflection. The North Georgia accent is a nasal mountain twang, in which hard *i*'s never close to an *e* sound (just "aye," instead of "aye-ee"), and words without *r*'s gain them ("wash" becomes "warsh"). It was not the prettier Middle Georgia accent, the sonorous southern drawl of the piedmont below Atlanta, where *r*'s fell away and words like dollar became "dollah" and soldier "souljah."

Regardless, Montanans were OK with southerners, as far as I knew. It was Californians they hated. And why shouldn't they? Rapidly outgrowing their own overcrowded state, with its wildfires and Santa Ana winds and earthquakes and mudslides and race riots, white Californians were rapidly colonizing what William Kittredge, among others, has called "The Last Best Place," Montana. They brought with them their Audis and Starbucks lattes and higher prices and sanctimony. And while I considered myself to be Georgian, my long hair, VW Bus, and California tags marked me as Californian.

Having reached another destination, I slowed down and enjoyed the drive, heading southeast from Coeur d'Alene roughly along I-90 through small towns and cities like Wolf Lodge, Canyon, Blackcloud, Smelterville, Spring Gulch, Quartz, and Cyr. Motoring into Missoula was like arriving in a mountain hippy Shangri-La. College students from the University of Montana were everywhere, not even bothering to leave downtown to enjoy nature. They didn't need to, with the beautiful Clark Fork River coursing right through the middle of this bustling little city. Driving over the Higgins Street Bridge offered an aerial view of the river. I pulled over and got out, amazed by what I saw. Fly-fishermen stood in waders, waist-deep, flicking their rods expertly, popping their lures into just the right spot. Kayakers, skirted into short brightly colored plastic kayaks, danced down rapids, and softly preened down deeper stretches between the shoals. In Missoula these whitewater kayakers are called "surfers"; every fifth or sixth car, it seemed, had a kayak strapped to its roof rack. Hiking boots and Tevas were the footwear of choice.

To the northwest, across Caras Park, was a lovely jewel-box carousel, spinning ferociously. A Carousel for Montana, handcrafted by a local cabinetmaker, is one of the fastest merry-go-rounds anywhere, its steampowered, leather-belted motor replaced with a humming ten-horsepower

THE M-FACTOR • 59

unit. Kids and parents alike clutched the grab rings, not just for show. To the southwest stood the Boone and Crocket Club, headquartered in a historic railroad depot, crammed with the taxidermied husks of Montana's wildlife, shot and stuffed by Teddy Roosevelt and his hunting buddies. On either side of the bridge, restaurants, cafes, coffee houses, bars, and breweries dotted the low-slung urban center, its old brick warehouses refurbed into hip hangouts.

Walking down the street, I eavesdropped on a couple of twentysomething guys strolling behind me. "I have a friend who's a cutpurse at ren faires," one was saying.

"A what?"

"A cutpurse. Like a thief."

"Yeah, I know that a cutpurse is. I meant a ren faire."

"A Renaissance faire. You know—where people dress up and eat turkey legs."

"Yeah, I've heard of it, just never been."

"Oh, it's wild. Everyone dresses up like medieval times: knights and ladies and squires and shit. There's merchants and peasants and wizards and ogres, maybe some fairies and elves, all sorts of stuff—comely wenches and all that. They watch jousts and get wasted on mead and ale and say 'Huzzah' and 'Well met' and 'The privies be yon, lubberwort.'"

"Sounds fun."

"Oh, it's *nuts*. And my buddy travels around the country going to these ren faires. He's dressed out too. Breeches and jerkin—a tunic or something, funny hat. And he's goofing and acting like this old-timey pickpocket, and talking like he's in Tudor England, and everybody thinks he's an actor, part of the show. But—get this—he's not. He's a goddamn thief. He's in there stealing people's purses and wallets for real. And when he gets caught, he just plays it off like it's part of the show. He laughs and returns everything and plays it off and moves on to the next faire. It's bananas . . ." The rest of the conversation drifted away as they crossed to the other side of the street. I considered following, wanting to hear more about the itinerant cosplayer with light fingers.

Perhaps it was the time of year, that last moment of balmy weather before the long winter, but everything felt right here. Like many college towns, Missoula had a good vibe. The students were outside, soaking up the sun: walking, biking, paddling, fishing, or just lazing about in the city

60 · CHAPTER 4

parks and spots of grass. I also knew a friend of a friend who lived here, offering a spare futon, a hot shower, and a soft landing spot. So I settled into Missoula, in no particular hurry to leave.

After a few days of R&R, I plotted an excursion to the north to see Glacier National Park, rumored to be one of the most beautiful places on the continent. Glacier had come into being in the same way as other national parks, imperiled and under threat. Humans had long inhabited this area, with Salish and Kootenai Indians occupying the valleys west of the Clark Range, Lewis Range, Livingston Range—all part of the Rocky Mountains—over which they traveled to hunt the great buffalo herds and other game on the eastern prairies, land of the Blackfeet. European explorers came in search of beaver and other fur-bearers, followed by miners and then land-hungry settlers. The Great Northern Railway, completed in 1891, allowed more people to enter northwestern Montana. Homesteaders settled in the valleys west of Marias Pass, and small towns sprouted. A few people, including George Bird Grinnell, noticed that the once limitless wilderness was quickly disappearing and pushed for the creation of a protected space, which in 1910 was signed into being by Pres. William H. Taft as the nation's tenth national park. In 1932 Glacier was joined with Watertown Lakes National Park in Alberta to create the first international peace park, which *National Geographic* has described as "a contiguous high-country wonderland of rock, ice, water, and wood." This "Crown of the Continent" contains some of the most impressive mountain scenery anywhere in North America.

I noted the dip in temperature as I headed north out of Missoula along Highway 93 toward the Flathead Reservation. Cold, I stopped at a western wear shop where I made my two biggest purchases of the trip: a thick, cable-knit, wool sweater and a Carhartt chore coat. The jacket, while "only" canvas, was made of triple-stitched, heavy-duty cotton duck with a blanket lining. It was water-repellent and wind-resistant, good enough for local farmhands and ranchers and therefore good enough for me. With its slightly longer cut, I thought it would keep my rear-end toasty while sitting and driving in the van. Between the sweater and coat I might, with any luck at all, not freeze to death.

A lovely church beckoned from the roadside in St. Ignatius, a small town built by Jesuit priests in 1854 on the Flathead Indian Reservation. Built in the early 1890s near the state's first Catholic school, the

St. Ignatius Mission Church was relocated a few miles south of a fur-trading post from its original site near Lake Pend d'Oreille, where the Jesuits furiously baptized as many local Indians as they could in the late 1840s. The current structure—a vernacular, Gothic revival building made of native clay brick—is notable for its fifty-eight original paintings by Brother Joseph Carignano covering its walls and ceilings; two of the most distinctive paintings depict the Salish Lord and Lord's mother in Native American form. I picked up a placard on the way out titled "An Indian Prayer," which read:

> O Great Spirit,
> Whose voice I hear in the winds,
> And whose breath gives life to all the world,
> hear me! I am small and weak, I need your strength and wisdom.
> Let me walk in beauty, and make my eyes ever behold the
>   red & purple sunset.
> Make my hands respect the things you have made and my ears
>   sharp to hear your voice.
> Make me wise so that I may understand the things you have
>   taught my people.
> Let me learn the lesson you have hidden in every leaf and rock.
> I seek strength, not to be greater than my brother, but to
>   fight my greatest enemy—myself.
> Make me always ready to come to you with clean hands and
>   straight eyes.
> So when life fades, as the fading sunset, my spirit may come
>   to you without shame.

It was different from anything I'd ever seen or read, but recognizing a great prayer when I hear one, I offered it up as my own, hoping the Salish wouldn't mind as I walked outside into the afternoon sun.

The presence of Native Americans in this part of the world was fascinating to me. I had grown up near New Echota, the historic capital of the Cherokee Nation, and my home state had many Indian place-names; the rivers of my youth were the Conasauga, Chattooga, Oostanaula, Chattahoochee, and Nantahala. Where I grew up, however, there were few Native Americans remaining, most having been force-marched along the Trail of

Tears in the late 1830s at bayonet point by the US Army (with some mixed-blood descendants staying behind). The Cherokee followed the other Civilized Tribes—the Creek, Choctaw, Chickasaw—westward to the Indian Territory, leaving only the unvanquished Seminole to the south in Florida. While their historical presence was still felt, and half the white folks you met seemed to claim some fraction of "Cherokee blood," in Georgia one couldn't easily find full-blooded Native Americans. In the Southeast they were everywhere yet nowhere; here in the Northwest they were omnipresent and irrepressible, even managing to "Indianize" the Catholic mission planted at St. Ignatius to civilize them.

From St. Ignatius I drove north through Kicking Horse toward Kalispell and Whitefish, veering off toward the park's west entrance at West Glacier. At the turn of the twentieth century, newspapers had touted Glacier's alpine scenery and plentiful glaciers as reasons to visit. Montana lured visitors with new hotels, chalets, and horse trails through the backcountry, and the Great Northern Railway offered a quick and convenient way to get to the park; but, in the century's second decade, automobiles were growing in popularity and motorists demanded new roads through the park. The plan for the first thoroughfare called for fifteen switchbacks to get up and over Logan Pass, but the final version, cut into the rock cliffs in the late 1920s, included only one switchback.

The result was Going-to-the-Sun Road, the only road that traverses Glacier National Park. The narrow, two-lane road winds for fifty miles, crossing the Continental Divide through Logan Pass at an elevation of 6,646 feet, the road's highest point. It is typically only open from July through late October; deep snowdrifts block passage the rest of the year. It is one of the most difficult roads in North America to plow in the springtime. On the east side of the Continental Divide, there are few guardrails due to heavy snows and the resultant late-winter avalanches that have repeatedly destroyed every protective barrier ever constructed. The speed limit is forty-five miles per hour in lower elevations and twenty-five in the alpine sections, where rockslides pose a constant threat. Not for the fainthearted, it is a harrowing road with steep drop-offs, hairpin turns, blind curves, rock overhangs, and vehicle restrictions by weight, height, and width. It is also one of the most spectacular roads anywhere, consistently rated one of the most rewarding mountain roads in America, a model for automotive touring. Going-to-the-Sun Road offers alpine lakes, scenic valleys, mountain peaks, waterfalls, glaciers, mountain goats, bighorn sheep, and majestic views in all directions.

From the park's western entrance, the road crossed the Middle Fork Flathead River, passed the Apgar Visitor Center and Campground, hugged the shore of Lake McDonald, and unwound to the northeast, gaining elevation with views of over a dozen peaks, including Gunsight Mountain, Little Matterhorn, Almost-a-Dog Mountain, and Mount Logan. It crossed Red Rock Point, threading between Glacier Wall and Bird Woman Falls, between Haystack Butte and Mount Oberlin. Carpets of mosses and ferns—bracken ferns, beech ferns, moonwort ferns, club mosses, and rough horsetail—blanketed the roadside beneath mixed conifer forests of cedar and hemlock, with a few lodgepole pines, Douglas firs, and Ponderosa pines for variety. Fungi ranged from edible morels and chanterelles to lethal deathcaps and the deadly fly amanitas. As the road climbed into the subalpine zone, spruce and fir predominated, with whitebark pine growing near the timberline. Lichens, those strange combinations of fungus and algae, covered the not-so-barren rocks.

One of the more interesting mosses in the park is sphagnum, an aquatic species whose competitive strategies include acidifying the surrounding waters to inhibit the growth of other plants. Growing in mats, sphagnum is superabsorbent, holding water many times its own weight. Its acidity makes it antiseptic, good for wound dressing, and resistant to decay, making it good for chinking log cabins. Native Americans once used it as a kind of disposable baby diaper.

The twenty-five-mile-per-hour speed limit was no inhibition because the Bus couldn't drive any faster. I slowed to a crawl, inching higher along this beautiful and terrifying road. If I didn't need both hands on the steering wheel I would have pressed on the dashboard for a little extra push. At one point I imagined pulling the vehicle, yoked to my shoulders like an Iditarod sled dog, mushing and straining up the incline. Mostly I just concentrated on staying in my lane while my head swiveled, marveling at the vistas and precipitous cliffs. In the Cascades I had felt scared *in* the Bus; on this leg of the journey I felt scared *of* the Bus. Driving it was strenuous on a regular day—no power steering here—but keeping it on the Going-to-the-Sun Road was a real challenge, a full-body workout. It seemed to want to lunge off the mountainside—a bulbous swan dive right over the edge—and at times it felt more like flying than driving. Swinging around sharp bends, I felt more air beneath the van than asphalt. Time and space slipped. Under my hands the steering wheel strained; under the van the road again assumed reality.

Cresting the Continental Divide, the Bus heaved into the parking lot at Logan Pass, the highest elevation reachable by car in the park, and I wiped my sweaty hands on my shirt. Diminutive wildflowers, many coated in waxy cuticles to conserve moisture and fine hairs to trap heat and diffuse ultraviolent light at high elevation, dotted the meadows here; northern eyebright, three-flowered rush, and false alphodel—the kinds of plants found in places like Greenland—are well adapted to the harsh conditions of the alpine zone. Visitors disgorged from their overheating cars, stretched their legs, sucked down soft drinks from the concession, and pointed at a pair of grizzly bears foraging a couple of hundred yards away on the far side of an alpine rift below the visitors center. While everyone else looked at the bears, I looked at everyone else: sizing up the other people looking across the ravine, mainly nondescript tourists excitedly snapping pics from too far away with disposable, yellow-cardboard cameras. One man stood out, wearing Merrill hiking books, khakis, a North Face parka, a crimped baseball cap. His clothes were muted in color, some of it camouflage. His array of equipment—Zeiss binoculars, a serious thirty-five millimeter camera with enormous telephoto lens mounted on a tripod, a spotting scope on a second tripod—was impressive. The crow's feet on his tanned face indicated a man who had spent considerable time squinting into the sun. It was not his first rodeo. That's him, I thought, that's my guy. I sidled over, and within moments, he asked if I wanted a closer look at the grizzlies through his scope. Yessir, I did.

We chatted as I zoomed in on the bears. Bill had worked for the USFS until he injured his back; retiring from the Forest Service, he had become a professional photographer, working in and around Glacier. He sold his pics to the government, to magazines and travel brochures, to anyone interested in high-quality photos of Montana's wild side.

The bears were a *lot* bigger and closer through the looking glass. One of them, looking for grubs, sniffed around a boulder the size of a large suitcase. Wedging its massive paw beneath the rock, the bruin flicked its paw and the boulder tumbled fifteen or twenty feet to the bottom of the rift. Casually, effortlessly, it flipped the boulder out of its way as if it were a garbage can lid.

It occurred to me as we talked that there was nothing separating me and the photographer from the two grizzlies capable of running at thirty-five miles per hour top speed. An observer once timed a grizzly traveling over a quarter mile at a sustained speed of thirty miles per hour. On multiple occasions, scientists in Yellowstone have clocked grizzlies running upwards of twenty-five miles per hour "at a rolling lope" over two miles. A twelve-second sprint to the bottom and up our side of the ravine would bring six hundred pounds of tooth and claw into our immediate personal space. Happy to view *Ursus arctos horriblis* from afar, I pulled away from the spotting scope and the beasts shrank to a comfortably small size, two brown blobs rummaging in the distance.

The peaks atop the pass cast knife-edge shadows, lengthening at dusk. We hung out with the bears until dark, at which point it seemed prudent to retire. I tucked the Bus into a corner of the parking lot as night fell, glad to be in a hard-sided vehicle rather than a nylon tent.

Watching the bears, I had felt for the first time in my life a bit like meat. Bears prefer grubs. The grizzlies would eat me instead of grubs should the opportunity arise, but here's the funny part—so would the grubs. I imagined that grizzly bear claws could make an effective can opener (or van opener), but whether the bears eat you or the grubs do, we're all just food in the end. There's nothing savage or horrible in this observation: it's a small fact that we are going to die. What is truly morbid is the inability to admit it—to deceive ourselves and act as if this existence is not fleeting, to be anything other than thankful for each moment in this exquisitely detailed and wondrous world. *Lesson # 7: Life is temporal. Be grateful for it.*

That night, beneath a nail clip moon and night sky as black as ground pepper, I slept soundly, dreaming of big things eating small things eating big things, a great wheel turning like a Volkswagen hubcap.

5

The Ghosts of Montana

Why I awoke thinking of pie, a nontraditional breakfast food, I cannot say, but I found myself like any good knight fixated on my quest. A quality coconut cream pie involves a light, fluffy center. It's different from a coconut custard pie, which has a baked filling made with an egg-and-milk-cream custard that sets up in the oven. Coconut cream pie is technically a custard too, but it's cooked on the stove and chilled until set. The key is proper thickening. While whisking, you pour one-half cup of nearly boiling milk into an egg yolk mixture, then—while still whisking madly—pour it all into a saucepan with a cornstarch slurry, cooking that until thickened, whisking constantly and vigorously to prevent curdling. If you get it right, it tastes like a day at the beach, ladies tanning on a cloud. If you don't, it's thin and watery—not unlike the reconstituted freeze-dried scrambled eggs I was currently pushing around a barely warm frying pan. Suffice it to say I was many, many miles from the nearest coconut cream pie and even further from the nearest beach.

From Logan Pass I enjoyed a couple of day hikes the next morning after the bears. I cut off a small piece of duct tape from a roll in the glove box and slapped it on a pink area on the side of my foot, beneath the plastic buckle of my Teva sandals. Friction is the hiker's worst enemy, with "hot spots" giving way to blisters, which give way to open sores and raw wounds. Moleskin is best, creating a second skin, and surgical tape works well too, but duct tape will do in a pinch, with the added bonus of serving multiple duties when called upon. With duct tape you can also repair a torn backpack, mend a broken tent pole—anything, really. I once saw my father, a firm believer in the restorative power of duct tape, reattach a trunk lid to a car with the stuff. I had learned from a master.

Cirrus clouds feathered like rolling breakers on a shoreline. On High Line Trail above the timberline, I was startled by a scrabbling sound on the talus alongside the trail: a group of bighorn sheep scrambled up the hillside behind me, shortcutting the switchback along which I had just hiked. The lead ram, with his massive spiraling horns, stood and stared at me with horizontal, rectangular pupils until he resumed his climb. A mile or so down Hidden Lake Trail, in a more thickly wooded section of the park, I came to a hot-pink paper sign, stapled to a wooden stake planted in the middle of the trail. WARNING, the sign cautioned, THIS TRAIL HAS BEEN CLOSED DUE TO GRIZZLY BEAR ACTIVITY. Wow, I thought, *now* you tell me . . . Why wasn't this sign posted at the trailhead? I did an about-face and hightailed it back to the visitors center, checking frequently over my shoulder for an ursine pursuer.

Leaving Logan's Pass, the road passed its namesake, Going-to-the-Sun Mountain. The dark, old-growth cedar and hemlock forests of the park's west side contrasted starkly with the more open forests, glades, and grasslands of the east side, where dry chinook winds bent trees into alien shapes along the high ridges above peaceful aspen groves below. Rough fescue, needlegrass, junegrass, timber oatgrass, and bluebunch wheatgrass cover the prairies. Clematis, pinesaps, Indian pipes, and purple asters offer subtle color amid the grasses.

The road spat me out in St. Mary, a tiny settlement on the edge of the Blackfeet Indian Reservation, about ten miles from the Canadian border. Southeastward toward Great Falls and Helena the traffic remained thin. Driving through Montana, one is struck by the vastness of the American West, a great plainscape of emptiness. It's the primary difference between the interior and exteriors: the wide-open, panoramic, agoraphobic enormity in between, easy to forget when glued to the coasts. I tried to imagine a sea of VW Buses covering the roadway, all rafted up, moving in sync across the Great Plains. It was difficult to picture, in part because physical spatiality has always fed the Dream. The United States is positively Texan in its dimensions. It must be a defining characteristic of America, this giant space without people and cars and habitation, and the solitude it affords. On a fundamental level, this country is about having the space, literally and metaphorically, to do your own thing.

Solitude and doing your own thing reminded me of a nineteenth-century easterner whose mind would have been blown by the western vistas I was seeing. In 1845, Henry David Thoreau set out from Concord, Massachusetts, to "live deliberately" in the woods by Walden Pond and to record his experiences in a volume simply titled *Walden*, which was published in 1854. A young New England essayist and poet, Thoreau heeded the call of his mentor, Ralph Waldo Emerson, to find inspiration not in the academic and aristocratic but in the unlettered and democratic. As Thoreau explains (in a passage responsive to Edmund Burke's eighteenth-century characterization of life being "nasty, brutish, and short"):

> I went to the woods because I wished to live deliberately, to front only the essential facts of life, and see if I could not learn what it had to teach, and not, when I came to die, discover that I had not lived. I did not wish to live what was not life, living is so dear; nor did I wish to practice resignation, unless it was quite necessary. I wanted to live deep and suck out all the marrow of life, to live so sturdily and Spartan-like as to put to rout all that was not life, to cut a broad swath and shave close, to drive life into a corner, and reduce it to its lowest terms, and, if it proved to be mean, why then to get the whole and genuine meanness of it, and publish its meanness to the world; or if it were sublime, to know it by experience, and be able to give a true account of it in my next excursion.

He lived there alone, subsisting mainly on the produce of his garden, from July 4, 1845, to September 6, 1847, roughly two years.

Despite Thoreau's hyperbolic descriptions of the perils and remoteness of Walden, he was never in harm's way. Neither an "errand into the wilderness" nor an expedition into the wilds, Thoreau's experiment was more of an extended nature visit: a respite in the woods. A casual twenty-five-minute stroll took Thoreau from his cabin to the main street in Concord, and he entertained visitors from town during his twenty-five month stay at Walden. Hostile Indians and large, dangerous animals had been driven from Walden long before Thoreau braved the little forest. Nor was he an accomplished outdoorsman. In one of the more unintentionally comedic scenes from *Walden*, Thoreau describes chopping a hole in the ice to fish during winter. After hacking his way into Walden Pond, he tosses the ax onto the ice, only to send it skittering across the frozen surface to plunge into a preexisting hole. He spent the rest of the day fishing—not for fish but for his axe, resting on the bottom of the lake.

At Walden Pond, Thoreau discovered a patch of nature in which God's splendor shone. His elegiac descriptions of the plants and animals and trees and lakes remain some of the most captivating examples of nature writing in American letters. For example, he describes a copse of trees as follows:

> Sometimes I rambled to pine groves, standing like temples, or like fleets at sea, full-rigged, with wavy boughs, and rippling with light, so soft and green and shady that the Druids would have forsaken their oaks to worship in them; or to the cedar wood beyond Flint's Pond, where the trees, covered with hoary blue berries, spiring higher and higher, are fit to stand before Valhalla, and the creeping juniper covers the ground with wreaths full of fruit; or to swamps where the usnea lichen hangs in festoons from the white spruce trees, and toadstools, round tables of the swamp gods, cover the ground, and more beautiful fungi adorn the stumps, like butterflies or shells, vegetable winkles; where the swamp-pink and dogwood grow, the red alder-berry glows like eyes of imps, the waxwork grooves and crushes the hardest woods in its folds, and the wild holly berries make the beholder forget his home with their beauty, and he is dazzled and tempted by nameless other wild forbidden fruits, too fair for mortal taste.

His writing elevates nature to mythic status, reiterating his notion that the natural world reflects the essence of the divine. In citing Druids and Valhalla and the "swamp gods," Thoreau invokes the holy. His description of forbidden fruits that dazzle and tempt recalls the Edenic nature of American wilds.

Thoreau's Walden was a fleeting wilderness, a vestige of an earlier period in American history. "When I first paddled a boat on Walden," he recounts, "it was completely surrounded by thick and lofty pine and oak woods, and in some of its coves grape-vines had run over the trees next the water and formed bowers under which a boat could pass." But in the time since he left "the woodchoppers have still further laid them waste, and now for many a year there will be no more rambling through the aisles of wood, with occasional vistas through you see the water." He rhetorically asks, "How can you expect the birds to sing when their groves are cut down?" and bemoans the fact that Concordians "who scarcely know where it [Walden Pond] lies" were considering channeling the pond's water "to the village in a pipe, to wash their dishes with!—to earn their Walden by the turning of a cock or drawing of a plug!"

In describing his life at Walden, Thoreau did not intend to advocate a hermit-like existence; instead, he sought to inspire his countrymen to seek deeper meaning in their lives through self-discovery and through communing with nature. "The mass of men lead lives of quiet desperation," he intones. "What is called resignation is confirmed desperation." Such characterizations won him few friends among his contemporaries, but his subsequent admirers recognized in his writings a clarion call to live more deliberately, cleanly, and simply. Thoreau's example presaged the stirrings not only of the conservation movement of the late nineteenth century but also the modern environmental movement. He continues to inspire and instruct those Americans seeking a more meaningful life, and what he did and observed at Walden continues to prick the conscience of Americans encased in lives of easy complacency and unadulterated materialism. He placed his faith not in mammon but in nature.

In homesteading at Walden, Thoreau defines two kinds of American Dream. His experiment in solitary living came to epitomize the American spirit of self-reliance and independence. It could be said that, in his embodiment of the pioneer spirit, Thoreau remains the most vivid example of American individualism. But there is another side to Thoreau. To read *Walden* as a paean to the self is a gross misreading of Thoreau's transcendentalist philosophies. While he is careful to encourage each person "to find out and pursue *his own way*, and not his father's or his mother's, or his neighbor's instead," Thoreau was not so individualistic as to shun what society required of responsible citizens. Part of living a fuller life is to challenge injustice whenever and wherever it crops up; his civil disobedience with regard to paying taxes to support the nation's war efforts in Mexico, and his outspokenness on the issue of slavery, testify to his compulsion to act not only as a moral *individual* but also as a good *citizen*. More importantly, he never loses sight of the communal dimension of life in the United States:

THE GHOSTS OF MONTANA • 71

> If a man has faith, he will cooperate with equal faith everywhere; if he has not faith, he will continue to live like the rest of the world, whatever company he is joined to. To cooperate in the highest as well as the lowest sense, means to *get our living together*. (emphasis in the original)

In this passage, Thoreau yokes individualism and communalism: faith enables a person not only to discover his or her own path but also to "cooperate" with others seeking their own paths. The emphasis is on "our" coexistence "together"—not on the individual. This reading of Thoreau is unconventional—most accounts highlight his emphasis on individualism, nothing more—but it's all there in the text. Marching to the beat of a different drummer, as Thoreau calls it, does not justify trampling the land or other people.

I had a professor at the University of Georgia, historian and biographer William S. McFeely, who liked to use the word *Thoreau* as a verb. Hiking across Oconee Forest Park, or walking along the river bordering the State Botanical Garden in Athens, Bill would Thoreau his way through the woods. When I came to the History Department at Le Conte Hall with mud on my boots, he asked if I'd been Thoreau-ing that day. While he never explicitly explained what he meant, I understood Thoreau-ing to entail a meandering yet mindful excursion, a kind of communing with nature, and I adopted that usage of the word as my own. I loved to Thoreau—and while it hadn't occurred to me before, perhaps this trip was a kind of Thoreau-ing too. If one can Thoreau by car, then perhaps the nomadic ambling and rambling of road trips reflect similar journeys roaming toward enlightenment.

Later that evening in camp, I looked up at the stars splashed across the sky: pinpricks in a theater backdrop, tiny holes in a black curtain. There was no moon. I could see the Milky Way, a rare treat in the East that's fairly common out West. I lay down staring up, trying to remember the constellations. I recognized Cassiopeia, the mother of Andromeda and vain queen who often boasted of her own beauty. She was easily recognizable, a lazy W anchored by five bright stars. It was an optimum time to see Cygnus the Swan, also known as the Northern Cross, the backbone of the galaxy within the Milky Way. There was the faint Aquarius, the simple angles of Aries, and the shallow V of Aquila, the eagle who bore Ganymede to Mount Olympus. I searched for the Gemini twins, Castor and Pollux, but couldn't find them.

Up or down, outer or inner, it seemed to come down to space. As Thoreau intuits, it's space that put the great in the great outdoors, giving the American landscape an incalculability and sublimity. Thinking under a big sky about the vastness of the American West, William Least Heat-Moon puts it this way:

> Space west of the line [between the East and the West] is perceptible and often palpable, especially when it appears empty, and it's that apparent emptiness which makes matter look alone, exiled, and unconnected. Those spaces diminish man and reduce his blindness to the immensity of the universe; they push him toward a greater reliance on himself, and, at the same time, to a greater awareness of others and what they do.

The paradox, which Least Heat-Moon recognizes, is that space out West also makes people and buildings and things more visible, more noticeable. As he puts it, "Things show up out here."

Visibility worsened as clouds rolled in, cumulonimbus piling like cotton candy. No more constellations tonight. I drifted inside and drifted off to the sound of rain falling gently on the canvas sidewalls of the pop top.

A crash of thunder jolted me awake, hard rain pounding on the camper roof. I lifted onto one elbow, parted the curtain, and peeped out the window. It was daytime, ostensibly, but a solid sheet of water was pouring off the roofline and visibility was nil, the rain a great loom stretching from ground to sky, reflecting the swordplay of lightning. Outside everything was green-grey and dark. In no hurry to hit the road, I reached above my head and fished around for a book. There were down days—nontravel days docked up in port—and today was shaping up to be one of them. My fingers clamped around an oversized paperback, and I pulled down John Muir's *How to Keep Your Volkswagen Alive*. Fine, I figured. There was a good chance I'd need this book sooner or later.

Life is probability, a game of likelihood. If you spin a roulette wheel, your odds are the same red or black, odd or even, low or high. If you walk out your front door, you might step into a giant sinkhole that opened overnight, but your feet will probably find solid ground. If you hike in the

Pacific Northwest you *might* see Bigfoot, but you're much more likely to see a squirrel. And if you drive an antique VW Bus cross-country, chances are you're going to have mechanical trouble at some point. Might as well read up and prepare for the inevitable breakdown.

John Muir the mechanic was born in 1918. He got an engineering degree from UC Berkeley and worked as a contractor for the US Air Force and for NASA on missile launch platforms. He eventually dropped out 1960s-style and settled in Taos, New Mexico, where he opened a garage.

In 1969 Muir approached one of his neighbors, Peter Aschwanden, with an idea for a book. He envisioned a repair manual for the mechanically disinclined VW owner, and he needed an illustrator. The illustrations, Muir explained, would allow someone who didn't know a crescent wrench from a socket wrench to make competent repairs. Aschwanden, a painter who was busy building a new goat pen, hesitated to commit to the project, but Muir persisted and Aschwanden eventually relented, taking three weeks to pen his illustrations by kerosene lamp at night.

What emerged in that first self-published edition was something more than a simple repair manual, though a simple repair manual it was. A user-friendly, step-by-step guide to everything related to air-cooled Volkswagens, *How to Keep Your Volkswagen Alive: A Manual of Step-by-Step Procedures for the Compleat Idiot* was meant to be used, as evidenced by its spiral-bound format. Where it differs from DIY shop manuals such as Haynes or Chilton or Bentley—no-nonsense mainstays of the automotive repair world—is in its lighthearted approach, its philosophy and humor, leavened with an empowering message of positive thinking. One would be hard-pressed to find advice in these other manuals like "talk to the car, then shut up and listen," as Muir instructs. "When you strip a thread, twist off a stud, drop a bolt into the engine and like that, don't freak out," he coaches. "Smile!" Jokes and anecdotes seasoned Muir's instructions, but it is his mechanical love ethic that suffuses this book. "If I get hung up with maybe a busted knuckle or a busted stud, I feel my tools, like art objects or lovely feelies until the rage subsides and sense and love return," he writes. "Try it, it works." On doing one's own valve adjustment and tune-up procedures, Muir writes:

> When you get interested in doing for your car as much as you would
> for a horse or mule, then some of the proper spirit will spring forth.

Translating words into actions is easy when you do it one step at a time. You are not going to intellectualize on these mechanical things, you are going to *do* them and that's different. The idea to grasp here is one of Return. You are going to return the car to a position of well-being by adjusting certain things that have worn, been used up, or been bounced out of alignment. As the I-Ching says, "Perseverance Furthers," and that is your thing.

In this sense, *How to Keep Your Volkswagen Alive* is as much a self-discovery guide—a tome of spiritual wisdom—as it is a fix-it book or how-to manual. The message? With a set of wrenches and the right attitude, anyone can fix anything. "Along with word problems in Math and Zen Principals [*sic*], the operation of a motor car seems to be a first water mystery," he admits, but Muir's bible stands ready "to help you put a little light on how a car runs so you can dig it."

His first edition—*For Sedan, Ghia, and Transporter*—was followed by a second edition, *For Beetle, Bus, Karman Ghia, Square, Fastback, Safari, and 411·412*. More editions followed, selling more than two million copies across nineteen updated versions. Muir died in 1977, but *How to Keep Your Volkswagen Alive* became a prototype of the existential repair manual, a tradition continued by Robert Pirsig in *Zen and the Art of Motorcycle Maintenance* (1974). Perhaps more importantly, it kept many, many vintage VWs on the road.

If he hadn't read Muir, then Robert Pirsig surely channeled the same tranquil repose in his own foray into meditative engine repair. *Zen and the Art of Motorcycle Maintenance* is the *Moby Dick* of road trip books: a big, dull, boring treatise about motorcycling and how to keep a motorcycle alive, interspersed with homilies and insights about the human condition. Like *Moby Dick*, it is ultimately lovable, rewarding those who burrow in, embrace its minutiae, and see it through till the end. Like *How to Keep Your Volkswagen Alive*, it affords transcendent contemplation born of muscle and grease: higher wisdom via the sweat equity of mundane wrench turning. It is the story of a seventeen-day motorcycle trip the author made in 1968 with his eleven-year-old son Chris from Minnesota to California. The journey is seasoned with a series of "Chautauquas": philosophical discussions about epistemology and being. Along the way, the author wrestles with his past self, an alter ego named Phaedrus, maddened by these questions of existence. Like *How to Keep Your Volkswagen Alive*, *Zen and the Art* is about making peace with technology rather than fighting it or, worse yet, avoiding it; the book touts rational problem-solving over a wait-and-see-and-hope-for-the-best approach to life's journey. It's about finding purpose—in work, in travel, in life. Pirsig aims "to see if in that strange separation of what man is from what man does we may have some clues as to what the hell has gone wrong in this twentieth century."

A motorcycle road trip is like a car-borne road trip, only more so. A motorbike rider is naked and exposed, closer to the road and closer to nature, bugs-in-the-teeth and all. For Pirsig, it's that exposure and vulnerability that allows better perspective. "You're completely in contact with it all," he writes. "You're *in* the scene, not just watching it anymore, and the sense of presence is overwhelming."

I ventured out when the rain subsided, comfortable in my vehicular cage. Later that same day, in another moment of serendipity, I found a treasure at a used bookstore in Helena. I couldn't believe it. There, in a box of discounted books, was another title by John Muir. This one was called *The Velvet Monkeywrench*, and I happily paid the one dollar price tag to free it from the bargain bin at Richard Van Nice Books, after double-checking to make sure it was the right John Muir (not that there's a wrong John Muir—I'd have read anything by the mechanic *or* the naturalist).

"Coming or going," Muir begins, "we must view the next century with an eye toward the possible continuence [*sic*] of our species on this planet and I'd rather be coming." *The Velvet Monkeywrench* is a bold articulation of the way society ought to work. It's a reenvisioning, an antiestablishment manifesto that centers power with the people, rather than with government bureaucracies or corporations. "This book presents a way for mankind to exist on *this* planet, in balance, sensibly using what Earth has to offer," he writes. "It explains a way to create a modern governmental structure, which gives the People, finally, the right to choose their present and their future: a blueprint for consental [*sic*] society." It is *not* a call for utopia, which the author views as limiting and ungrounded in reality. It is instead a template for an alternate way of existence. "We need a leaderless, bloodless riot free change to a People's Establishment and Society: one in which we have something to say and which we have a part in forming," Muir suggests. "**Complete directions enclosed**," he boldly emphasizes.

Muir aims to restructure governance, societal norms, living arrangements, law, money, business, transportation—everything. "The kind of changes that we People can make are in the direction of harmony, humor, helping and honor among ourselves, which simply means feeling good together," he suggests. "All the changes proposed in this book head in that direction." For him, government is "the science of finding out what the people want and then helping them to do it," which "allows it to be two-valued instead of the single valued *Might is Everything*." This quest must be informed by the needs of the planet:

> The major problem of today is misuse of our ecology. So while we're changing everything, let's consider ourselves Ecologists and see what division of the planet Earth would make the most sense ecologically in order to provide a way of life for us and our jillions of descendents [*sic*]. We gotta think big.

Drawing on political theory, city planning, environmentalism, and a host of other fields, Muir offers nothing short of his own complete and total guide to living in harmony with one another.

Unfortunately, *The Velvet Monkeywrench* is kind of a garbled mess. It meanders and rambles, never landing on any singular topic long enough to detail the author's views fully. The tone is casual and loose, very different from the precision of Muir's auto manual. There is a wide paranoid streak, perhaps reflective of the author's countercultural worldview, throughout the entire work. "When I speak about *Them* with a capital T," Muir writes early in the text, "it indicates a Power Group, a bunch of people acting together to program *US* into doing what *THEY* want done." Much of his ponderings seems unnecessarily complicated, reinventing the wheel. He champions "Credits" instead of money, "Customs" instead of laws, "Councils" instead of voting districts, identification numbers to pinpoint individual citizens (whom he characteristically terms something other than citizens). A central tenet is something Muir calls "timebinding," the human system of data storage that distinguishes us from other organisms. His mantra, repeated at the end of each section and liberally seeded throughout, is "mankind must learn to progress without contention." It's a noble goal, but the end result is a byzantine, 247-page clutch of countercultural hippy speak, a language that nicely seasoned a period auto manual but muddied a seemingly genuine attempt to reorder societal norms.

Better written and organized are the writings of another John Muir, an earlier guru and namesake of John the mechanic. John Muir the naturalist was born in Scotland in 1838. Emigrating to central Wisconsin in 1849, his stern Calvinist parents kept him and his seven siblings busy doing farm chores and clearing land. He left home in 1860, studied for two years at the University of Wisconsin, and flirted with careers in inventing, medicine, and teaching. A conscientious objector, Muir fled to Canada in 1864 to avoid conscription in the Civil War. He returned to the United States in 1866 and worked for a year in a carriage factory in Indianapolis, where he was temporarily blinded in a serious industrial accident. On a lark, at the age of twenty-nine, he left for an impromptu hike across the southeastern United States, a journey he later described in *A Thousand-Mile Walk to the Gulf* (1916). Leaving on a whim to walk from Louisville, Kentucky, to Savannah, Georgia, then boating to Fernandina Beach, he walked across Florida to Cedar Key, on the Gulf Coast. A bout with malaria cut his adventure short but awakened in him an unquenchable wanderlust. He arrived in San Francisco by ship in March 1868 and began a lengthy period of wilderness sojourns, roaming the Sierra Nevada Mountains from Tahoe south to Mount Whitney, and north to Mount Shasta. In the last quarter of the nineteenth century, he became the best mountaineer in the United States, not only an accomplished rock and ice climber but also a well-rounded alpinist. An athlete and a philosopher, he led the life of an ascetic, "sauntering" as he calls it with no gear or provisions: no rope, no blankets, no food, few creature comforts.

Weaned on hard work, he survived on hardship and perseverance, his physical prowess surpassed only by his powers of observation, his ecological awareness, and his unusual outlook on people and nature. He saw manifestations of God everywhere in the natural world; for him, climbing mountains was a way to be closer to the divine. He was also mildly insane: talking aloud to plants and animals, rushing headlong into the forest with no preparation, losing himself in the wilds. He studied the wilderness, immersing himself, allowing it to strip him of the conventions of civilization. If Thoreau dipped his toe in nature, then Muir hurled his whole being into it. He became half wild, the Bigfoot of the Sierras—but he also became the biggest champion of wilderness. When he returned to civilization, he fought to protect what he had found—not conserving natural resources for humankind's use, as was becoming vogue among Progressive politicians and policymakers such as Teddy Roosevelt and Gifford Pinchot, but preserving the wilderness for its own sake, apart from any utility assigned to its commodification and commercialization. Muir's efforts led to the creation of Yosemite National Park in 1890 and, two years later, the Sierra Club. Books such as *The Mountains of California* (1894) articulated his passion for nature. In *Our National Parks* (1901), Muir relishes in the back-to-nature craze that he had helped to create, seeing a way to rescue a materialistic nation from the narrow concerns of the Industrial Age:

> The tendency nowadays to wander in wilderness is delightful to see. Thousands of tired, nerve-shaken, over-civilized people are beginning to find out that going to the mountain is going home; that wilderness is a necessity; and that mountain parks and reservations are useful not only as foundations of timber and irrigating rivers, but as foundations of life. Awakening from the stupefying effects of the vice of over-industry and the deadly apathy of luxury, they are trying as best they can to mix and enrich their own little ongoings with those of Nature, some are washing off sins and cobweb cares of the devil's spinning in all-day storms on mountains; sauntering in rosiny pinewoods or in gentian meadows, brushing through chaparral, bending down and parting sweet, flowery sprays; tracing rivers to their sources, getting in touch with the nerves of Mother Earth; jumping from rock to rock, feeling the life in them, learning the songs of them, panting in whole-souled exercise, and rejoicing in deep, long-drawn breaths of pure wilderness.

It was a passion that would consume Muir, who fought to stave off plans to dam the Tuolomne River in Yosemite. Where Muir saw a beautiful, glacier-carved river in no need of "improvement," officials in San Francisco saw a solution to the city's water shortage. A dam at the mouth of the Hetch Hetchy Valley would not only create an immense reservoir to supply San Francisco with all the water it needed but also pay for itself as a hydroelectric power source and a recreational destination for fishermen, boaters, and swimmers. With Secretary of the Interior James Garfield's support,

Congress in 1913 passed the Raker Act, which authorized the dam and reservoir. Exhausted and demoralized, Muir died a year later.

Exploring south of Missoula, I was pondering the two Muirs when I came to a place called Big Hole, the site of an infamous Indian battle. On August 9, 1877, the US military closed in on an overnight encampment of Nez Perce passing through the Bitterroot Valley after crossing Lolo Pass into Montana. The Nez Perce did not believe they would be pursued. "Going to buffalo country!" a Nez Perce named Yellow Wolf later described. "War was quit. All Montana citizens our friends." But the Seventh Infantry Regiment attacked, surprising the sleeping men, women, and children in a sunrise raid. Three volleys shattered the chilly dawn—then, a charge by the column of foot soldiers. By the time the smoke cleared on August 10, almost ninety Nez Perce were dead along with thirty-one soldiers and volunteers. Big Hole National Battlefield was created at Nez Perce National Historical Park to honor all who died there.

I had grown up in the middle of Civil War battlefields—Chattanooga, Missionary Ridge, Chickamauga, Dalton, and Resaca, among others—but I had never visited a battlefield like this one. The field was dotted with teepee frames without covers, the effect like so many skeletons. The military historians and park rangers, presumably using archaeological finds as evidence, had mapped where bodies had fallen in battle and placed wooden, two-dimensional cutouts on the spots. For every dead soldier, a blue-brimmed cavalry hat was staked; for every Indian brave, a white eagle feather. The effect was chilling. In certain spots there were clusters of blue hats, in others feathers. In some places there were pairs, one blue hat and one feather together, where two men obviously killed each other in hand-to-hand combat. The hats and feathers were everywhere, scattered across the entire area. A tactical victory for the Nez Perce, who managed to slip away, Big Hole was simultaneously a defeat. Two months later, the Nez Perce—exhausted, cold, hungry—surrendered. "Hear me, my chiefs," proclaimed Chief Joseph. "I am tired; my heart is sick and sad. From where the sun now stands I will fight no more forever."

There was a sense of historical presence at Big Hole, a feeling that something momentous had happened here. One might call it sense of place, this solemnity that blankets battlefields and monuments and memorials. One feels it at Shiloh and Appomattox—but one also feels it at Kittyhawk, where the Brothers Wright cheated gravity for a few seconds in

Fig. 5: Big Hole is dotted with teepee frames without covers. Photo by author.

1903; or at Apgar's Farm in upstate New York, where the liberated, free-thinking youth of 1969 gathered for three days of peace, love, and music. Sense of place need not be tragic, but the fact that it often is tells us something about what we assign historical value to. Death affords reverence: if loss of life occurs, that spot can almost instantly achieve historical significance. Abraham Lincoln dined all over Washington, DC, but it is Ford's Theatre that still draws crowds of tourists.

Are these places haunted? Perhaps, sort of—but one need not believe in ghosts to appreciate the nature of hauntings, which are inherently linked to sense of place. Paranormal investigators describe hauntings as worldly visitations by otherworldly beings: recurring, quasi-corporeal manifestations of spirits in a given place. Less spooky definitions simply describe a place habitually frequented; accordingly, we call places we used to visit our old "haunts" and hangouts. On yet another level, a haunting is little more than a lasting impression; in this sense we speak of being "haunted" by a painful memory or incident. Central to any definition of haunting, however, is the sensation of remembrance occurring in a given locale—the notion of place. Certain localities evoke more of a sense of place than others, perhaps because of certain memories lingering there; therefore, we might think of a haunting as a memory imprint, a time stamp on a particular place. Few would deny that places such as Big Hole or Senlac Hill, where English knights locked shields to face the Norman advance at the Battle of Hastings in 1066, have more historical weight—more *gravitas*—than other places that conjure less emotion or sentiment. Are they not haunted—not because of the large-scale loss of life that occurred there but rather because they keep a certain historical memory? In visiting the site of the greatest American Civil War battle, for example, it is easy to feel the ghosts of Gettysburg—not as apparitions or spirits, per se, but as a uniform atmosphere thick with presence and past meaning. Such hauntings are not limited to battlefields or sites of great tragedy. Walden Pond, for example, is haunted by Thoreauvian descriptions of quiet beauty; Muir Woods by the statuesque majesty of redwoods; and the US Capitol in Washington, DC, by palpitations of weighty decisions, of political power wielded by influential statesmen.

Where there are ghosts, or at least the suggestion of ghosts, one is mindful of ghost towns, and I found myself driving from Big Hole to Bannack and Nevada City, two of Montana's best-known and best-preserved ghost towns. Symbols of the Old West, ghost towns evoke frontier images of tumbleweeds and weather-beaten storefronts long abandoned to the ravages of time. Hollywood Westerns have made ghost towns iconic, and while fewer and fewer remain, some still dot the American West. A few locales have even actively preserved them: Bannack, the territorial capital of Montana, and Nevada City, a re-created settlement, now draw tourists as a state park and tourist attraction, respectively.

Ghost towns come in different flavors. First, there are what most people imagine as classic ghost towns, places like Bannack, which flourished then died with few traces of former existence. Second, there are towns once thriving and prosperous, now dwindling in decline with a handful of residents still living there. Third, there are named spots on maps—railroad stops, junctions, and so forth that needed to be called something—that were never really towns at all. Fourth, there are towns swallowed by other towns, now superimposed on top of preexisting communities. Fifth and finally are "living historical museums" like Nevada City.

They are interesting because they are so rare. A few ghost towns remain but most disappeared totally; on the frontier entire settlements—houses, hotels, businesses—simply vanished, so that subsequent visitors are hard put even to find the spot where they existed. Perhaps there was a storm or bad winter. Perhaps the railroad (or later, the interstate) bypassed the town, or perhaps an anchor or flagship business, key to the regional economy, failed. Regardless, it was usually hard economics that killed towns.

These places serve an important function, beyond any inherent architectural value or significance as economically viable heritage sites. As traces of earlier built environments, as repositories of memory, and as tangible links to past human presence, ghost towns signify a lack of constancy while still often providing a means to imagine a bygone era. They are the liminal spaces between living present and dead past, between rapid expansion and sustainable development, between amnesia and remembrance.

Nevada City is a tourist attraction, an outdoor museum with many original log structures and a collection of old-time music boxes, player pianos, and calliopes. Restored between the end of World War II and the late 1970s by Charles and Sue Bovey, who relocated many historic cabins and buildings to the site, Nevada City gives you an idea of what it would have been like to live in the Alder Gulch area during the 1860s. The kind of place one might see a staged showdown at high noon, it is geared toward family fun, playing to the town's rough past, as evidenced by the main sign:

> NEVADA CITY. A ghost town now but once one of the hell roarin' mining camps that lined Alder Gulch in the '60s. It was a trading point where gold dust and nuggets were the medium of exchange: where men were men and women were scarce. A stack of white cost twenty, the sky was the limit, and everyone went heeled. The first Vigilante execution took place here when George Ives, notorious road agent, was convicted of murder and hanged. The gulch was once filled with romance, glamour, melodrama, comedy and tragedy. Its plumb peaceful now.

Bannack, by contrast, was downright eerie. Here visitors could stroll through an entire town frozen in a state of arrested decay. No kitsch, no humor. Only wind-stripped dilapidated buildings, venerable structures, many with false fronts, everything deadwood grey, wind whistling through the chinks in the walls.

Founded in 1862 when John White discovered gold on Grasshopper

Creek, Bannack quickly lured prospectors hoping to strike it rich. The Grasshopper gold was different from other gold—99 percent pure, it was rumored—and miners flooded this new El Dorado of the north, a lawless, violent place. When Henry Plummer was elected sheriff in 1863 shortly after his arrival, few of the townspeople—mostly men, with a few saloon girls and painted ladies to entertain them—suspected that he also led the Innocents, the area's largest gang of bandits. Locals doled out vigilante justice, hanging road agents—including Plummer—by the neck at the gallows; however, the vigilantes themselves were eventually warned by concerned citizens to cease or face retaliation. Bannack's population fluctuated between the 1860s and 1930s; by the 1950s, the gold was gone and so were the people. The town itself—houses, sheds, a courthouse, a Masonic lodge, a hotel, a saloon, a jail—remains disconcertingly whole, as if the residents stepped out for a short while, never to return. If there were actual ghosts in Montana, they were here.

After Nevada City and Bannack, I cruised toward the world's first national park, a place where hot springs percolated and buffalo roamed. With any luck at all, I'd see some deer and antelope playing too.

6

On the Road in Yellowstone

October 1998: The rain fell in a splatter on the windshield as petrichor wafted through the driver's side valance, a whiff of ozone mixing with the smell of old dashboard vinyl. Low, bruise-purple clouds scudded past, dragging the sky like Portuguese man o' wars. I drove slowly, scanning the horizon for more bison.

Earlier that day, I had seen a single animal standing by itself halfway up a shallow rise, in the middle of a golden plain stretching in all directions as far as I could see: one buffalo, kind of mangy and utterly alone. I think it was the saddest thing I had ever seen. Every American school kid knows the story of how this proud animal had once roamed the grasslands of North American in massive herds numbering in the millions. Indiscriminate hunting and widespread slaughter had nearly brought it to extinction; only in protected pockets like this one were they able to repopulate and escape annihilation. To see one in the wild was a thrill, but to see *one* in the wild was jarring. I thought of the well-known photograph from the Michigan Carbon Works of the mountain of bison skulls—not entire skeletons, just skulls—piled to the sky, ready to be ground into fertilizer. One man stands in front, dwarfed by the skulls; another stands atop, easily thirty feet in the air. Things are, of course, better now. I knew that there must have been more animals nearby—in fact, there was probably an entire herd just over the rise—but that day all I saw was that lone buffalo. I drove on, thinking that herd animals should never be so solitary.

I'm not sure why, but before I had arrived, I had not expected much from Yellowstone. Yes, it was the world's first national park, and yes, it was renowned for its geothermic activity—its volcanos and hot springs and mudpots and geysers. But I think I considered it more of a tourist destination than a wildland, more theme park than wilderness. I had already visited Yosemite, where rock meets sky, and had only recently seen Glacier National Park, whose expansive views were the most incredible I'd ever seen. Both of those places were spectacular. In Yosemite Valley, God had seemingly jumbled together all of the best scenery in one place so that you could see it all in a glance. Any single piece on its own would be impressive, but taken together the elements of Yosemite Valley—El Capitan and Half Dome and Yosemite Falls—are truly magnificent. "Yosemite Valley, to me, is always a sunrise," writes Ansel Adams, who captured the place in stunning black-and-white photographs, "a glitter of green and golden wonder in a vast edifice of stone and space." As John Muir the naturalist writes, "it is by far the grandest of all the special temples of Nature I was ever permitted to enter." About Glacier, Muir writes that visiting there would lengthen one's life, a cure-all for modern problems:

> You will find yourself in the midst of what you are sure to say is the best care-killing scenery on the continent—beautiful lakes derived straight from glaciers, lofty mountains steeped in lovely nemophila-- blue skies and clad with forests and glaciers, mossy ferny waterfalls in their hollows, nameless and numberless, and meadow gardens abounding in the best of everything.

With astonishing 360° panoramas, no matter where one looks on the ascent up the Going-to-the-Sun Road—north, south, east, west—the eye falls on a remarkable vista. The effect is breathtaking. Between these two parks, I knew that I had seen the best America had to offer.

Fresh from Glacier, I planned to spend only a day or so in Yellowstone; but, ten days later, I was still finding more to see. Yellowstone was mind-blowing, unlike any place I had ever been. If Yosemite is a carefully proportioned composition, then Yellowstone is abstract art by Jackson Pollock, with barely tamed colors and savage brushstrokes. Not jaw-dropping in panoramas and vistas in the fashion of Yosemite and Glacier, Yellowstone is instead a place of discovery, a wonderland of hidden and fearsome treasures, "magnificent to behold but fretful to engage," according to writer David Quammen (this time writing for *National Geographic*). The paradox of Yellowstone, according to him, is "the paradox of the cultivated wild": that is, "wilderness contained, nature under management, wild animals obliged to abide by human rules." Quammen asks:

> Can we hope to preserve, in the midst of modern America, any such remnant of our continent's primordial landscape, any such sample of true wildness—a gloriously inhospitable place, full of predators and prey, in which nature is still allowed to be red in tooth and claw? Can that sort of place be reconciled with human demands and human convenience?

If the answer is yes, he writes, then the answer is Yellowstone.

Every year millions of visitors from around the world crowd into Yellowstone via the park's three main entrances. Despite the warning signs and brochures disseminated by the park's rangers, many of these visitors expect a managed and curated experience, more city park than national park. Perhaps because motorists are used to experiencing the park two-dimensionally through the lenses of their car windows, a surprising proportion of those who do exit their vehicles do so with unchecked hubris and a perilous sense of invulnerability. Accidents abound, including falls and drownings and rockslides and lightning strikes, but it is the tales of human folly—the man who dove headfirst into a 202-degree-Farenheit hot spring to save his dog, or the ranger and naturalist who mistakenly poisoned themselves with hemlock—that comprise the most morbidly compelling stories in Lee Whittlesey's *Death in Yellowstone: Accidents and Foolhardiness in the First National Park* (1995). This book by Whittlesey—not only an author but also a staffer, guide, ranger, and historian at the park—serves as a reminder that calling an area a national park in no way tames it.

The history of Yellowstone is a history of this clumsy, violent interaction between people and land and animals, and of course, it is the land and animals that have historically suffered the most. Protecting wildlife was an afterthought when Pres. Ulysses S. Grant signed a bill creating Yellowstone as the world's first national park on March 1, 1872. Despite the law's prohibition of "wanton destruction of the fish and game" within park boundaries, a lack of staff, budget, and clarity of purpose spelled disaster for the park's nonhuman inhabitants, now penned like so many fish in a barrel. The destruction wrought by Native Americans, the Shoshone and Crow hunters who recognized no rectilinear boundaries, paled in comparison to the white market hunters who "operated brazenly" in the park, according to Quammen, "killing elk, bison, bighorn sheep, and other ungulates in industrial quantities." Small in number but great in impact, tourists did their part too, breaking off geyser cones as souvenirs, carving their initials into rocks and old-growth trees, and killing waterfowl for fun. When the National Park Service took over park operations from the US Army in 1916, officials still distinguished "bad" wildlife (predators) from good (herbivores); as a result, coyotes were poisoned and shot until 1935, about five years after wolves had been eliminated not only from Yellowstone but also from the entire American West. Otters, skunks, and beavers were all deemed bad; they were trapped and shot accordingly. Interestingly, grizzlies and black bears were tolerated and even encouraged, recognized as important tourist draws in the 1890s. For eighty years, until the early 1970s, the bears consumed human refuse at garbage dumps by the hotels at Old Faithful, at Yellowstone Lake, and at other locales where tourists provided handouts, sat on bleachers, and watched the bears fight for scraps.

This tortured history brings into sharp relief the difference between Yellowstone the national park and Yellowstone the ecosystem. The former is delineated with official boundaries, signs, and fences; the latter subsumes the park itself, a vast ecological web of national forests, wildlife refuges, public and private holdings, transition lands, and buffer zones in which land, wildlife, and people are connected. The tourists and hikers and hunters and fishermen and ranchers and suburbanites and stockmen and conservationists and activists and scientists and wolf lovers and coyote haters are all constituents of the Greater Yellowstone Ecosystem, but they are not the only ones. Indeed, Yellowstone belongs to the nation and to the world—and to the plants and animals and rocks and waters there too.

The rain was intermittent. My van rocked back and forth like a ship making headway in calm seas, lulling me as the suspension shifted beneath, the springs and dampers moving left then right at regular intervals as the two-lane ribbon of asphalt unspooled in curls ahead. I drove

Fig. 6: On the road in Yellowstone. Photo by author.

slowly, well below the posted forty-five mile-per-hour maximum speed limit. For hours I had been gaining altitude while driving further into a more heavily wooded section of the park. Douglas firs gave way to Englemann spruce, subalpine firs, lodgepole pines, and a few whitebark pines, whose seeds provide important food for grizzlies. An understory of pinegrass and grouse whortleberry blurred past on either side. As late afternoon approached, I drove for an hour without passing another car. Patches of grey sky appeared sporadically through the canopy.

Then, as I rounded one curve to the right, something loomed in my path and I stood on the brakes, coming to a quick stop. *Lesson #8: Test your brakes before you need 'em.* There across the middle of the road stood two enormous elks, a male and a female. They looked as if they had been crossing the road, the bull in front and the cow behind, then lost interest halfway across. The two of them covered the width of an entire lane.

I had never seen an elk before. They were like deer, but much, much bigger. The velvet from his antlers, big and spiky, had been stripped in violent combat for the cow beside him. I studied their fur, the same fur that had brought six to eight dollars per hide in the late nineteenth century, when an ambitious hunter might kill between twenty-five and fifty elk per day. I couldn't believe how big they were. The bull was five feet high at the shoulder, his eyes on the same plane as mine, his rack extending another four feet above his head; all in all, the animal towered nine feet in height. My reveries ended when the bull turned toward me, took four steps forward, and peered through the windshield. We were eye to eye, his breath fogging the glass. With too many points to count, the bull's rack spread majestically, as wide as the van and much higher. Imagining being speared, skewered to the driver's seat backrest by those impressive horns, I put the van in reverse and slowly backed away, then carefully turned across the double-yellow lines into the far lane, giving the elks as wide a berth as I could. When last I saw them in my rearview mirror they were still standing there, unmoving and unmoved.

The sun sank lower, a faulty lamp flickering through the thick wall of pines. Tired but not sleepy, I drove a while longer then pulled into a turn-out. No campfire tonight: a witch's wind whipped up from the northwest and off-and-on rains kept me "indoors." After a quick supper that required no cooking, I bedded down in the back of the Bus. Nestling into my mummy bag, I groped around in my duffel for one of the paperbacks I'd brought along and pulled out a tattered copy of Jack Kerouac's best-known novel.

On the Road (1957) is both perfect and flawed, an iconic midcentury American novel. Many of the Beat generation's key players appear in it in fictionalized form. There's Kerouac himself as the narrator, Sal Paradise; Neal Cassady as the book's main character and driving force, Dean Moriarty; poet Allen Ginsberg as Carlo Marx; the writer and drug sponge William S. Burroughs as Old Bull Lee; and others. They freebase experience, mainlining as much as they can in an open-throttled series of journeys crisscrossing the United States. Women, music, words, food, drink—all are consumed in a rush of speed and amazement. It is a manic book of jazz and cars and movement and wonder.

At its best, *On the Road* channels the great American literature that came before it. Refrains of Mark Twain and Walt Whitman echo throughout the book, and Henry David Thoreau casts a long shadow over the entire madcap proceedings. Twain can be heard in the author's description of the Mississippi River, "the great brown father of waters rolling down from mid-America like the torrent of broken souls—bearing Montana logs and Dakota muds and Iowa vales and things that had drowned in Three Forks, where the secret began in ice." Transcendentalism is here too, as when Kerouac describes New Orleans. In this scene Old Bull Lee is trying to persuade Sal to stay with Jane and him, noting, "If you go to California with this madman you'll never make it":

> There was a mystic wraith of fog over the brown waters that night, together with dark driftwoods; and across the way New Orleans glowed orange-bright, with a few dark ships at her hem, ghostly fogbound Cereno ships with Spanish balconies and ornamental poops, till you got close and saw they were just old freighters from Sweden and Panama. The ferry fires glowed in the night; the same Negroes plied the shovel and sang. Old Big Slim Hazard had once worked on the Algiers ferry as a deckhand; this made me think of Mississippi Gene too; and as the river poured down from mid-America by starlight I knew, I knew like mad everything I had ever known and would ever know was One.

Whitman might have been quite flattered by (or taken great umbrage at) Kerouac's description of the New Orleans waterfront, which echoed his own descriptions of New York's docks and stevedores. Like the Net of Indra, the metaphorical net in Vedic mythology whose every vertex contains a gem reflecting all of the other gems, Kerouac's epiphany of interconnectedness (that everything he "had ever known and would ever know was One") echoes Ralph Waldo Emerson's concept of the oversoul, joining all things in holy unity.

The most Whitman-esque part of the book comes in Sal's encounter with "the Ghost of the Susquehanna": a wraith-like old man who appears one night in the wilds of the Alleghanies, on the road from Harrisburg,

Pennsylvania, to Pittsburgh. The wizened rambler regales Sal with a few stories before vanishing into the night, leaving our narrator to wonder if the man had really been there at all:

> I thought all the wilderness of America was in the West till the Ghost of the Susquehanna showed me different. No, there is a wilderness in the east; it's the same wilderness Ben Franklin plodded in the ox-cart days when he was a postmaster, the same as it was when George Washington was a wild-buck Indian-fighter, when Daniel Boone told stories by Pennsylvania lamps and promised to find the Gap, when Bradford built his road and men whooped her up in log cabins. There were not great Arizona spaces for the little man, just the bushy wilderness of eastern Pennsylvania, Maryland, and Virginia, the backroads, the black-tar roads that curve among the mournful rivers like the Susquehanna, Monongahela, old Potomac, and Monocacy.

It is these long, rambling passages, in which Kerouac free-associates, gathering up all of the familiar names and places of American folklore and piling them together as Whitman was wont to do, where the author shines brightest.

Jazz music fuels the Beats, propelling the characters forward as much as the gasoline in their big guzzly cars. More than a musical form, jazz is a motivation, a destination, and a form of movement in the novel. The characters sprint from nightclub to nightclub to hear it; it carries them until their next fix. Kerouac's descriptions of musicians like pianist George Shearing, playing and rocking and sweating, mirror his descriptions of Moriarty, who rocks and sweats "from pure excitement" when digging a new place with new people, sights, and sounds.

At its worst, *On the Road* suffers from the male excesses it seeks to chronicle. The boys-gone-wild aspects of the novel—the whiskey runs and piss calls and one-night stands and discarded girls—beat down even the least feminist of readers. The men are piggish, chasing sex at every turn, impishly and impulsively abandoning objectives in pursuit of "that little sumpin down there tween her legs, boy," as Moriarty puts it. They are vampires, parasitically bleeding the women they encounter of time, energy, and money in their own selfish quests for fulfillment. When Kerouac calls Dean Moriarty and Ed Dunkel "two mindless cads" who coax one poor girl to join a leg of the trip to "have her foot the bill," the reader understands that Sal recognizes the manipulative, opportunistic chauvinism of it all. Yet neither Sal nor Kerouac can distance themselves from the scene; both narrator and author are, knowingly and willingly, along for the ride. The trips are testosterone fueled, and *On the Road* is, at base level, a misogynistic fantasy that women (and many men) may struggle to enjoy.

Furthermore, as much as Kerouac admires jazz and the artists who created it, true understanding of people of color evades Kerouac. Seeing African Americans as simple, trouble free folk, Sal Paradise admires Black people and their cultural expressions but paradoxically reduces them to simplistic projections of his own desire to free himself of inhibitions and hang-ups. Naive and essentialist, Sal's "wishing I were a Negro" is the kind of sympathetic but surface-level empathy one might expect from a privileged white northerner in the 1950s. Sal never pauses to consider that being a Black man in the Jim Crow era is its own special hell, and Kerouac's attempts at cracking the color line, at breaking through midcentury barriers of race ("they thought I was a Mexican, of course; and in a way I am"), seem destined to fail.

Finally, as a book about travel and discovery, Kerouac's opus leaves much to be desired. Roaring from place to place in big-engined Hudsons and Cadillacs and Fords—cars that become minor characters in the story themselves—Sal and Dean careen across the continent at breakneck speed even as their companions attempt to slow down and enjoy the ride. The 1960s hippy mantra "the journey is the destination" would not have registered with the book's protagonists—not yet. *On the Road* works from the assumption that the American Dream is *out there*, waiting to be discovered like gold in the South Fork at Sutter's Mill. Kerouac wants to celebrate America but blasts through it at ninety miles per hour, catching only bits and pieces in his wide-woven net.

That said, in its excesses and speed the book does capture something quite, well, *American*. The elegiac descriptions of the land, the deep appreciation of the nation's peoples and cultural output and variety, and Dean Moriarty's thirst for experience propel the reader along a white-knuckle ride into the bigger-better-faster-more of American life. And Kerouac sprinkles in enough glimpses of his own sensitivity as a writer and observer of the human condition to keep the reader engaged and wanting more. "I preferred reading the American landscape as we went along," Sal tells the reader. "Every bump rise and stretch mystified my longing." It is the great American road novel, and those who take to the nation's highways with anything other than a desire to get from Point A to Point B follow in Kerouac's tire tracks.

In 1906, Upton Sinclair wrote *The Jungle*, which he intended as an exposé of the plight of the working class. The book missed the mark: instead of the exploitation of American workers, readers could focus only on the filthy factories of Chicago's meat-packing industry. They were outraged and disgusted—not about how their fellow man was treated but rather about where their meat was processed. "I aimed for the public's heart," Sinclair lamented, "and hit it in the stomach." Much like *The Jungle*, *On the Road* misses its mark. Kerouac wanted to write a book about the divinity of the everyday; a paean to the fellahin, the enlightened poor; and an exploration of *beat*, not only a word meaning down-and-out, busted, or exhausted but also a shortening of beatific, an expression of holiness in daily living. Instead, the reading public found a handbook of hedonism, the hipster's Bible. The people who went looking for Neal Cassady after the publication of *On the Road*—searching for the patron saint of road trips and digging life—missed the end of the book, the punchline: Dean Moriarty is mad, broken. Kerouac himself was not prepared and in fact never intended to be an ambassador of debauchery and self-gratification.

Dharma Bums (1958) is the book Kerouac intended to write, the book he wanted to write. A rapid follow-up to *On the Road*, this sequel gets at the issues important to Kerouac: the spirituality and longing and asceticism lost in the freneticism of his first book. As a work of Beat literature, and as a window into the author's worldview, *Dharma Bums* is superior to *On the Road*. If the 1957 manuscript is a book of jazz and cars and movement and wonder, then the 1958 one is a book of hikes and rituals and visions and prophecies that delves further into the experience and meaning of Beat enlightenment.

Harbingers of the second book are evident throughout the first but appear mainly toward the end, as when Sal describes the "final development" of Dean Moriarty, who "no longer cared about anything (as before), but now he also *cared about everything in principle*; that is to say, it was all the same to him and he belonged to the world and there was nothing he could do about it" (emphasis in the original). Dean becomes what Sal calls "the HOLY GOOF," a phrase only partially explained in the text:

He [Dean] was alone in the doorway, digging the street. Bitterness, recriminations, advice, morality, sadness—everything was behind him, and ahead of him was the ragged and ecstatic joy of pure being.

He is, in other words, *beat*, "the root, the soul of Beatific." It was a concept he would explore further in his next book.

Dharma Bums has more of the same "Three Stooges adventures," as Kerouac calls them—the sophomoric binges that made him famous. But on the whole it is a much more serious work than its predecessor. Nowhere is this seriousness more evident than in its focus on the Japanese tea ceremony. In this novel, Kerouac as Ray Smith pals around with Japhy Rider, a character based on real-life Berkeley student and scholar of East Asian languages, Gary Snyder, who taught Kerouac the Japanese way to consume tea ritualistically. "The first sip is joy," Rider tells Smith, "the second is gladness, the third is serenity, the fourth is madness, the fifth is ecstasy."

It is with Rider that Smith goes backpacking in the Sierra Nevadas. Upon summiting a peak, Rider passes Smith while flying in a dead sprint down the mountainside:

I looked up and saw Japhy *running down the mountain* in huge twenty-foot leaps, running, leaping, landing with a great drive of booted heels, bouncing five feet or so, running then taking another long crazy yelling yodelaying sail down the sides of the world[,] . . . and with a yodel of my own I suddenly got up and began running down the mountain after him doing exactly the same huge leaps, the same fantastic runs and jumps, and in the space of about five minutes I'd guess Japhy Rider and I . . . came leaping and yelling like mountain goats or I'd say like the Chinese lunatics of a thousand years ago. . . . With one of my greatest leaps and loudest screams of joy I came flying right down to the edge of the lake and dug my sneakered heels into the mud and just fell there, glad.

Like his racing across the country, Kerouac's/Smith's running down the mountain evokes Whitman's barbaric yawp, or John Muir's climbing the tallest lodge pole pine, waving back and forth while riding out a terrible mountain gale: moments of pure joy, born in primal abandon and loss of control.

The Beats, of course, were ahead of their time in this quest, and the novel offers glimpses of things to come, most notably the rejection of bourgeois respectability and economic conventionality by the 1960s counterculture. This new sensibility, focused by an appreciation of nature, will bring a "great rucksack revolution," as Japhy portends, "a world full of rucksack wanderers," or Dharma Bums. "Why, do you realize the Jurassic pure granite of Sierra Nevada with the straggling high conifers of the last ice age and lakes we just saw is one of the greatest expressions on this earth," he marvels. "Just think how truly great and wise America will be, with all this energy and exuberance and space focused on the Dharma."

While there are occasional sightings of Thoreau in *On the Road*, the nineteenth-century transcendentalist and protoenvironmentalist takes center stage in *Dharma Bums*, in part because so much of the book takes place in the wildernesses north and south of San Francisco. If Kerouac raced from city to city in *On the Road*, then he lingers in the hinterlands in *Dharma Bums*. One sees a writer more attuned to nature, as in this Thoreau-mimicking passage:

> I wanted to get me a full pack complete with everything necessary to sleep, shelter, eat, cook, in fact a regular kitchen and bedroom right on my back, and go off somewhere and find perfect solitude and look into the perfect emptiness of my mind and be completely neutral from any and all ideas. I intended to pray, too, as my only activity, pray for all living creatures; I saw it was the only decent activity left in the world. To be in some river-bottom somewhere, or in a desert, or in mountains, or in some hut in Mexico or shack in Adirondack, and rest and be kind, and do nothing else, practice what the Chinese call "do-nothing."

This statement of intent recalls Thoreau's explanation in *Walden* of why he came to Walden Pond. In *Dharma Bums*, Thoreau's cabin has become a backpack. This deliberate attempt at distilling the essence of life is largely absent from *On the Road*. Thoreau's asceticism holds deeper meaning for the *Dharma Bums* protagonist, who is more interested in solitude and communing with nature than Sal Paradise ever could be.

The Beats may be commended for trying to bring the East to the West; however, they may also be accused of what Edward Said has termed

"Orientalism," a source of inaccurate cultural representations based on perceived differences between "the Orient" and "the Occident." Kerouac attempts to import Eastern sensibility into the Western orthodoxy of 1950s America; but in doing so he, perhaps inescapably and unavoidably, simplifies and reduces complex ontologies and epistemologies rooted in China, Japan, and the Indian subcontinent. The Beat outlook, as conveyed by Kerouac in these two novels, offers a kind of pop Buddhism, a shallow understanding born of the Beats' own blitzkrieg attack on experiential learning. One wonders if something has been lost in translation in their earnest but hurried studies of not only Zen but also Hinduism and Sufism.

A parallel can be seen in *wabi-sabi*, the supposedly Japanese notion of finding perfection in imperfection. A popular design concept in contemporary America, the term was popularized by art publisher Leonard Koren in the 2000s. Rather than trying to cover the blemish or flaw, wabi-sabi showcases it. Rather than trying to mask the signs of age, or scrub away patinas, wabi-sabi embraces them. It's the pine-knot whorl in the tabletop, the crack in the raku glaze. It is that which affords comment, the beauty mark on the supermodel's impossible face. It is Siddhartha, the bodhi, the Buddha Becoming. It is as it is and it is perfect as such.

In offering a way of making peace with imbalance, flaws, and the slow deteriorations of aging, wabi-sabi offers a Zen-like path to harmony with life's bumps and the passage of time. *Kintsugi*, a related concept, is the Japanese art of repairing ceramics with gold filler, which emphasizes the mended crack and transforms the broken object. A broken vessel thus becomes whole again, with the gold not only fixing what's broken but also transforming it aesthetically by emphasizing and beautifying its brokenness. Rather than *in*visible, the cracks are rendered overly visible: one cannot help but notice the now golden seams where the repair has occurred. Both wabi-sabi and kintsugi are fascinating to Americans and Europeans attuned to alternative ways of understanding the world.

Wabi-sabi, however, is not what it seems. More Western design aesthetic than Eastern philosophical concept, wabi-sabi is more Californian than Japanese—which is to say it's not authentic. In researching the history of the term, one finds no ancient texts or related religious treatises; the only dictionary references and definitions are in the past fifteen years or so. There are older Japanese allusions to what might be termed wabi as a kind of austere beauty in traditional Japanese architecture, and there are evocations of sabi in the seventeenth-century haikus of Matsuo Bashō, but there is no such thing in traditional Japanese writings as wabi-sabi, per se. In fact, Koren seems to have made up wabi-sabi, much like he made up "gourmet bathing" in the late 1970s when he founded his groundbreaking New Wave art journal, *Wet*. In other words, it's bullshit.

But just because it's bullshit doesn't mean it isn't useful. In fact, wabi-sabi is akin to one of the noble lies described in Plato's Republic: with little authenticity in Japanese tradition, it still carries utility for Westerners trying to apprehend something very different from their own cultural values and paradigms. To an American mind, Buddhist notions of impermanence and imperfection juxtapose sharply—and valuably—with Western ideals of geometric perfection and symmetry. In this space, the broken flower pot becomes an *objet d'art*, not a castoff; the wrinkles of the elderly become badges of wisdom; and the dilapidated building a historical treasure, rather than an eyesore. It is a compelling contrast to the raze-and-pave norm demanded by American emphasis on unmarred newness and youth.

In this sense, Kerouac's brand of Eastern mysticism is similar to wabi-sabi: at times oversimplified, corrupted in its exportation to Western thought, rootless and somewhat inauthentic, but also sincere and instructive to those who would study it. It is genuine insofar as he believed it to be an admirable counterpoint to an American ethos mired in conformity and materialism. If wabi-sabi can be considered seriously, then *On the Road*—in its East-meets-West striving, perfect in its imperfection—may be its prime example.

Were there any connections between Kerouac and Yellowstone? Was it mere chance that drew my hand to *On the Road* that night? I later learned that Kerouac had, on July 9, 1956, sent Malcolm Cowley, an editor at Viking Press, a postcard from Yellowstone that depicted the Lower Falls in Yellowstone National Park. Frustrated by the slow turnaround and seeming lack of interest in *On the Road*, which had stalled at Viking, Kerouac threatened to sell the manuscript elsewhere if Cowley didn't send him a contract and advance. Cowley would become his editor at Viking, which shortly thereafter published *On the Road*.

How many travelers and seekers has Kerouac inspired? How many Ford Econolines and Chevrolet Greenbriers and Dodge A100s and Mystery Machines and VW Buses have lumbered forth in his tire tracks? Remembered as King of the Road Trip, he deserves credit as a seeker and explorer, someone who tried to break through the ordinariness of his environs into a deeper level of understanding, someone who tried to filter his comprehension of the American character through insights from other cultures and philosophies, however abridged or generalized. Like many of us, he fumbled his way toward knowing. And he chose the highway as his path to enlightenment.

Was Kerouac crazy? Perhaps a bit. He seemed to admire crazy, using the word "mad" in his writings to describe those who were furious to live, furious to know, furious to experience as much as they could in this brief, sputtering existence. If that's what it meant to be mad, then perhaps (*Lesson #9*) it was okay to be slightly shattered, a tad jangled and imperfect. These thoughts turned as I drifted off, dreaming of buffalo floating past in low clouds of broken pottery.

7

Land Bad

Yellowstone conjured an unfamiliar feeling, a swelling of appreciation for natural beauty incongruously mixed with patriotic pride. The words to "America the Beautiful" turned in my head as I finally drove out of the park after much exploring:

> O beautiful for spacious skies,
> For amber waves of grain,
> For purple mountain majesties
> Above the fruited plain!
> America! America!
> God shed His grace on thee,
> And crown thy good with brotherhood
> From sea to shining sea!

Inspired by a cross-country train trip to Colorado in 1893, the lyrics were written by Katharine Lee Bates, a professor of English literature at Wellesley College. The gleaming alabaster buildings constructed for the World's Fair in Chicago that year, the wheat fields of Kansas, the majestic view atop Pike's Peak . . . all made their way into the poem that eventually became a favorite patriotic hymn when set to music composed by Samuel A. Ward, an organist and choir director at Grace Episcopal Church in Newark, New Jersey. Bates seemed to get it, seemed to recognize that it was

North America itself, the land and sky and waters and plains, that made the United States exceptional in equal measure with our democratic ideals; the two have in fact been tightly entwined throughout US history. As much as any other factor, the nation's natural resources—its towering mountains and flashing rivers, its deep forests and deeper harbors—have seeded whatever claims to greatness its people could honestly make. Accordingly, in much the same way that Ben Franklin preferred the turkey to the bald eagle, I'd always felt that Bates's celebration of America's natural splendor would make a more apt national anthem than "The Star-Spangled Banner," a bellicose martial tune.

After Yellowstone, I headed from Wyoming back up into Montana, through Billings. Twiddling the radio dial, I joined a preacher in midprayer: "And we ask, O Lord, that you help us to help ourselves and, more importantly, to help each other in recognizing Your will and serving You to our fullest potential." Amen to that, I thought, lightly slapping myself once or twice to wake up. More us, less them. More we, less me.

Ours is an individualistic society—an oxymoron—and that self-contradiction infuses the American Dream. The Dream is individualistic rather than communalist, more often articulated in terms of equality of opportunity rather than equality of condition. In theory everyone has a shot at middle-class comfort, if not upper-class wealth; therefore, the United States has been a place where anyone (though not everyone) can succeed. For some the Dream becomes reality, but it's a dream or hope for all: *anyone* can achieve therefore *everyone* believes. Betterment and improvement are not particularly or exclusively American, but we deeply believe that the Dream, any dream, is more attainable here. The exceptional part of the Dream may not be its Americanness but rather the depth of our belief in it, even in its selfishness.

It was St. Jean de Crèvecœur, a French-born essayist and planter, who first described the American cult of the self in *Letters from an American Farmer* (1782). The newly independent states were a place where religion "demands but little of him [the American]," who seemed to place faith in something else, according to Crèvecœur, a self-described "cultivator of the earth" and "simple citizen." "Here the rewards of his industry follow, with equal steps, the progress of his labour," he writes. "His labour is founded on the basis of nature, *self-interest*: can it want a stronger allurement?" In this new republic, work—rather than birthright or status—would determine wealth and success. Moreover, that work would be grounded in concern for one's own welfare; the success of the whole would stem from each person working toward his or her own individual success. In defining Americans' work ethic, it was Crèvecœur who first articulated the selfishness of the American Dream.

Like Crèvecœur, Alexis de Tocqueville saw the well-being of society in the well-being of its individual citizens. It was the individual visions—the aspirations of tens of thousands of planters, farmers, craftsmen, artisan-inventors, storekeepers, manufacturers, and other entrepreneurs—that combined to launch the country into a vigorous new economic frontier. The ethic of enterprise fed American growth; but, unlike Crèvecœur, Tocqueville saw an ominous undertone in this self-interested enterprise. "The Americans," he writes in *Democracy in America* (1835):

> enjoy explaining almost every act of their lives on the principle of self-interest properly understood. It gives them pleasure to point out how an enlightened self-love continually leads them to help one another and disposes them freely to give part of their time and wealth for the good of the state. I think that in this they often do themselves less than justice, for sometimes in the United States, as elsewhere, one sees people carried away by the disinterested, spontaneous impulses natural to man.

He distrusts Americans' heightened "taste for physical pleasures" and questions their compulsive ambition. "It is odd to watch with what feverish ardor the Americans pursue prosperity," he writes, "and how they are ever tormented by the shadowy suspicion that they may not have chosen the shortest route to get it."

At the root of American enterprise, according to Tocqueville, lay desire for riches. "To clear, cultivate, and transform the huge uninhabited continent which is their domain," he observes, "the Americans need the everyday support of an energetic passion; that passion can only be the love of wealth." In "no other country in the world," he writes, "is the love of property keener or more alert than in the United States." He adroitly understands the treadmill-like quality of American industry, writing, "There is perhaps no country in the world with fewer men of leisure than America, nor one in which all those who work are so keen on making themselves prosperous"; everyone works hard, few reach the top. Furthermore, he seems to understand the relationship of individualism and national prosperity embodied by the American Dream:

> Sometimes he [the American] seems to be animated by the most selfish greed and sometimes by the most lively patriotism. But a human heart cannot really be divided in this way. Americans alternately display passions so strong and so similar first for their own welfare and then for liberty that one must suppose these urges to be united and mingled in some part of their being. Americans in fact do regard their freedom as the best tool of and the firmest guarantee for their prosperity. They love them both for the sake of each other.

In other words, it is the very possibility of progress—the American Dream—that makes Americans so industrious. For Tocqueville, Americans do not work to attain the American Dream so much as the American Dream works to attain them.

He celebrates individualism and considers it a key ingredient in American success but also worries about its natural conclusions and how it might mix with Americans' love of materialism. According to him, the "common man" in the United States understands the simple but elusive idea of "the general influence of the general prosperity on his own happiness"; yet, he is "accustomed to regard that prosperity as his own work." Therefore, he "sees the public fortune as his own," and "works for the good of the state, not only from duty or from pride, but, I dare almost say, from greed." Still, Tocqueville assures himself and his reader, "Every American has the sense to sacrifice some of his private interests to save the rest."

It is no surprise that these insights derive from Frenchmen, one an eighteenth-century planter and the other a traveler in the early nineteenth century. The French were perspicacious in their observations of American polity and society not only because of their own interests in *liberté*, *egalité*, and *fraternité* but also because of their nascent experiments with democracy, realized in the French Revolution of 1789 and in the creation of the French republic in 1792. What's more surprising is how Americans continue to grind harder and harder in the workplace as individuals in pursuit of financial security with little sense of shared endeavor. Like Tocqueville's laborers, we assume that if individuals take care of themselves, the collective will prosper, and for most of us, the possibility of success, rather than its assurance, is enough. The tension between opportunity and condition, between anyone and everyone, between enough and too much, stretches and tightens.

On the Crow Indian Reservation, I walked into a nondescript gas station/convenience store/garage and got a cup of coffee, the color of light crude oil. Old car chassis were parked three-deep around the lot's fence line. I greeted the man behind the counter. "How's it going?" I said absentmindedly, fishing in my pocket.

"Living the dream," he replied, and I looked up to meet his gaze before counting out some change for the coffee. He was, not surprisingly, Native American, his round face and ruddy complexion framed by long, straight, black hair. "Nice van."

"Thanks. Your place?" I asked, dropping coins into his palm. He nodded silently. I paused. "Hey, would it be OK if I parked in your lot overnight?"

He looked at me. "Sure," he allowed. "You might want to try that far corner, under the sign. Might be a little quieter." I squinted through the front picture window and studied the parking lot dotted with jalopy bones— rusting car hulks and pickup frames—my head gently bobbing as I tried to imagine this parking lot as anything other than quiet. We were the only two people in sight. It was deader than a cemetery, his garage more automotive graveyard than service station.

"Thanks," I said. "Wanted to be sure to ask. Didn't want to presume anything."

"No problem. Let me know if you need anything."

"Thanks again, I really appreciate it. I'll stay out of the way." Turning away, I spun around again. "Say, you don't have any coconut cream pie, do you?" He shook his head. I bought a microwavable pizza pocket for dinner, a pint of milk and a cellophane-wrapped package of mini chocolate donuts for breakfast the next morning, and a soda before backing the van between two oxidizing heaps: a 1948 Ford F-1 pickup and a 1962 Dodge Dart, both see-through lattice, more rust than metal. In the automotive litter around me I spied two Volkswagen Buses, both Type 2s, including a First-Gen Split-Window dating from the 1950s. That night I dined at sunset in an old polyethylene school chair, leaned back on two corroded steel tubes, propped against the front of the store, watching the sun spray shades of ginger and pink and crimson over the reservation. The black vault of night soon arched overhead, dotted not only with stars but also with what I knew must be entire galaxies.

I thought of the St. Ignatius paintings, the red Jesus and red Virgin Mary, and the prayer to the Great Spirit. In Seattle, Spokane, Coeur d'Alene, Missoula, and elsewhere, First Peoples were a visible minority, present and noticeable; in and around the Blackfeet and Crow Reservations they were majorities. The reservations were impoverished and grim but real, and for easterners who'd never seen them it might be easy to forget that Native American history didn't end in 1890 at Wounded Knee. American Indians were still in and of the West. No ghosts were they.

I slept soundly that night. The next morning the store owner walked over as I gassed up. "Heading out?" he asked.

"Yep, heading over to the Little Bighorn," I said, referring to the Little Bighorn Battlefield National Monument, site of Custer's Last Stand.

He nodded quietly, looking at the ground. He smiled, looking up. "Custer lost, you know," he grinned. "Sitting Bull kicked his ass."

"Yeah, I heard," I laughed.

"You'd be surprised how many people don't know," he asserted.

"Not around here, I'll bet."

"No, even here people get the facts mixed up."

I nodded. "I went to Big Hole. Pretty somber place. The caps and feathers."

"Yes," he agreed. "Lots of people died there too."

A few quiet seconds passed. I scuffed some gravel with my foot to erase the silence. "You gonna fix up that ol' microbus? The splitscreen?" I asked.

"One day," he nodded. A few more seconds passed. "Travel is good," he offered. "Time unfolds in a straight line. As it passes it constricts, becoming smaller, a narrowing of choices. Not so with travel. It's the opposite. As you travel, the world expands, opportunities and experiences multiply, flaring out like the bell of a trumpet—a cornucopia, you know? Spilling ahead, big. Not like time."

I nodded, trying to follow. "Travel is good," he reiterated. We shook hands, and I thanked him again and drove off after assuring him that I'd be traveling for a while yet.

Little Bighorn was disappointing. The visitor center was worn and tired, dated to the point of being embarrassing. The exhibits were collection focused rather than historically interpretive. There was little explanation of

LAND BAD • 105

Fig. 7: Like the teepee frames at Big Hole, the grave markers at Little Big Horn were disquieting. Photo by author.

why the two sides were fighting, no contextualization of the Battle of the Little Bighorn in the greater Indian Wars of the 1880s. There were only various artifacts—bits of uniforms, belt buckles, weapons, and so forth— in Plexiglas cases with minimalistic script to accompany it. The soldiers came off as good guys and the Indians as bad guys. Since passage in 1990 of the Native American Graves Protection and Repatriation Act (commonly called NAGPRA), museums have done better with Indian artifacts and sacred cultural objects. They had begun to consult with cultural committees from the various tribes in an attempt to be more sensitive to Indian concerns, attempting to explain Indian cultures and history from a perspective that takes Indian viewpoints into account; but, Little Bighorn still had some catching up to do. The best part was getting outside, walking down the hill away from the visitor center toward the actual battle site, but even this experience was anticlimactic, particularly after Big Hole. I understand that the experience later improved, but when I visited it wasn't much.

From Little Bighorn, I headed east, dipping down into Wyoming again, approaching Devils Tower National Monument from the north. The first national monument in the United States, Devils Tower was set aside in

1906 not as a park or a nature preserve, but as a place that Pres. Teddy Roosevelt and other US officials simply recognized as remarkable and worth preserving. Sacred to Native Americans, the massive rock spire goes by many names. The Arapahoe call it Bear's Tipi. The Kiowa refer to it as Aloft on a Rock or Tree Rock, and the Lakota know it as Bear Lodge, Bear Lodge Butte, Grizzly Bear's Lodge, Mythic-Owl Mountain, Grey Horn Butte, and Ghost Mountain; however, it is commonly referred to as Mateo Tepee, which is Sioux for Bear Wigwam or Bear Lodge. Many First Peoples hate the name Devils Tower, bequeathed in 1875 by Col. Richard Irving Dodge, who led geologist Walter P. Jenney's scientific expedition through the region. Towering 1,267 feet above the plains of northeastern Wyoming and the Belle Fourche River, the rock is still the site of many Native American ceremonies, including sun dances and sweat rituals: a holy place for winter camps, vision quests, and summer rites.

Made famous by Steven Spielberg's 1977 feature film *Close Encounters of the Third Kind*, Devils Tower is an astounding geologic feature. The largest example of columnar jointing in the world, the spire is formed of a rare igneous rock, phonolite porphyry. It is a mystery to geologists, who have studied the mountain since the late 1800s and still don't know how it formed. Most agree that Devils Tower began as magma: molten rock buried beneath the Earth's surface. What they cannot agree upon are the processes by which the magma cooled to form the tower, or its relationship to the surrounding geology of the area, which is mostly sedimentary. The simplest explanation is that Devils Tower is a stock—a small intrusive body formed by magma that cooled underground and was later exposed by erosion—but some have suggested it is a volcanic plug or the neck of an extinct volcano. Today it is contested rock: scrutinized by scientists, valued by climbers as one of the finest crack climbing ascents in North America, and revered by Native Americans as hallowed ground. All share it in an uneasy truce.

I hiked around the base, from which the climbers looked like specks, flies crawling up the rock face in immeasurably tiny movements. "The tower is sacred to Native Americans," a sign cautioned. "Please stay on trail." Around the base I found prayer bundles and prayer cloths, tied to trees along the Tower Trail. The brightly colored cloths, fading in the cool sun, fluttered reverently, lapping in the breeze. Out of respect I did not touch or even photograph any of these items.

LAND BAD · 107

Driving eastward from Sundance, Wyoming, I crossed into South Dakota, toward Spearfish, and dipped into the Black Hills, the mountainous region between the Cheyenne and Belle Fourche Rivers. From a distance, the rounded hilltops, well-forested slopes, and deep valleys present a dark appearance, giving the Black Hills their name; however, the color black mostly hides behind granite grey, pine green, and sprays of red, orange, brown, and gold, depending on the time of day. The grassland prairie gave way to ponderosa pine, with a few hardwoods—aspen, bur oak, and birch—visible too, and spruce at higher elevations. Mule deer and white-tailed deer flitted through the trees.

In the northern Hills, completely surrounded by the Black Hills National Forest, lies Deadwood, a town whose reputation precedes it. The gold rush of 1876–77 provided ample wealth to construct a thriving commercial center in the heart of this small and isolated mountain range in western South Dakota. With impressive Victorian architecture, the entire city is now on the National Historic Register, but it is the town's history rather than its buildings that garnered notoriety. The gold rush brought not only miners seeking a quick buck but also larger-than-life figures such as Wild Bill Hickok and Martha "Calamity Jane" Canary, who drank, gambled, fought, and shot their way into American legend. Playing five-card stud at Nuttal & Mann's Saloon, Hickok was murdered here, shot in the back of the head while holding two pairs, black eights and black aces, now known as "the dead man's hand." Wild Bill and Calamity Jane lie interred next to one another in Mount Moriah Cemetery, Deadwood's Boot Hill.

Sturgis, infamous in its own right, is a few miles down the road. Every August, Sturgis transforms from a sleepy town of a few thousand residents into a wild motorcycle rally of hundreds of thousands of bikers. I had just missed the annual gathering, one of the biggest motorcycle events in the world. Even now, Harleys and Hondas lined up outside the Full Throttle Saloon like horses at a hitching post.

A short drive down Route 16 would have taken me to Mount Rushmore, but I didn't go. I came within a stone's throw but didn't see it, mainly because Rushmore didn't seem to fit into this trip. It seemed like a giant granite tourist trap, cloaked in Lee Greenwood patriotism, and frankly it was: South Dakota's state historian Doane Robinson blasted this colossal set of presidential busts into the impressive granite of the Black Hills with the express goal of luring tourists to this remote corner of the nation.

I viewed it as a defacement, the antithesis of the parks and natural scenery that I'd been seeking, and I was OK with not seeing it. The massive sculpture of four American presidents draws approximately three million visitors from around the world each year, mostly during the summer, so I figured George, Tom, Teddy, and Abe wouldn't miss me much.

In Rapid City, South Dakota, I stopped in a frame shop called Graphic City at 3471 Sturgis Road. I had bought two postcards at Little Bighorn: one of Custer, one of Sitting Bull. "Could you frame these?" I asked the lady behind the counter.

She took the cards and disappeared into the backroom for a few minutes, came back, and gave me a price for a custom frame job, one that I couldn't afford. I started to leave. "Wait a sec," she advised.

She went to the front of the store, beneath a giant Frederic Remington repro, and rummaged in a box of mismatched frames. She came back with a weathered, rustic, wood frame, stained dark with a light tan mat cut to bracket two postcard-size pictures, vertically arranged. Perfect, right outta the Old West. "How do you want them?" she asked.

"Sitting Bull on top, Custer on bottom, please."

She popped them into the frame and charged me ten dollars. It looked like a custom job.

That night after some cheap grub at a forgettable diner, I lay atop a twin bed at the Town House Motel in downtown Rapid City. Thinking about Native Americans, I scrounged another book out of the Bus: William Least Heat-Moon's *Blue Highways: A Journey into America* (1982). Thirty-eight-years old, recently separated, and newly unemployed, the author set out on a long, circular trip over the backroads of the nation in a van he called *Ghost Dancing*, a 1975 half-ton Econoline (Ford's smallest production van at the time, "a basic plumber's model," according to the author): two seats, with a box bed in the back, tricked out for camping. He carried two books he considered essential: Walt Whitman's *Leaves of Grass* and John Neihardt's *Black Elk Speaks*. Soon his worries were reduced to simple questions: When's the rain going to stop? Who can you trust to fix a water pump around here? Where's the best pie in town? He sought out not only the less traveled blue highways (to escape the "tyranny of the freeway") but also "where-you-from-buddy restaurants," as he calls them, and "seven-calendar cafes," which indicate honest food and a degree of authenticity quantifiable by the number of calendars hanging on the walls.

LAND BAD • 109

Born William Trogdon, the author changed his name after finishing the manuscript for *Blue Highways*. Part Osage Indian, his father, Ralph Trogdon, had adopted the name Heat Moon, based on Sioux tribal lore. He called his eldest son Little Heat Moon and young Bill Least Heat Moon, which the author would later hyphenate to avoid being called Mr. Moon. While the family did not use these names publicly, the author felt compelled to change his name to William Least Heat-Moon (which was not a given tribal name) to avoid giving readers the impression that he possessed a wholly "Anglo point of view," as he explained in an interview with *People* magazine. By today's standards, the author might be accused of trading on a cultural identity that was not his fully to claim; but, at the time of publication (when cultural appropriation did not exist, as least not in its currently recognizable form), he saw little to gain other than a more truthful rendering of his identity, seeing himself as a "mixed-blood," a "contaminated man who will be trusted by neither red nor white." His heritage and self-perception as a man in-between give the author a unique perspective on all things American.

His renaming also indicates a man in turmoil. Having lost his teaching gig, his marriage foundering, Trogdon found himself at a crossroads. He chose to drive—from Columbia, Missouri, eastward toward the coast, then clockwise around the nation's edge. He stuck to the sideways and byways, the blue highways. Three months and thirteen thousand miles later, he stopped to write, culling through his journals and tape-recorded interviews for four years to craft the manuscript. William Least Heat-Moon created *Blue Highways*, but *Blue Highways* also created William Least Heat-Moon.

In this book, Least Heat-Moon slows down—way down—to experience whatever the journey brings. No agenda, no route, no destinations. "Maybe a tonic of curiosity would counter my numbing sense that life inevitably creeps toward the absurd," he writes. "Maybe the road could provide a therapy through observation of the ordinary and obvious, a means whereby the outer eye opens an inner one." Most striking is the way the author talks to everyone he meets. "Being alone on the road makes you ready to meet someone when you stop," he maintains. "You get sociable traveling alone." He talks to monks at a monastery outside Conyers, Georgia; the "Duchess of Dare," North Carolina; the Boss of the Plains; a Black air force vet outside Brown's Chapel in Selma, Alabama; and countless bartenders, restauranteurs, saloon keepers, and waitresses. He talks to farmers and fishermen and students and factory workers and hitchhikers and runaways. He talks to cops and rednecks and hillbillies and Cajuns and boatbuilders and soldiers and merchants and carpenters and mechanics and hang gliders. He talks to preachers and prostitutes and programmers and pilots. He talks to white folks and Black folks and Hispanics and Native Americans. *Blue Highways* is one of the most exploratory and complete road trip books out there. In many ways it is also the best and greatest. It is full of the wisdom of all sorts of Americans, including plenty from the author himself.

I wondered what Least Heat-Moon would've thought about Rapid City. Originally called Hay Camp, Rapid City began along a picturesque creek in the 1870s as a supply stop for miners. In June 1877, the townspeople apprehended two horse thieves, Red Curry and Doc Allen, along with a hapless eighteen-year-old who happened to get caught up in the fracas. A vigilante mob hanged all three men—or tried to. Whether the noose was incorrectly tied, or the distance was incorrectly calculated, the result was still a botched execution with no broken necks. The three slowly strangled to death atop a mountain overlooking the town that's still called Hangman's Hill. Over the next hundred years, the town grew slowly, square blocks of square houses replicating in pleasant sameness, her denizens eventually uniting in the 1980s to preserve and restore its historic downtown buildings. The city had left its rough origins behind, or at least developed on a trajectory comparable to other South Dakota towns, agreeable and charming.

The line between urban and rural comes into sharp relief when leaving small cities like Rapid City, the quick drop-off between somewhere and nowhere. No gradual transitions here. One minute there's houses and buildings and development, then nothing man-made at all, just the Black Hills to the west and small grass prairie to the east. It's like passing through an invisible wall or driving off a cliff—quite literally, in some places. The roads in Bakersfield, California, for example, end in a huge cliff overlooking the Kern River Oil Fields, littered with wells all the way to the horizon: pumpjacks or "nodding donkeys" they're called, bobbing up and down, slurping oil from the desert. The steep Panorama Bluffs drop off sharply, 250 feet to the oil fields below, where 75 percent of California's oil production happens.

LAND BAD · 111

When driving out of Rapid City, or peering over the edge of Bakersfield, the answer to the question "why road trips?" becomes self-evident. One *has* to explore what lies beyond, has to see what comes next. The gnawing sense that there's more ahead—not just more, but *better*—looms large, inversely proportional to the size of one's current environs. It was kind of like the store owner on the Crow Reservation had said. Time and space are narrow, constricting, but travel opens and widens.

There is also a sense that the nation's in-between spaces—the places between cities, between the coasts, the heartland—hold answers. That perception, however, parallels a contradictory and paradoxical notion, which is the sense that the middle of the country is barren. "In the United States there is more space where nobody is than where anybody is," wrote Gertrude Stein in 1936. "That is what makes America what it is." When watching TV it's easy to get the impression that the United States is quite empty. The Weather Channel—where meteorologists brush across the entire continent to show weather patterns, casually sweeping their hands from the Pacific Northwest across the Rockies and Great Plains to trail off somewhere in Missouri or Arkansas—feeds the impression that no one lives in the vast expanses of the "real" America. The Weather Channelification of America demeans those who live beneath the sweep.

Of course, there really *are* empty places in America, and one of the most famous lay ahead, east on I-90 then south on State Highway 240 from the town of Wall, South Dakota, a tiny town most famous for the Wall Drug Store: a pharmacy (the only one for forty miles in any direction), restaurant, souvenir shop, barroom, Western wear store, theme village, animated display, bookstore, museum, art gallery, and more, all rolled into one. If you've driven on I-90 anywhere in the American West, then you've seen the signs imploring you to visit Wall Drug. Ted and Dorothy Hustead opened a small pharmacy in Wall in 1931 during the Great Depression. Desperate for business, the Husteads advertised free ice water to parched travelers. It worked—they were able to drum up some business. The Husteads lobbied the federal government in the 1950s to route the new interstate through Wall. More people came. Through shrewd and shameless promotion, their drugstore eventually developed into a large roadside tourist attraction, an oasis on the High Plains and tourist trap of the first magnitude. It's the signs—at first tactically deployed at nearby crossroads, then liberally seeded along I-90 for hundreds of miles:

291 Miles to Wall Drug . . . U Wall Come . . . Wall to Wall Fun at Wall Drugs . . . 5 Cent Coffee . . . Homemade Pie . . . It's Cool . . . Refreshing . . . Blucher Boots . . . Wild West Museum . . . Travelers' Chapel . . . Steaks and Cakes . . . Buffalo Burgers . . . 6-Foot Rabbit, See It Free . . . Wall Drugs, Strongly Recommended . . . As Told by Irish Independent . . . As Told by London Telegraph . . . As Told by Wall Street Journal . . . Just Ahead . . .

By the 1960s there were signs in all fifty states. These signs have a magnetism, eroding the will of the most determined motorists, lured off the interstate to see what all the fuss is about.

A cup of ice water from Wall Drug is much needed before or after a visit southward into one of the most foreign, foreboding terrains on the continent. One of those places where motorists pray not to encounter mechanical trouble, the Badlands consists of 244,000 acres of sharply eroded buttes, pinnacles, and spires: an arid, wind-swept land wickedly barbed with rock. Extreme temperatures, lack of water, and the exposed, rugged terrain led the Lakota Sioux to call this place *mako sica*, or land bad. French Canadian fur trappers called it *les mauvais terres pour traverse*: bad lands through which to travel. "The Bad Lands grade all the way from those that are almost rolling in character," said Pres. Theodore Roosevelt, "to those that are so fantastically broken in form and so bizarre in color as to seem hardly properly to belong to this earth." Indeed, the Badlands seems like a desert planet from a sci-fi film, an apotheosis of wastelands: waterless, plantless, barren, blinding. Amazingly, some Native Americans call it home.

Exit 110 off I-90 leads into Wall. From there, driving south on State Highway 240 brings intrepid motorists into Badlands National Park along the Badlands Loop Road, a scenic byway winding through the eastern part of the park. It takes an hour to drive the forty-mile stretch without stopping, which no one does; instead, it's a two-hour trip with intermissions along gob-smacking turnouts and overlooks. Pausing at Big Badlands Overlook, Pinnacles Overlook, and Yellow Mounds Overlook, this two-lane road snakes through ancient rock formations, sharp cliffs, and colorful pinnacles. A careful eye might pick out an occasional sign of life: a prairie rattler, pronghorn antelope, mule deer, prairie dog, or even a buffalo in the western reaches. The overwhelming impression, however, is one

LAND BAD • 113

of being dropped in the middle of a place people and animals shouldn't be. It's hard to imagine anything living in this sea of arid rock, whose wind-cut stonescape tops some of the harshest environments on earth.

In *Travels with Charley*, John Steinbeck notes that he was unprepared for the Badlands. "They deserve this name," he writes. "They are like the work of an evil child."

> Such a place the Fallen Angels might have built as a spite to Heaven, dry and sharp, desolate and dangerous, and for me filled with foreboding. A sense comes from it that it does not like or welcome humans.

Like many visitors, Steinbeck may have overlooked some of the natural history here. Much of the inhospitable rock beds are blended in Badlands National Park with the largest protected mixed-grass prairie in the United States. One of the world's richest fossil beds, it is one of the most complete fossil accumulations on the continent, where archaeologists continue to coax entire mammoth skeletons from the ground. The habitat of North America's most endangered mammal, the black-footed ferret, it is also home to two of the longest cave systems in the world: Wind Cave National Park and Jewel Cave National Monument.

Unlike its natural history, however, the place's human history is every bit as terrible as its name suggests. Paleo-Indians first hunted the prairie—their arrowheads and tools visible today in eroding stream banks alongside the charcoal of their campfires—long before the Great Sioux Nation arrived, its seven bands displacing other tribes on the northern plains. The Sioux existed unperturbed until 1874, when Lt. Col. George Armstrong Custer led an expedition from Bismarck, North Dakota, to find a suitable site for a fort in the unmapped Black Hills. Rumors of gold discovered by Custer's troops brought miners. Greedily eyeing the land granted to the Sioux by the federal government in the Treaty of Fort Laramie in 1868, prospectors stumbled upon rich deposits in the creeks around Deadwood, which sprang up overnight into a lawless, thriving town located on tribal lands. Tensions grew between white settlers and Native Americans, stripped of their territory by the federal government, which used the US military to pen Indians on reservations. Placer mining gave way to more invasive forms of extraction, the end result being the largest and deepest mine in the Western Hemisphere, the Homestake Mine. The Black Hills

Gold Rush peaked in 1876–77, but rustlers and bandits found the arroyos, box canyons, and caves of the Badlands perfect for outlaw roosts and robber dens.

Deadwood and the Badlands are not unique in their ominous sounding names. There are many across the American West. Little Hope, Texas. Tombstone, Arizona. Cripple Creek, Colorado. Devil's Den, Wyoming. And it wasn't just town names. In South Dakota alone there's Go-To-Hell Gulch, No Water Lake, Lost Dog Creek, Miring Mule Creek, Burnt Ranch Draw, Broken Nose, Hardscrabble, and—in addition to Deadwood—Dead Dog Hill, Deadlog Canyon, Dead Ox Campground, Deadman Creek, Dead Irishman Gulch, and Deadman's Lake. Perhaps life on the frontier was truly terrible for the people who named it, or perhaps the old prospectors were trying to scare interlopers away from their claims with foreboding names, or perhaps giving a bit of wilderness a terrifying name and then conquering it lent a sense of empowerment. But even if some of these names are fanciful and imaginative, there are undoubtedly pockets of desolation and misery where nature stacked the deck against human habitation.

One of them lies forty-five miles south of Badlands National Park: the Pine Ridge Indian Reservation, one of the largest reservations in the United States, bigger than Delaware and Rhode Island combined. The four counties that comprise it are among the poorest in the nation. Only 340 square kilometers of its 9,000 square-kilometer total area are suitable for agriculture. Its poverty is rivaled only by its history of violence. It was here that tensions culminated around the Ghost Dance in the fall and early winter of 1890, when thousands of Native Americans, including many Oglala Sioux, followed the Paiute prophet Wovoka, who prophesied a return of ancestral spirits, a reunion of dead and living to expel white people from the land and bring prosperity and peace. In Wovoka's vision, the white man would vanish and hunting grounds would be restored. To make this vision a reality, hopeful followers danced, wearing blessed shirts they believed would make them impervious to army bullets. Under the leadership of Chief Spotted Elk, allied with his half-brother Sitting Bull and nephew Crazy Horse, prophecies and visions mobilized skilled fighters into holy warriors: a threat the United States could not abide. A botched attempt to disarm the Lakota became the Wounded Knee Massacre, a slaughter of several hundred Indians, about half of whom were women and children, on December 29, 1890.

During World War II, the US Army Air Force (USAAF) seized over five hundred square miles of the Pine Ridge Indian Reservation to make a gunnery range. Families were relocated. Gunners and bombardiers aimed at giant bullseyes scratched into the earth; they blasted old car chassis and fifty-five-gallon drums, painted bright-yellow for contrast. Today the area is littered with discarded ammo casings and unexploded ordinance, some of it dating back to the Indian Wars.

On some level those wars never really ceased, flaring again a century later in 1973, when over two hundred tribal activists in the American Indian Movement (AIM), unhappy with tribal governance, seized and occupied the town of Wounded Knee within the reservation. Federal agents moved in and, in a scene eerily reminiscent of the 1890 massacre, encircled the outgunned and outmatched Indians. The standoff ended, but two years later, two FBI agents were shot and killed on the reservation after tailing a carload of AIM members. One AIM member, Joe Stuntz, was killed by police and another, Leonard Peltier, was convicted on two counts of first-degree murder for killing the agents. Another prominent AIM worker and suspected informant, Anna Mae Aquash, was found murdered in 1976.

Alcoholism continued to take its toll, a problem at Pine Ridge since its founding. Though prohibited, booze flowed onto the reservation from nearby border towns in Nebraska. High mortality rates, depression, substance abuse, malnutrition, and diabetes plagued those who lived at Pine Ridge, their lives circumscribed by poverty. With no banks and few stores, what little money they had was spent in stores located "off the rez" in Nebraska, a spending pattern that created no benefit for the tribe. Many families had no electricity, telephone, running water, or sewage systems; many used wood stoves to heat their homes, depleting limited wood resources. The people of Pine Ridge have among the shortest life expectancies of any group in the Western Hemisphere: approximately forty-seven years for males and fifty-two years for females. The infant mortality rate is five times the US national average, and the adolescent suicide rate is four times the US national average.

How much of this misery was created by American mobility? Plains Indians were always in motion, tracking herds and seasons, but the larger history of white-Indian relations is a history of white encroachment on Indian land, the displacement of Native Americans from that land, and the forced migrations of Indian peoples. Drawn into capitalist markets via trading with white men, Plains peoples in the 1860s and 1870s hunted more and more buffalo, the hides of which they traded for Euro-American trade goods, including metal wares and guns and liquor. That overhunting depleted the number of buffalo, forced the Indians to follow the great herd further and further, and ultimately undercut the Indians' way of life. Reservations like Pine Ridge arose from white envy of Indian land; the federal government's best answer to the land greed of nineteenth-century settlers was to relocate Indians and herd them into designated areas in the Indian Territory or Upper Great Plains, out of the way of white progress. From the Cherokee, removed from Georgia and East Tennessee against their will and marched along the Trail of Tears in 1838, to the Navajo, removed from Arizona to New Mexico on the 250-mile-long "Long Walk" and forced to fight not only US troops but also Paiute, Apache, Utes, Mexicans, and Zunis in their new home, to the Winnebagos, removed from Wisconsin to Minnesota to South Dakota, the history of Native Americans is itself a history of migration. From Sacagawea, who guided Meriwether Lewis and William Clark across the Louisiana Purchase to the Pacific Ocean and back, to Least Heat-Moon, who followed Sacagawea's moccasined footprints along now paved trails in his van, Native Americans have searched for solace "out there" as much as white people have, both historically and in modern times. In San Francisco in the late 1960s and early 1970s, AIM was made up of Indians who left their reservations and moved to the Bay Area for work and education. Migration, whether chosen or forced, anchors US history, but the latter seems to define Native American history in profound ways.

I knew that there was beauty and good and hope at Pine Ridge, but I didn't see them in my brief skirting of the reservation there. I put this sad place behind me, knowing that the problems of some were mitigated by a promising new vice industry: gambling. Prairie Wind Casino began operation in 1994 in three doublewide trailers, where white and Indian people alike could court chance to improve their fortunes. The revenues helped to support education and social welfare efforts, and lined the pockets of a few tribal leaders, but gambling had yet to cure the problems of most of the poor, proud Indians stuck out there in mako sica.

8

Crossing Over

"We were somewhere around Barstow on the edge of the desert when the drugs began to take hold." So begins Hunter S. Thompson's *Fear and Loathing in Las Vegas*, which, as the subtitle admits, is "a savage journey to the heart of the American Dream." Sent to cover a motorcycle race in the Nevada desert, the journalist Raoul Duke—a not so thinly disguised Thompson—rockets across the sunbaked Southwest with his lawyer in a battleship-sized Chevy convertible with a trunkful of drugs and booze to Sin City, where things get crazy. "Every now and then," the author explains, "when your life gets complicated and the weasels start closing in, the only real cure is to load up on heinous chemicals and then drive like a bastard from Hollywood to Las Vegas." They attack this simple journalistic assignment with gusto and an elevated sense of purpose. "Old elephants limp off to the hills to die; old Americans go out to the highway and drive themselves to death with huge cars."

> But our trip was different. It was a classic affirmation of everything right and true and decent in the national character. It was a gross, physical salute to the fantastic *possibilities* of life in this country—but only for those with true grit. And we were chock full of that.

While they miss the mark of right and true and decent, there *is* something weirdly affirming and unmistakably American about their drug-fueled swan dive into hedonistic excess.

Thompson seems to intuit how postwar American exceptionalism, so powerful through the 1950s and 1960s, had waned by 1972—even before Watergate. In the mid-1960s, there was "a madness in any direction, at any hour.... You could strike sparks anywhere," he writes.

> There was a fantastic universal sense that whatever we were doing was *right*, that we were winning.... Our energy would simply prevail.... We had all the momentum; we were riding the crest of a high and beautiful wave.

Five years later, from a steep hill in Las Vegas "with the right kind of eyes" looking west, "you can almost see the high-water mark—that place where the wave finally broke and rolled back." The strength and limitless resources that most Americans claimed as a birthright were receding into US history.

Fear and Loathing is *On the Road* dialed up to eleven without the introspection and elegiac landscape descriptions. Bigger, better, faster, more. As with *On the Road*, in which Kerouac's alter ego is overshadowed by his larger-than-life sidekick, the real star of *Fear and Loathing* is not Thompson as Duke but rather his madcap traveling companion and attorney, a giant Samoan named Dr. Gonzo. The real-life inspiration for the character was Oscar Zeta Acosta, a Mexican American lawyer and prominent activist in the Chicano movement. Thompson and Acosta had an enormous falling out when the book came out in 1972. Interestingly, Acosta apparently had few qualms about Thompson's portrayal of him as a drug-addled maniac. As the "300-pound Samoan," Acosta felt anonymized, erased, and robbed of his contributions to the book. In his telling he was a cocreator of Gonzo journalism, not a comedic sidebar. Acosta was becoming a writer of note in his own right, the author of *The Autobiography of a Brown Buffalo* (1972) and the roman à clef *Revolt of the Cockroach People* (1973).

In April 1972—at the same time that Thompson and Acosta were screaming across the desert in the *Great Red Shark*—another traveler began a very different sort of pilgrimage. John Francis, a twenty-seven-year-old African American man originally from Philadelphia, decided to stop using motor vehicles. Living a hippie life in a tiny seaside village north of San Francisco, Francis found himself in crisis after a friend's unexpected death and after an oil spill spoiled the beautiful bay where he lived. He began to walk everywhere he needed to go, including a twenty-five-mile hike to Petaluma for a needed surgery. What began as a kind of protest became something else. "In the walking I discover a thread that runs through time," he would later write, "beyond the need of personal protest." Less than a year after he stopped traveling by car he also stopped speaking, a one-year pledge that turned into an eighteen-year vow of silence. A solo cross-country trek begun in 1983 ended in Atlantic City, New Jersey, in January 1990, though Francis's journeys would carry him by sail to the Caribbean, to South America, and eventually to Antarctica and back. These ramblings and what he learned along the way are described in *Planetwalker* (2005), in which Francis investigates "the ethical justification of my choices and actions through a method of 'experiential reflection' on the life experience that awakened and delivered me onto this path of a pilgrim."

In describing his pilgrimage, Francis invokes the Belgian ethnographer Arnold van Gennep, who defines three phases through which every pilgrim must pass in his 1908 tome *The Rites of Passage*. First, there is separation or detachment from the familiar; the second, a liminal phase, "a sort of ambiguous state during which the pilgrim is part of no fixed social structure"; and third, "the reaggregation," when the pilgrimage is finished and the traveler returns. Francis's odyssey is all of these things and more, a journey of peril—dehydration in the high desert of Idaho, grizzlies in Montana, malaria in Bolivia—and of learning, both informal and formal (he managed to earn a master's degree and PhD along the way).

Whether he walks because he chooses not to speak or vice versa is not an unimportant question. When Francis first begins to walk, he finds it easier to walk in silence. He grows tired of having to explain his perambulations to those who do not or cannot understand. Early in *Planetwalker*, he describes how people constantly question his motives, some even challenging him confrontationally, threatened by his choice not to drive or ride in a car. It becomes much easier to go mute, rather than constantly explain and defend his actions. Is he a prophet? A saint? A nut? Like those who encountered him on the open road, the reader is left to decide.

Planetwalker raises another interesting question: Is a road trip a road trip without wheels? If we expand the definition of road trip to include means of transportation other than cars and motorcycles, then there's room in the road trip canon for books such as *Planetwalker*, or *A Walk across America*, or *Mississippi Solo*, or even Robin Lee Graham's *Dove*, the

1972 round-the-world teenage sailing saga first serialized in *National Geographic*. The road can be loosely defined, as can the means of traveling it. Strictly construed, however, a road trip involves a person (or persons) and a car—and not even a very roadworthy car at that. Some of the best tales, including *The Cruise of the Rolling Junk* and *The Lost Continent*, involve beaters and jalopies that leave the reader wondering if the protagonist will perish on the side of the road somewhere.

Like Francis, I understood the difficulties in articulating the compulsion to go, and I also came to appreciate quietude. On long drives, one can enter a fugue state, the cars and billboards and dotted yellow lines ticking by hypnotically, somnambulantly. At other times a kind of mania kicks in. And sometimes it's a bit of both. More often than not I enjoyed the silence, but I also furiously filled it. I found myself singing along with the radio unabashedly. The Dave Matthews Band, Phish, and other jam bands moved me down the road. There were familiar R&B favorites from Otis Redding and Marvin Gaye and Gladys Knight, and new alt-rock earwigs like "Volcano Girls" by Veruca Salt, "Flagpole Sitta" by Harvey Danger, "One Headlight" by the Wallflowers, and "Banditos" by the Refreshments. I couldn't get away from "Bittersweet Symphony" by the Verve. Avoiding talk radio, I was indiscriminate in my choice of tunes, everything from rock and alternative to hip-hop and rap. I kept time on the steering wheel and dash and floorboard and headliner, playing the van like a drum kit. The spectacle of a long-haired white guy thrashing to Ice T's "Body Count" in a VW Bus must have been quite a sight, had there been anyone there to see it, at least until Jimmy Buffett's *Coconut Telegraph* album got stuck in the tape deck. But mostly I listened to country because that's what the AM/FM radio consistently afforded, reminiscent of the classic line from *The Blues Brothers*: "We've got both kinds of music, country AND western." Willie and Waylon and Hank and Dolly and Reba and Garth all made the trip.

At times I yelled and cussed and screamed while driving. I found myself belting out obscenities at no one in particular, a kind of road-borne Tourette's syndrome. It wasn't angry, and it wasn't directed at other motorists. It just . . . was. I shouted the F-word, getting creative with its applications, but mainly I just shouted, loudly and joyously: "AHHHHHHHHH!!!" I cursed because I could, screamed because no one else was there to hear it. It was cathartic, hopeful, and cleansing.

To stay awake and keep focused, I read the bumper stickers of passing cars (and all cars are passing cars when driving a VW Bus—I lived in the right-hand lane). The pro-gun guys were everywhere—"They Can Have My Gun When They Pry It from My Cold, Dead Fingers," "If Guns Are Outlawed, Only Outlaws Will Have Guns," and the ubiquitous "Guns Don't Kill People, People Do"—but the vast majority of stickers announced school or sports team allegiances. There were fraternity and sorority letters in Greek. There were a number of political pronouncements. Some stickers were dedicated to trashing damn libruls, some dedicated to bashing lunkhead neocons. Some supported particular political candidates. One sticker said, "I'm Proud to Be an American"; another tagged the driver as a "Nature-Loving, Tree-Hugging, Dirt Worshipper." I saw a couple of stickers with a Nike swoosh that read "Just Do It" and a couple that read "Shit Happens."

I noticed a "Keep Christ in Christmas" sticker, which I pondered thoughtfully as a born-and-raised Presbyterian. As a protest against the commercialization of the holidays, I applauded the sentiment, but, as part of a mounting perception that Christians (particularly evangelical Christians) were being marginalized and threatened in the United States, these stickers bothered me. There was no war on Christmas. There was no war on the US flag or the Pledge of Allegiance either. If non-Christians are troubled by the placement of a nativity scene on a town green in front of a courthouse, then I respect their vocalization of the need to separate church and state. If someone's homeowner's association limits the dimensions of flags flown in the neighborhood—allowing a five-foot-long flag but restricting, say, a fifty-footer—it's not "un-American" to restrict the one that blocks out the sun. Neither is a portent of the demise of Western civilization, but the quickness of white middle-class Americans to defend their institutions against imagined threats surely spoke to the manufactured outrages of our times.

I saw an "Eracism" sticker whose clever enjambment spoke to me—at least it did at first. I was all for erasing racism, but I wondered if the driver was one of those "I-don't-see-color" folks whose attempts at overcoming bigotry shaded into severe egalitarianism, one that caused as many problems as it corrected. If you can't see race, you can't see racial inequality. If you can't see race, you miss out on some wonderfully scintillating cultural nuances too—differences that make the United States an exciting and vibrant place to live. In a pluralist, multicultural America, color was fine as a positive demarcation, I reasoned. Only when used as a negative delineation ("No Negroes Allowed," "Orientals Need Not Apply," etc.) did it become problematic.

After a while, I began to read bumper stickers—these public declarations of belief and loyalty and self—like tea leaves, scrying wisdom from America's tailpipe pulpit for immutable truths. I'm not sure if I found any, but I did decide that there are two kinds of people: those who see problems that need to be addressed and those who look around and say, "Things are pretty good, largely because they are good for me, and therefore nothing should change." This latter group lacks empathy, in part because they perceive that empathy costs them something. They are right, of course: it *does* cost them something. It pierces their self-assuredness that everything is OK and forces them to consider that the American Dream may not be all it's cracked up to be, at least not in equal measure for all dreamers. And that's a terrifying prospect for those who've never contemplated it. Could meritocracy be a myth—not in the good sense of myth as founding story of common origins, but in the negative sense, as a falsehood or lie?

Somewhere outside the Twin Cities, I began to make up stories about my fellow motorists. Some profiles were easy, based on the drivers' stickers. There was the troubled vet, whose life peaked with his military service; everything since had been disappointing, less meaningful. There was the Big Ten university grad, whose life peaked with his collegiate experience; everything since had been disappointing, less meaningful. There was the misogynist gun-nut divorcé, the animal lover, the cat lady, the anarchist. Their stickers told the tale. Other bios were more speculative. I saw a woman in a BMW. No political decals, no collegiate vanity tags, no nothing. But the factory-stock sterility of her coupe spoke volumes, her story in the absences and silences. Her whole life was a bonsai garden where everything was cultivated and beautiful and twisted and stunted.

There went a retired oil tycoon, there a teacher who moonlighted as a Watkins salesperson to make ends meet. There was a German couple on holiday, touring the American West in a rented Class-C RV—childless, unmarried but steadfastly devoted, environmentally conscientious . . . spies, perhaps? The American West was crawling with German tourists whom I imagined as foreign operatives amassing a fifth column, scouring the New Mexico desert for nuclear secrets, probing the Hoover Dam for structural weaknesses. There was a hospitality-industry tycoon touring his hotel chain. A nondescript Ford sedan carried a highway serial killer to his next victim.

While my little game passed the time, it also forced me to ponder a paradox: Bumper Sticker America did not correspond with the America I saw on the open road or in port. To judge from the plastered chrome of their cars, many Americans were malcontented, the pronouncements on their vehicles strident and angry; but, the people I met were not, being generally neighborly and warm. I didn't understand. There seemed to be an undercurrent of hostility and mistrust, a river of acrimony flowing everywhere at once, flooding its banks in all directions, that receded and disappeared with the first human contact.

Could it be that the very thing that differentiated us as Americans also tore at the fabric of community that knit us together? How can one build a society on individualism? The nineteenth-century Confederate experiment did not offer much hope on this front; in that case, a nation organized around states' rights proved to be unsustainable (a shortcoming hastened by the South's stubborn adherence to human trafficking and unfree labor). Hopefully our proclivities for self-sufficiency, self-determination, and self-improvement wouldn't short-circuit our communal experiment in democracy. These competing Americanisms often seemed at odds.

When I wasn't singing or projecting biographies onto passersby, I sometimes communed with the Bus. Sweet-talking it and whispering into its air vents, I implored it to keep chugging along, willed it to roll forward, begged it not to quit on some forsaken backroad. I prayed to Saint John the Mechanic and the road gods for safe passage and garage-free travels— all of which, it turned out, was quite unnecessary. The Bus was the most reliable vehicle I ever owned. I turned the key and it cranked and went everywhere I asked it to go. Perhaps it heard my pleas.

The sing-screaming and yelling and car talk might have indicated a mind unspooled, a lonesome traveler lost in the byways of his mind, his van turned rolling sanitorium. But I felt great—much better, in fact, than I had at the beginning of the trip. There's a profound difference between being alone and being lonely. I didn't mind being alone, and I didn't feel lonely. I was enjoying my own company, and the trip was healing me by degrees.

In Minneapolis I saw my college friends Chris and Julie, who offered a spare bed, a hot shower, and a warm meal. Chris was my fraternity pledge brother, Julie his college sweetheart. They sagely married after we graduated, and I missed them both. We reminisced and did a little sightseeing, including the original Red Wing Shoe Company, founded in 1905 in nearby Red Wing, Minnesota. The name Minnesota comes from Dakota Indian words meaning "sky-tinted waters," and I made a mental note to come back to the Land of Ten Thousand Lakes for a more in-depth visit. I wanted to stay, but I needed to get to Michigan to do some academic research.

Somehow I managed to drive across the United States without crossing "the great Mississippi," as Mark Twain called it, or if I did I have no memory of it. I must've crossed somewhere between the Twin Cities but I didn't commemorate this crossing or even mentally note it to myself. I was probably swept along in heavy traffic, too preoccupied to notice, tumbled like a log rolling downstream, but it's possible that the Great Father of Rivers did not make the same impression here as it does further south. Indeed, the Mississippi varies in grandeur. The same river that Twain called "the majestic, the magnificent Mississippi, rolling its mile-wide tide along, shining in the sun," Charles Dickens called "the hateful Mississippi . . . an enormous ditch."

Southeast of Minneapolis and St. Paul, Dickens's "foul stream" separated Minnesota from Wisconsin, whose natural beauty surprised me with its green, rolling hills, its lush farmland, and its open vistas. Dotted around the state, particularly on the outskirts of towns, I encountered strange eateries, part restaurant and part tavern. Many were low-slung, nondescript buildings with signs advertising a particular make of regionally brewed beer (Leinenkugel, Old Style, Pabst, Schlitz, Rhinelander). A few had neon signs advertising "Food" or "Cocktails," but most of them advertised themselves as "supper clubs." These establishments were a mystery to me. Were they primarily restaurants or bars? Were they actual clubs—exclusive, members only—or could anyone go there? Were they racially segregated "whites-only" clubs, intended to keep out people of color? I pulled over and peaked in the window of one, sitting empty on a country road outside Oshkosh. Inside was nothing special: wood paneling, vinyl tablecloths, fake flowers, country-kitsch décor. A bar extended down one side of the dining room. I concluded (wrongly) that the supper club was some sort of legal dodge around local liquor laws, Wisconsin's answer to the honky-tonk or Prohibition-era roadhouse, situated outside city limits to thwart town ordinances. Only later did I learn about Wisconsin's proud tradition of supper clubs: homey, welcoming restaurants, some fancier than others, where anyone could enjoy generous portions of prime rib, steak, fried fish, or roast duck after a mixed drink and a pants-popping helping of iceberg salad, soup, breadsticks and dinner rolls, kidney bean salad, shrimp cocktail, pickles, relishes, and cheese spread. It's little surprise that the term "doggie bag" is attributed to Wisconsinite Lawrence Frank, who in 1938 in Beverly Hills founded Lawry's, which many consider to be the first supper club in the United States. Since then, generations of Wisconsinites have enjoyed special occasions or a simple night out at their local supper club: eating heartily, washing down mountains of delicious homestyle food with a Manhattan, an Old-Fashioned, or a glass of wine. New Jersey has its diners, Georgia its BBQ shacks, Wisconsin its supper clubs.

I reached the banks of Lake Michigan below Green Bay at the shore town of Manitowoc, where I faced a choice: I could drive southward through Sheboygan, Milwaukee, Racine, and Kenosha into Illinois on my way to Chicago; or I could forego Chicago and head straight across the water into Michigan. I chose the latter, driving my car onto the SS *Badger*, a car ferry between Wisconsin and Michigan. Built in 1951, the *Badger* was the last coal-fired, steam-powered passenger ship sailing on Lake Michigan and the largest car ferry to sail the Great Lakes. It had recently been named a Registered Wisconsin Historic Site. Over four hours, the *Badger* cruises sixty miles from Manitowoc to Ludington, Michigan, across the lake. I would be catching one of the last shuttles of the year. The ferry stops running in October due to high seas and ice in the winter months.

At the end of Highway 10 is a staging area where cars and trucks cue to board the ship. A professional driver loads and unloads all vehicles. Indeed, one of the strangest parts of the trip was handing over my car keys to a stranger. Could he manage the manual transmission? Could he drive up the gangway while handling the finicky clutch? I realized that I had not been away from the Bus for any appreciable length of time, had certainly never allowed anyone else to drive it. Passengers are not allowed in their vehicles once underway—not even allowed on the car deck except along some side stairs while boarding and disembarking. I was experiencing separation anxiety, something I had not anticipated. I missed my Bus.

I explored the ship, its steel bulk impossibly staying afloat. It was huge.

Hanging from overhead racks were rows of strange, bright-red, hooded suits, with little round cutouts for the face. They looked like something from a Ray Bradbury novel—Martian space exploration gear—or maybe the standard diving dress of a deep-sea diver, sans brass helmet. Scarlet Gumby or Diver Dan, it was hard to say. Closer inspection revealed these weird, one-size-fits-all body sacks to be safety gear: neoprene survival suits in case of cold-water immersion, one for each person. I gulped, imagining a plunge into the icy waters of Lake Michigan in October. Hegel calls the sea "flux, danger and destruction," and while this lake was no ocean, it was big water. My thoughts turned to an old Gordon Lightfoot song, commemorating the sinking of a freighter on Lake Superior in 1975. Written in the Dorian mode, a minor scale that gives it a haunting quality, "The Wreck of the *Edmund Fitzgerald*" topped the charts in Canada and the United States ("that good ship and true was a bone to be chewed / when the gales of November came early"). The entire crew of twenty-nine perished in the storm. The SS *Edmund Fitzgerald* was the largest ship on the Great Lakes, and it remains the largest ship to have sunk there: a lake-borne *Titanic*, claimed by an inland sea.

Moody and somber, I tried to think of something other than drowning full-fathom-five. I had grabbed a book from the glovebox before embarking, an old Bantam Books paperback edition of John Steinbeck's *Travels with Charley*, first published in July 1962. A Book-of-the-Month Club selection by a Nobel Prize–winning author, my copy was from Bantam's twenty-first printing in late 1966 or early 1967. It had already traveled, with a smeared, illegible inscription on the title page from a previous owner: "For [smear], who always [smear] . . . Enjoy!" With my feet propped on the deck railing, I settled into a nonskid chair to read a chapter or two from this dog-eared softcover.

Steinbeck's premise was simple. After years of success as a novelist, he found himself out of touch with "this monster land":

> I discovered that I did not know my own country. I, an American writer, writing about America, was working from memory, and the memory is at best a faulty, warpy reservoir. I had not heard the speech of America, smelled the grass and trees and sewage, seen its hills and water, its color and quality of light. I knew the changes only from books and newspapers.

CROSSING OVER • 127

He therefore sets out with his French poodle, Charley, to rediscover the nation—its people, food, landmarks, customs, but most of all the desire of its people to be *out there*. His friends gathered to see him off:

> I saw in their eyes something I was to see over and over in every part of the nation—a burning desire to go, to move, to get under way, anyplace, away from any Here. They spoke quietly of how they wanted to go someday, to move about, free and unanchored, not toward something but away from something. I saw this look and heard this yearning everywhere in every state I visited.

"Nearly every American hungers to move," he concludes, citing a wanderlust he terms "the virus of restlessness." The pioneers and immigrants who peopled the continent were transplanted and wayward Europeans; "the steady rooted ones stayed home and are still there [in Europe]." We Americans are therefore "descended from the restless ones." It's in our blood—in our national character—to move and travel. And so Steinbeck becomes *vacilador*, going without urgency or purpose, but picking a direction and going nonetheless.

After a couple of hours, I looked up, realizing that the freshwater spray on my lips lacked even a trace of brine or salinity. It was a strange reminder that I was in the middle of an enormous lake. It felt for all the world like I was crossing an ocean.

"You must be an English major," a voice drawled. I turned to see a lean, tan gent with longish grey hair and droopy mustache. Beneath a crushed trucker's cap, he wore a small gold hoop in one earlobe. He looked a bit like Sam Elliott, the actor. Standing next to him was a pleasant-looking middle-aged woman, like him wearing a T-shirt, blue jeans, and light jacket. They smiled amiably, leaning over the ship's rail. I stuffed Steinbeck in my daypack and the three of us struck up a conversation, passing the last half of the trip in good-natured chitchat. Where was I going, they politely inquired. Eventually aiming for Ann Arbor, I told them. Where had I been? I told them.

Though I was in fact not an English major, I had always loved language arts and taken lots of lit courses in college. I had wanted to follow in the footsteps of my grandmother, an English teacher in middle and high school—a true grammarian who never met a sentence she couldn't diagram—but two things happened in college. First, I was ensnared by some particularly compelling history professors; and second, I became enthralled with the idea of becoming a professor myself. I knew that meant earning a PhD, but in what subject? I couldn't decide between English—my first love—and history, my new flame. I remember playfully flipping a coin, which my mom snatched out of the air as it flipped and arced downward. "No," she said somberly. "Don't do it that way." I did a cost-benefit analysis, weighing pros and cons, but the real reason I didn't pursue becoming an English professor was that I didn't want to think too much about literature, didn't want to overanalyze it. Like Whitman with his stargazing, I didn't want to attend symposia, listen to lectures, or discuss it in seminars. I loved literature too much to study it closely, to scrutinize it clinically under a microscope. What I wanted to do was to sit and read, to clutch my chest and keel over in a dead swoon like Jane Austen's Musgrove Sisters when the words fit together just so. It seemed frivolous when I thought about it, and I wasn't about to confess as much to my newly met shipmates. Happily, we didn't get into it on our brief cruise across Lake Michigan. We just talked.

Tom and Jean lived in Pentwater, Michigan, where she kept house and he worked odd jobs as a handyman. Like me, they were sightseeing, exploring the Upper Midwest. We talked and talked, and they both seemed really interested in my travels. The more we chatted, the more something maternal seemed to kick in with Jean, a concern for this wayward grad student. Confusing "traveling" with "homeless," she asked more and more questions about my destination on the other side of the lake. Tom seemed less worried, maybe even a bit envious of my meanderings; however, after conferring briefly, they insisted that I spend a few nights with them in Pentwater. Jean saw a thin student that needed fattening, a tired traveler that needed a rest, but Tom took a different tack. He suggested I come back and work alongside him a few days in exchange for room and board. He'd taken a job painting an office and needed some help. They wouldn't take no for an answer. Charmed by their hospitality, I agreed.

They wanted me to sleep in the house in a bed, but in the name of not inconveniencing them, I stubbornly refused, preferring to sleep in the Bus in their driveway (I may have been semiferal at that point in the trip). Jean did her best to fatten me up. I took all my meals there in their house, and they fed me well. But I was working too hard to put on much extra weight.

Fig. 8: Jean and Tom aboard the SS *Badger*. Photo by author.

For three days we painted eight or nine hours a day: rolling our rollers, cutting in perfectly with fully loaded sash brushes, listening to the radio, smoking cigarettes and loafing during the occasional break. We talked about everything and nothing at all.

"So," Tom said, during one smoke break. "Whatcha lookin' fer?" I instantly understood what he was asking.

"Truth, beauty," I replied, no hesitation. "Same as everyone else."

"Bah," Tom snorted. "It's the same all over. Get born, get slapped. Suck air, suck milk. Grow, study, learn, work. Taste pleasure, live pain, struggle, gain wisdom. Perish."

He was right, of course, this painter-philosopher. Clearly it was Tom who should be the professor, not me. I was reminded of Ferris Bueller, Matthew Broderick's character in *Ferris Bueller's Day Off* (1986). "Life moves pretty fast," Bueller observes. "If you don't stop and look around once in a while, you could miss it." Truer words had never been spoken, at least to many Gen Xers like me.

After three days we finished. Tom paid me a little, I thanked them and promised to write and backed out of their driveway after a weirdly sentimental goodbye. It was the longest the Bus had sat in one place since I'd bought it. *Travels with Charley* remained buried in my daypack, where it stayed for the rest of the trip.

9

Homeward Bound

Driving after dark could be dicey. Bad things happen at night, when something as simple as a flat tire becomes more dire, sable angels and devils reaching, tree limbs clawing from the shoulder, the stars above drowning in darkness. The evening after leaving Tom and Jean I was driving half-asleep down a two-lane highway in Michigan, chugging along at fifty-five miles per hour. I glimpsed a billboard out of the corner of my eye. "You are not dreaming . . ." was all I registered before vrooming past. I drowsily noted an eighteen-wheeler a few hundred yards ahead whose headlights suddenly divided, a dangerous mitosis. Someone was passing the truck. Now they were hurtling toward me in my lane at ninety miles per hour. I was a target, a sitting duck. "Watch out!" I cried, but not aloud (or maybe I did). The oncoming car swerved back into its lane at the last second, a second in which I may or may not have squinched my eyes shut, the van rocking in a meteoric contrail. I pulled over, coasting to a stop on the shoulder, and there I spent the rest of the night. Exhausted, I didn't sleep much at all, putting a dent in my minibar after a much-needed drink or two (or three).

I developed predilections for where I spent the night. I preferred, in order: federal land, national parks, state parks, county parks, rest stops, city streets (dead ends, cul-de-sacs, etc.), parking lots. Initially I sought out established parks—federal, state, or local—but I soon came to appreciate the public domain, particularly land under the jurisdiction of the Bureau of Land Management (BLM), which was unrestricted, open-access, and free. Parks had rangers and fees, and towns had nosy constables, but one could stay on BLM land relatively unmolested by authorities—a freedom that cut both ways, positively and negatively. The BLM refers to camping on public lands away from developed recreation facilities as "dispersed camping," which was generally secluded and agreeable; however, after that first night in Oregon when I nearly lost myself in the Cascades, I realized there was such a thing as too much privacy, too much isolation, and after months on the road, I still made errors in choosing where to sleep.

Sleeping on the Crow Reservation had been pleasant. County parks were unpredictable; some saw little use and some saw a lot. Certain parking lots invited visitors to peek in the window. Rest stops could be sketchy; for a potty break and a quick rest they were fine, but they ranged in quality from interstate oases with full services to pull-offs on state and county roads with a picnic table or two. City streets could be OK, but like rest stops, one never really knew what to expect; homeowners tended to dislike strange vans parked near their houses. I wondered if I could sleep through a towing, chains clacked around the undercarriage as I slept soundly a few inches away.

I spent an entire week sleeping in different residential neighborhoods in Ann Arbor while visiting an archive at the University of Michigan. Eating most of my meals there in restaurants, I moved the Bus from neighborhood to neighborhood, never spending the night in the same place so as not to arouse suspicion. By day I did research at the Bentley Historical Library; by night I camped in the Bus with the curtains drawn tight. After a week I urgently needed a bar of soap and a good scrubbing. I was pretty funky by the end of my visit to Tree Town, the Ace Deuce (as *Ann Arbor* was sometimes called). I rarely went a full week without bathing, but I did at UofM and I know I was rank.

One evening in Ohio I pulled over at a rest stop at dusk. I had the place to myself. I popped the top, ate leisurely, read for a while, drew the curtains, and bedded down. When I closed my eyes, rings of color shimmied upward like rings on a Tesla coil, morphing into nebulas of light, pinks and oranges against the dark curtain of my eyelids. Sleep came in rainbows.

A few hours later, I awoke to car doors slamming and gravel crunching. Light was pouring into the van—lancing the thinly veiled windshield and windows, flooding the interior, tracking across the glass as headlights crisscrossed from multiple angles. The light fried my eyeballs. Figures were silhouetted against the curtains, people moving and talking and shouting. The place was abuzz. I cautiously lifted one curtain and peeked out. Someone—a young, hair-gelled guy with a cigarette—was staring back at me, trying to see into the van through cupped hands, leering like Hokusai's ghost. I twitched back instinctively, dropping the curtain. There were a lot of guys out there, groups of men, milling around, leaning into car windows, laughing and flirting. They were cruising. I had somehow made camp in the middle of the local gay pick-up spot, disguised by day as a peaceful rest stop.

In 1998, men across the United States still met up for sex in highway bathrooms and rest areas. Part of being a gay man in America—a part that was by no means universal, but a historically undeniable part nonetheless—was seeking sex in unsexy places: anonymous meetups in bathrooms, waysides, roadside parks, picnic areas, and lay-bys, public (or semipublic) places where one can get in and out discreetly and quickly. This rest stop was apparently one such place. With my top popped and curtains drawn, I was clearly there to party—or so it must have seemed ("If the van's a-rockin'"). I was most certainly *not* there to party, and once I figured out what was happening, I quickly dropped the roof, cranked the engine, and left hurriedly.

Did homophobia speed my exit? Probably. But I didn't want to explain myself to the guy peeking in my van window, or to whatever local law enforcement officers might come along to break up the gathering, or to my parents after being rounded up and slapped with a misdemeanor "morals charge," that McCarthy-era holdover created to harass and embarrass gay men. So I peeled out and slung gravel, putting distance between me and the rest stop scene.

And as I did my initial alarm faded, morphing into embarrassment and then sadness. I was embarrassed by my reaction, but I was mainly sad that gay men had been so ostracized and marginalized that they had to meet up for sex in highway bathrooms and rest areas. I doubt it was a circumstance they preferred. Who would willingly choose to find companionship or seek intimacy in a roadside pit-stop? The moral majority's fear and intolerance had pushed them into these spaces.

I had grown up in a gay-fearing, gay-loathing world, one that labeled homosexuality deviant and aberrant, a world in which we flung words like *faggot*, *queer*, and *gay* as casual put-downs. Things had changed, things were changing, and it struck me as an enormous step forward that the public sphere was opening to make space for gay men and women. It represented the next evolution of national development, the ongoing experiment in broadening democracy to all Americans, the quintessential advancement of egalitarianism.

America itself is the story of expanding civil rights, a Big Bang set off in the 1700s by the Founding Fathers that, over the course of US history, has reached further and further to more groups and more individuals—to racial and ethnic minorities, to women, to others. The United States had always embraced a strange mix of sexual license and prudery, and perhaps with its puritanical roots, it's understandable that some (especially conservative Christians with their scriptural heritage) had expressed apprehension about gay equality. But what really did they have to fear? And what business was it of theirs what happened between consenting adults behind closed doors? Perhaps the key was to help those who're worried to see equality and civil rights as something other than a zero-sum game. More freedom and opportunity for one person doesn't equate with less for someone else. It's not coconut cream pie. In fact, more security and happiness for some can only equal more security and happiness for all. Inclusion is funny that way. I drove on, a straight man pondering crooked taboos, eventually finding somewhere else to pull over and spend what remained of the night.

The next day I delved further into Ohio. I had turned, one of the big directional shifts on this trip, now making my way southward toward home. I had expected the differences between East and West to be stark, but this land was still open, wide open, domed skies and languorous grasslands. I had entered the Midwest, a place-name used by land surveyors in the 1880s to mark the plains between the Great Lakes and the slaveholding South (but also a term not officially adopted by the US Census Bureau until 1984), a place we now call the heartland: notable in its ordinariness, a place of genuinely kind people that the rest of us like to imagine as living in pastoral insularity. And maybe they are. People I'd known from this part of the world were in fact wholesome, practical, pragmatic . . . Don't many stereotypes often contain a seed of truth? Midwesterners had earned their reputations by looking out for each other and for those who passed through their bucolic midst—though it's also possible that many of us live out the regional stereotypes that others attribute to us, we stoic Yankees and laconic westerners and unreconstructed southerners.

The Midwest is a place defined as much by what it's not as by what it is. It's not puritan New England, nor the Spanish-Catholic- and Indigenous-- flavored Southwest, nor the paradoxically pugnacious yet hospitable South. It's neither crunchy-granola California nor un-messed-with Texas, neither taciturn Wyoming nor mouthy New York. It's overwhelmingly white but also ethnically mixed, a land settled by hard-working Swedes and Germans and Poles and Irish, whose descendants seem humble and often happy. Its cities vacillate between vitality and dereliction: in good times they vi- brate, pulsing with life; in hard times they wear their patinas of wear and tear more visibly, like a well-used, patchy overcoat. The region's regularity is both boon and curse: boon because of its attractiveness, curse because those who live there (and many who don't) often view it as bland and unre- markable, even in its beauty and diversity. To be so "normal," it's notable in its history of radical politics, including abolitionism in the nineteenth cen- tury, when intentional utopian settlements also sprang up across the region.

I had read somewhere that Ohio is the least expensive state in which to live, based on cost of living and housing expenses, and the Ohioan sub- urbs seemed to confirm this rumor. Outside Dayton, the housing develop- ments grew, providing shelter for those who would enjoy a bit of midwest- ern ordinariness. Residential architecture norms seemed to have changed little since the first suburban development in Hempstead, New York, where Levitt & Sons construction company followed a precise, twenty-seven-step building process using prefabricated materials to churn out more than thirty houses per day between 1947 and 1951. As Henry Ford had done to the automotive industry, the Levitts brought assembly-line production to housing: bulldozing the land and covering it with standardized units with uniform floor plans. Cost-saving measures meant that the American Dream had suddenly become much more affordable. Other Levittowns fol- lowed, changing the American landscape in their sprawl as middle-class, mostly white families moved out of cities into new "collar" or "bedroom" communities, replete with not only schools and churches but also shopping centers, grocery stores, and restaurants—all the conveniences of modern life within a short drive.

What was it about single-family dwellings that spoke to Americans? For many of us a house with a white picket fence is synonymous with the American Dream, an idealized symbol of freedom and accomplishment. As Delores Hayden has noted, most American housing is based on Levitt's

136 · CHAPTER 9

model of the home as a haven for the white-collar male commuter and his family. This design choice lends a certain uniformity, in which the outskirts of Sacramento look similar to the outskirts of Seattle, which look similar to the outskirts of Minneapolis and Dayton. "Many American towns and cities look very much alike, and they look different from towns and cities elsewhere in the world," writes Craig Whitaker in *Architecture and the American Dream.* "American values, more than any other attribute, underpin the singularity of American architecture." The values reflected in single-family dwellings are presumably independence and self-sufficiency, hearkening back to the pioneer's sod house or woodsman's log cabin, themselves testaments to the frontier spirit of autonomy and self-reliance. Here controlling one's destiny has meant having a plot of land and a place of one's own.

The irony, of course, is that in our eagerness to own freestanding houses and thereby taste the American Dream, we've sequestered ourselves in sometimes sterile built environments where all the houses look alike and the inhabitants think and talk and act alike, the very opposite of individualism. Plus, with everyone concentrating on their own dwellings—focused on creating cocooned, idealized, private domiciles—it becomes easy to ignore the crucial spaces of public interaction and community: the town commons or village green or neighborhood park. At some point the "dream home" replaced the American aspiration of the "city upon a hill," the wants of the individual again supplanting the needs of the collective, perhaps to our shared detriment. New Urbanist designers such as Peter Calthorpe notes that sprawl is not a choice: it is rather the entropy of unchecked development, what Howard Kunstler calls "the geography of nowhere." Redesigning the American Dream on this front would involve, according to Calthorpe, moving away from the single-family-dwelling ideal; creating neighborhoods rather than subdivisions; minimizing automobile use; investing in public transit; planning around people, not cars; recentering pedestrians and cyclists in city planning; and revitalizing urban centers while changing patterns of growth at urban peripheries.

That night I pulled over to spend the night in a county park, a lovely place with a large pond in the middle glinting like a pane of glass, and picnic sites dotted around its perimeter. The sky cleared at nightfall, the vainglorious stars a bit harder to see in the cool light of a full moon. The temperature was dropping. Somewhere a train whistle wailed. As I studied the dim stars—small as a hobbit, slowly pirouetting, mouth agape—I heard behind me the strangest sound, like soup being ladled into a giant bowl. A flock of Canada geese had landed on the pond, *glissando diminuendo*. They now paddled in lazy curlicues, gently honking to one another. The moon swam just below the pond's surface, a white koi winking up from below.

The weather turned frigid that night, becoming the Coldest Night of My Life, surpassing that first night in the Cascades. I thought I knew what it was to be cold, but I didn't—not until then. I felt like a polar explorer locked in pack ice, where the ocean turns solid and the mercury freezes in the thermometer and breath falls like hoarfrost. I put on my warmest clothes, burrowed into my sleeping bag, and debated piling my wool blanket on top of me or putting it underneath, where the backseat's cold vinyl leached body heat. *Lesson # 10: Always have an extra blanket.* I shivered violently, pondering what else I had learned on this trip.

Steinbeck explains it as a "virus of restlessness," this itch to move. Twain and Fitzgerald felt it, as did Peter Jenkins, Bill Bryson, and others. It was real, as real as warm blankets. "The American has not root in the soil, he has no feeling of reverence, and love for the natal spot and the paternal roof," notes Michel Chevalier, who visited the United States in 1834. "He is always disposed to emigrate, always ready to start in the first steamer that comes along, from the place where he had but just now landed." *That* it existed was less mysterious than *why* it existed. Was it nationalistic, this desire to be "out there"? Patriotic? Pierpont concludes that "our excessive mobility" is a fundamental characteristic of "Americanism," this "rich and strange" American character. Colonization, immigration, westward movement, and internal shufflings all play a role in Pierpont's theory of American growth and progress; for him, migration is a "great stimulant to action," the "Destroyer, Distorter, Conservator, Atomizer, and Energizer," the most effective "Optimizer." Restless to begin with, a nation of immigrants, "we have become more so with repeated displacement," he posits. The "wandering mania" has "got into our blood, our houses, our attention, our very ways of speech":

> Come on! Get going! Don't be a stick-in-the-mud! You don't want to get left, do you? It's a good year to make the move. So long! I don't know where I'm going, but I'm on my way. Anywhere I hang my hat is home, sweet home, to me.

The American vernacular, defined in terms of movement, reflects our collective transience.

That vernacular seldomly points to a sinister side to American travel, often ignored in our romanticization of the open road. The ubiquitous cow skull, tumbleweed, and cactus alongside the desert highway speak to the harshness of travel, and the many hazards—bandits and highwaymen, flat tires and boiling radiators, rockslides and washed-out bridges—belie our preference for carefree, drop-top travel down Nostalgia Lane. Unvarnished histories remind us of the real costs of travel in social, racial, and environmental damage.

Today we tend to associate mobility with opportunity and fresh starts and betterment, but mobility is only positive when voluntary; *choosing* to move and *having* to move are two very different things. The darker side of mobility encompasses not only restricting some peoples from moving but also forcing others to move. Euro-Americans historically told themselves that Native Americans were mobile, itinerant, unrooted—but were they? Certain Plains Indians followed the migrations of buffalo, and others followed seasonal migrations (as described expertly by William Cronon in his 1983 book *Changes in the Land*); however, many eastern tribes were quite rooted and stationary, becoming migratory only when uprooted by Indian fighters like Andrew Jackson, Martin Van Buren, and Winfield Scott. The Cherokee—an advanced, sedentary, agricultural people who had assimilated and adopted white folkways, up to and including a written language and political constitution—were still forced to leave their native Georgia at bayonet point for the arid climes of the Indian Territory.

In the nineteenth century there was a conservatism to American mobility, in which antirooting justified clinging to old ways, bad habits, and antiquated methods. For many pioneers and westward migrants, acclimating to the frontier's boom-and-bust economic cycles, it became easier to relocate than to learn a new vocation. When they'd cut down a forest, loggers would move to the next glen; when a mine played out, miners moved toward the next whispers of gold (or silver or copper). The cheap lands of the West made it easy to continue clear-cutting and dry farming and strip mining, thereby avoiding the painful choices necessitated by crop rotation, soil management, conservation, and sustainability. So American wanderlust is historically linked to environmental degradation.

It also seemed to be something that resonated with white folks more than people of color. Yes, William Least Heat-Moon and Eddie Harris had chronicled their journeys, but most American travel writers were white. One need look no further than *The Negro Motorist Green Book* to realize that travel for Black folks was a different ballgame, until very recently fraught with danger and still a dicey proposition at times. Compiled and published during the Jim Crow era from 1936 to 1966 by Victor Hugo Green, an African American mailman in New York City, the *Green Book* served Black motorists facing hardships such as white restauranteurs who refused to serve them, white mechanics who declined to repair their vehicles, white hoteliers who refused accommodation, and threats of physical violence and forcible expulsion from white-only "sundown towns." Confronted with the alternative indignity of segregated public transportation, many Black Americans used their own cars to travel between cities for work, but racial profiling could be even worse out there, where Black mobility was severely restricted by hostile sheriff's deputies. So fraught with danger were their road experiences that African Americans prayed that they'd never by pulled over by a law enforcement officer. All road trips are not created equal, and Green's book, which enabled Black travelers to find lodgings, restaurants, and service stations, made trips less embarrassing, more enjoyable, and safer.

Even before auto travel, white supremacists had found ways to harass and hassle African Americans whether they were coming or going, leaving or staying. After the Civil War, bitter plantation owners, in desperate need of labor to replace the fieldhands they had previously owned, passed vagrancy laws and other Black Codes that deterred freemen from moving away to find work. The Thirteenth Amendment to the US Constitution, ratified in 1865, prohibited slavery and involuntary servitude; however, it explicitly exempted those convicted of crime. As a result, southern state legislatures rapidly passed new laws that explicitly applied only to Black people and subjected them to criminal prosecution for a variety of "offenses." Mississippi's Vagrant Law of 1865 and Virginia's Vagrancy Act of 1866 allowed anyone who *appeared to be* unemployed or homeless to be arrested and sentenced to hard labor for no compensation. Loitering, breaking curfew, vagrancy, and failing to carry proof of employment were all punishable crimes; violators were hired out to white employers to "work off" their sentences and fines. It was the high-water mark of the convict lease system, in which states lent prisoners to private railways, mines, and large plantations.

During the Jim Crow era, the next generation of African Americans were similarly targeted when the sons of planters who had passed vagrancy laws now passed segregation laws that further circumscribed Black travel, dictating not only where Black folks could eat and spend the night but also where they could go, period. Convict labor came in two flavors: the prison farm (like Mississippi's infamous Parchman State Penitentiary, immortalized in blues music and movies like *Cool Hand Luke* and *The Defiant Ones*) and the chain gang, which started in Georgia in 1908 as a progressive penal reform measure to replace the convict lease system. The chain gang coincided with a public demand for improved transportation, and it soon became common to see chained prisoners, mostly Black, shackled together along southern roadways. As maintaining roadways became a priority, the chain gang morphed into the "good roads movement." Reformers told themselves that prisoners were trading cramped cells for fresh air, exercise, and sunshine, but chained Black roadworkers looked a lot like twentieth-century state-owned slaves. As the saying went in Georgia, "Bad boys make good roads," and Georgia indeed boasted some of the finest roads around. In this way, Black folks enabled better travel for white folks while they were inhibited from traveling themselves. Road travel was thus very much racially bound and circumscribed.

It furthermore seemed to be a largely male phenomenon, this wanderlust. The word *patriotism* comes from the Latin *patria*, which means homeland or fatherland. In *Women, America, and Movement: Narratives of Relocation* (1998), Susan Roberson notes how women experience mobility and movement through time and space differently than do men, "in large part because of constraints placed on them by patriarchy and their traditional roles as wives and mothers." Was the desire to be "out there" gendered in some way, or was it simply more convenient for men to pick up and hit the road? I wondered if women felt the same as men in this regard, this compulsion to roam, and it was this question that led me to a brand-new book by two young filmmakers, Shainee Gabel and Kristin Hahn.

It would be a mistake to argue that Gabel and Hahn's *Anthem: An American Road Story* (1997) is one of the few American travel narratives by female authors. Marilyn C. Wesley, author of *Secret Journeys: The Trope of Women's Travel in American Literature* (1999), reminds readers that there have always been women who traveled and many who have written about that experience, though these narratives have been traditionally

HOMEWARD BOUND • 141

undervalued. Their challenges to dominant social values organized by gender and conveyed by culture are "secret," according to Wesley, in the sense that they have not been fully recognized and acknowledged. From Mary Rowlandson's seventeenth-century captivity narrative through Eudora Welty's short stories and Elizabeth Bishop's poems, representations of the woman traveler "have provided expressions of contradiction of the dominant culture and projections of ethical and political alternatives," she writes. "To read about her journeys is to uncover a complex and dynamic pattern of women's agency and revolution." As road-tripping cinematographers and female storytellers, Gabel and Hahn would seem to represent what Wesley terms "a species of scandal that rewrites the travel narrative and disputes the social values it structures in a variety of contexts."

Hungry to make a film and eager to get out of Los Angeles, Gabel and Hahn interviewed Americans across the country, mainly VIPs and celebrities, and in the process created a "time capsule road movie" about "the American Dream, the American hero, the land, and the lingering influence of the founders of the country":

> If we could distill America into one collective voice, a song, a composition, what might it sound like and what would it tell us? If we could tell the story of the American Dream—by living our own—how many voices would we meet along the way?

Their year-long quest to capture these voices began in 1996 with written invitations to leaders in education, conservation, science, medicine, entertainment, literature, politics, and religion. Ben Cohen and Jerry Greenfield, the ice cream moguls, replied affirmatively. Ben & Jerry's acceptance was followed by one from politico George Stephanopoulos, though their first interviewee was actually historian Douglas Brinkley, who provided mentorship and advice based on his experiences aboard the Majic Bus, a mobile college classroom he had conceptualized as a young professor at Hofstra University. The list cascades from there: Rita Dove, John Waters, John Irving, Charlayne Hunter-Gault, George McGovern, Studs Terkel (whose work clearly influenced their own), Hunter S. Thompson, Michael Stipe, Chuck D, Geraldine Ferraro, Tom Robbins, Willie Nelson, Robert Redford, and others. I wondered how two struggling young filmmakers could amass such a list of luminaries, only later realizing that they must have had major connections. Brinkley took an interest and opened some doors, but Hahn, I learned, had been living in LA with actress Jennifer Anniston (already famous from the TV show *Friends*, which debuted in 1994) until 1996, the same year they began *Anthem*. Hahn would go on to become executive producer of Martin Scorsese's *The Departed* (2006), and Gabel would write and direct *A Love Story for Bobby Long* (2004), starring John Travolta and Scarlett Johansson.

Nineteen ninety-six was an auspicious year for two young women like Hahn and Gabel to hit the road. It was a Super-Woman-ish moment in US history, or so it felt. The daughters of second-wave feminists were delaying marriage and children, joining the workforce, and launching out independently. Janet Reno, Madeleine Albright, and Hillary Clinton modeled powerful femininity in politics. In pop culture, strong female role models abounded, from Scully on *The X-Files* to *Xena: Warrior Princess*, from Buffy the Vampire Slayer to Hermione Granger, from Gwen Stefani to Missy Elliott. Sex positivity was strong. Angry women rockers decried violence against women and championed Girl Power. Riot Grrrls reclaimed girlhood and bashed patriarchy. Women had such a strong presence in rock 'n' roll that they commanded their own music festival, Lilith Fair. Whether these signposts were harbingers of a permanent and empowering shift for American women or not remained to be seen, but if ever there were a moment for two young women to undertake such a project, it was then.

It may be surprising, then, that the story that emerges from *Anthem* is that of two earnest filmmakers whose gender seems ancillary to the stories they are trying to bottle. That is, *Anthem* is not a self-consciously feminist piece made by women activists so much as an engaging oral history project engineered by filmmakers who happen to be women. The most striking feature of their study is not the authors' femininities but rather their youthful enthusiasm for the people and places they meet; as filmmakers/writers, Hahn and Gabel display little trepidation in running down their interviewees. Of course, the fact that they exhibit no inhibition or self-consciousness—only autonomy, confidence, and grit—may in the end make *Anthem* the most feminist of endeavors.

Like gender, personal safety recesses into the narrative, but there are moments of concern. Gabel and Hahn pique the interest of construction workers at a motel in Alabaster, Alabama, after accidentally barging into their room. They're pulled over by a Texas Ranger who suggestively inquires if they are related "or are you *friends*?" If they are harassed by Hunter S. Thompson in the six days they spend with him at the Owl Farm in Aspen, then they leave it out of their book. In Chattanooga, they're approached at a gas station by "two toothless young men with unfortunate haircuts and tobacco-stained T-shirts who inquired if we were traveling alone":

> Kris kept her eyes on the gas pump's handle when she answered, "Yep, just us and our dead boyfriends in the trunk." They went away.

The reader believes the authors when they say, as they assured Douglas Brinkley at the start of the trip, that they are capable of taking care of themselves. "One thing I knew about Kris before we entered into this partnership was that she was not big on caution," Gabel writes. "I had learned not to waste energy or worrying about her decisions to endanger her own physical well-being, because she was always fine." Carrying heavy camera equipment while handicapped by scoliosis, however, Gabel also confesses to wishing they had "a boyfriend or two around to lug things for us." It was an "ugly, unfeminist longing," she admits, "but one to which we readily subscribed."

They visit Dollywood but make no attempt to interview Dolly Parton, whom Gabel begrudgingly respects. They marvel at former US poet laureate Rita Dove's fingernails, each one an ornately painted work of art, and Dove's admiration of Thomas Jefferson, but note that her accessibility was the exception to the rule: more often than not, they are stonewalled in trying to interview women. "From Governor Ann Richards to the astronaut Dr. Mae Jamison to the musician Melissa Etheridge to the poet Dr. Maya Angelou," Hahn admits, "we found it more challenging to penetrate women's camps of schedulers, assistants, agents, and publicists." Men, for whatever reason, were more available and willing to be interviewed. Perhaps as women they were able to penetrate *men's* camps of schedulers, assistants, agents, and publicists in a way male interviewers could not. Theirs is a story of interviewees hunted and meals missed and low blood sugar.

If you read *Anthem*, or a similar oral history collection like Studs Terkel's *American Dreams: Lost and Found* (1980), you get the sense from many interviewees, both famous and not-so-famous, that a sense of community is important, "being supported in times of crisis *and* celebration," as Gabel and Hahn put it. It is a curious thing to ponder while "out there," but perhaps it is out there on the road where one is reminded of the ties that bind us as Americans. To roam is not only to assert one's independence but also to accept one's reliance on total strangers. Being out there is a weirdly communitarian act of surrender, as these two aspiring filmmakers intuitively understood—a stripping of identity, an un-naming.

In *Road Frames: The American Highway Narrative* (1997), Kris Lackey argues that road books share certain conventions, including not only examinations of self and possession of the land but also discovery—or, more accurately, an *illusion* of discovery that reconstitutes older American myths of discovery, conquest, and possession. Motoring lends itself especially to transcendentalist imaginings filtered through subjectivity, observation, bohemianism, and less-traveled roads. There are even older forms, including the knight errant of medieval lore and the picaro of sixteenth-century Spanish literature, but in America, it is the automobile that has most effectively (and quickly) brought travelers into intimate contact with pastoral settings where reflection can occur via altered states (what Lackey terms "highway consciousness") and altered views (related to how the speeding eye perceives the world through the windshield, or what Lackey terms "road phenomenology"). There is a tension, obviously, between machine and nature, between spectator and participant, between transience and permanence; but it is the auto that facilitates solipsistic inquiries into self-discovery and self-knowledge. For those who drive and write about it, the road inscribes the autobiographical self.

The same age as Gabel and Hahn, I, too, was fumbling toward knowing. I'm not sure if I ever satisfactorily found the answer to "why out there?" but a theory was emerging, however half-baked and untested, a bit different from Lackey's. When "the center becomes decentered," as Susan Roberson puts it—that is, when a person is mobile and migratory and displaced from home and that which is familiar—the task of locating and finding oneself becomes more complicated but also paradoxically simpler. My own sense was that a person on the road never really adapts to his or her surroundings. Existence "out there" is experiential; there is shockingly little contemplation or solipsism. The lens never turns inward, never stops long enough to let the mind stew in its own juices. It never gets past "where am I?" to the who, what, when, and why. On the road, you are first and foremost a spectator. And while sometimes exhausting—a filmstrip of ever-flitting frames, a constantly scrolling backdrop—that circumstance

HOMEWARD BOUND • 145

can also be healing, the difference between fresh, flowing water and a stagnant pool (it also explains why chain restaurants have their appeal, affording an oasis of familiarity in the unfamiliar, putting the "rest" in restaurant). While there are more variables—where to go, where to eat, where to sleep—the mobile life is paradoxically simpler, *less* introspective. The newness of surroundings sharpens the senses even as it relaxes them. It is this simplicity, as Least Heat-Moon intuits, that renews and rejuvenates the spirit.

The question of out there also relates to perspective and vantage points. Some move to be in motion, others because something's up ahead. Some drive to arrive, some to get away. Some never look in the rearview mirror and some might as well be driving in reverse. I was doing all at once. I wanted to go with nowhere to go—to sort out some stuff, to get to know the driver. I wanted to see what's out there; but I also wanted to see what's in here. In this way travel frees the sculpture in the stone, chipping away the negative to reveal a preexisting form, not creating so much as releasing what's already there.

I had heard various quotations over the years about travel, all profound, none that I could remember precisely or quote verbatim. Henry Miller, for example, had noted that the destination is not a place but a new way of seeing things. As Proust put it, the real voyage of discovery consists not in seeking new landscapes but rather in having new eyes. Descartes believed traveling is like conversing with people from different centuries. Flaubert said it makes you modest because you see what a tiny place you occupy in the world. Twain felt that travel destroys prejudice, bigotry, and narrow-mindedness. Trying to recall these quotations, I was reminded that, knowingly or not, those who travel enter a standing conversation with other travelers, past and present, who may understand the act of traveling differently but still agree upon its transformative power. There was only one travel-related quote I could recite from memory. "Once you have traveled, the voyage never ends, but is played out over and over again in the quietest chambers," writes Pat Conroy in *The Prince of Tides* (1986). "The mind can never break off from the journey."

Somewhere outside Cincinnati I pulled over at a roadside diner for a bite to eat. There were cars and pickups but also a wide variety of eighteen-wheelers rafted up on the far side of the gravel lot: bobtails, day cabs, reefers, sleepers, doubles—even one massive B-train with two trailers linked like lovebugs—but mainly just standard dry vans hauling general freight, an even mix of fleet trucks and owner-operated vehicles lovingly bedazzled with cursive script, gleaming chrome, and extra reflectors and running lights. If you've ever seen the old Westerns where a stranger enters a saloon and the piano player stops abruptly, or the needle scratches across the phonograph and every head in the joint swings around, then you can picture the scene when I flung open the door and let in a blast of frigid air. Muttered curses and cold glances. I smiled meekly and shouldered my way to an open spot at the counter. The diesel men sized me up as I sat down. Their mesh-back baseball caps were emblazoned with names like Peterbilt, Mack, Kenworth, and CAT—even though some of the grill badges and hood ornaments outside now read Isuzu, Mitsubishi Fuso, and Volvo.

A giant human being—at least I think he was human—walked in the door behind me. His sequoia-sized T-shirt read "Hard Times Don't Last, Truckers Do." He quickly scanned the diner. "Hey pardner!" he shouted. "You!" He pointed, striding the length of the counter in four steps. I nearly choked when I realized he was talking to me.

He clamped an iron mitt onto my shoulder. "You left your lights on, buddy," he said, clapping me on the back. "Figured that's your van outside."

"Oh, thanks," I burbled, slinking out to flip the switch and save the battery. Good people everywhere.

A short, dyspeptic waitress slid a cup of coffee at me without my asking. She was crone-like, bosomy, mouth slashed with lipstick, a pile of platinum blonde hair. "What'll you have?" she growled. I looked unsuccessfully for a menu. "Just tell me what you want, honey," she instructed gently, seeing my rising panic. Four minutes later she brought a plate heaped with hash browns, two eggs sunny-side-up, rye toast, a rash of bacon, and a large glass of frothy orange juice. She didn't bat an eye when I chased it with a slice of coconut cream pie.

Plunging temperatures chased me southward as my route straightened. These roads were recognizable, the passes blasted through the Appalachians by highway workers to lay the interstate. In the rocky bluffs through Kentucky and Tennessee one could still see the lines where they had drilled and dynamited the mountains to make I-75. There are no easy merges in a VW Bus, but I poked into traffic, slipping into a stream of cars, pickups, and tractor trailers migrating southward through familiar idioms—Pilot Flying Js and Days Inns and Walmarts—past tacky billboards advertising carpet and A/C repair and slow-cooked BBQ and fast

HOMEWARD BOUND • 147

Fig. 9: Barns painted with Rock City ads pointed the way toward Chattanooga. Photo by author.

food, past longleaf pines and dogwoods and eastern redbuds, toward the screech of bluejays and scarlet flash of cardinals and red-bellied woodpeckers, whose *jub jub* song marked a return to the familiar.

I chugged past the Kentucky limestone that made good water and better bourbon, that state's bluegrass farms and blooded thoroughbreds a verdant blur, into the wine-dark East Tennessee hills, where the road hugged the crests of steep ridges. The familiar lyrics of the Allman Brothers, Lynyrd Skynyrd, and the Black Crowes filled the FM airwaves, carrying me southward. Winding through the hills and rills in autumn colors, drifting in and out of woodsmoke, and the smells of root vegetables and fowl and meats on cookfires and breads and pies and cakes wafting through barely cracked screen doors, a realization stirred that the vastness of southern vistas, once inviting exploration and possibility, were now largely closed off and fenced in. The "Private Property" and "Keep Out" and "No Trespassing" signs now really meant it. The sightseeing fell away as I zeroed in like a homing pigeon sensing its destination, and in early November I glimpsed the familiar swells of Tunnel Hill, Rocky Face, and Mount Sinai as I rolled into North Georgia for Thanksgiving and Christmas, happy to be home with my family and friends for the holidays.

10

The Last Road Trip

Back in Georgia, I visited the King Library and Archives in Atlanta, locally known as the King Center, where I hoped to accomplish some research. It was a bit of a bust. The King Center calls itself the largest repository in the world of primary source materials on Dr. Martin Luther King Jr. and on the civil rights movement, but I discovered (as other scholars have too) that those materials are notoriously difficult to access. Proprietarily guarded by the King family, whatever was kept at the King Center was locked up tight along with his legacy. I had better luck when I later visited Boston University, where King became Dr. King after earning a doctorate in systematic theology in 1957. His papers—including his office files, lectures, correspondence, telephone call records, general correspondence, student exams and term papers, and clippings—are housed at BU's Howard Gotlieb Archival Research Center. They are the Gotlieb Center's most used archive.

I was in a strange space in Georgia, having come off the road and landed in familiar environs. While I was working hard at my scholastic endeavors, I looked and felt like a bit of a ne'er-do-well, a vagabond in a VW Bus. My friends were all working, earning money, from the ones who had attended graduate school to become lawyers or architects, to the ones working in local factories who had never gone to college. "Still in school," I told people who politely inquired at church and the grocery store. I saw some close friends but also skipped a few get-togethers. I didn't feel right. My stomach and bowels were giving me trouble. After a couple of weeks of gut problems, I went to the doctor, who diagnosed me with a parasitic infection, probably from drinking contaminated water somewhere while camping (the only thing I could think of was a questionable spigot in Ohio). I started a round of Flagyl, a powerful antibiotic, to kill whatever was camped in my gut. It worsened. On Christmas Eve, my throat swelled shut, and I had difficulty breathing, an apparent allergic reaction to the Flagyl. I needed a doctor, but they were all at Christmas parties, and I stopped shy of going to the emergency room after my throat relaxed enough to take in air. After recuperating for a while at my parents' house, I made preparations to hit the road once more to head back to California.

The trip to California from Georgia was much different from the first half of the journey. It was faster, more direct, less exploratory. The return trip tracked from I-20 to I-10 and across the Southwest, more or less. I trucked across the endless, awful length of Texas. Past Abilene I trekked through Midland and Odessa, where I pondered H. G. ("Buzz") Bissinger's *Friday Night Lights* (1990), his touching and disquieting account of the 1988 Permian High School football season in Odessa, Texas. The book renders the denizens of Odessa not only abnormal and fanatical in their football obsession but also ubiquitous and emblematic, their hopes and civic pride pinned to a squad of high school athletes in a place of diminished hope, like many other small towns across the region and the nation. In West Texas, football is a religion, much like the Dream itself. In fact, under the Friday night lights, football *is* the American Dream. For townspeople, the Permian Panthers are a wellspring of civic pride; for the players, football is a passkey to opportunity and glory, however fleeting. The players at Permian High believe in the Dream with a certain degree of naivete—and why not? The American Dream is childlike insofar as dreaming itself is the perquisite of childhood. First Corinthians 13:11 decrees that kids dream and adults don't ("When I was a child I spoke as a child"), but in Odessa the players and parents and fans all believe alike, lured by a dream "as beautiful and elusive as the green light at the end of Gatsby's dock," as Bissinger puts it. From the highway I searched for the famous metal-halide floodlights illuminating resplendent stadiums, but the Friday night lights had recently dimmed, another season of high school football concluded.

I drove through the other Twin Cities, El Paso and Ciudad Juárez. Near the southern border I was stopped at a police roadblock. Whether it was a sobriety checkpoint or a US Border Patrol sting, I wasn't sure. Perhaps it was part of the new 287(g) program codified in the Illegal Immigration Reform and Immigrant Responsibility Act (IIRAIRA) of 1996 that allowed state and local police officers to collaborate with federal agents to enforce federal immigration laws. Regardless, the officers waved me over to the side of the road for a closer inspection.

The Fourth Amendment to the US Constitution holds that people have a right against illegal searches and seizures. Generally speaking, police are required to obtain a search warrant before conducting a search. There are, however, certain circumstances under which a police officer can conduct a legal search and seizure without a warrant as long as it's "reasonable." With my long hair, VW Bus, and California plates, I'm sure the officers felt they were acting with probable cause. It must have seemed too easy in a way. I was a stereotype, an overblown caricature of a 1960s-era, drug-running pothead, smuggling marijuana from Mexico back to Cali—only I wasn't that guy. There was no ganja in the Bus. With the easy confidence of a white, middle-class, twenty-something American man who knows he's innocent, I never felt alarm or concern. I never felt inconvenienced, only oddly detached, like Meursault in Albert Camus's *The Stranger*. I didn't resent the intrusion nearly as much as I might have, but I *was* reminded of the fine line between proactive policing and profiling. I realized how different I would feel if I were a person of color, less sure that the wheels of justice were turning as they should, more vulnerable to the system. Finding no drugs or other incriminating evidence, with no proof of any wrongdoing whatsoever, they put me back on the path to Berkeley, a turtle scooped from a busy highway and deposited back on its plodding course. Behind me America's constabulary stood vigilant, ready to detain drug offenders, deport Mexicans, and, after moderate hassling, wave through young white southern men.

I moseyed across the deserts where thunder lizards once strode, now buried in deep sand. I slowed down late one evening at a last-chance gas station somewhere outside Sonora. A perimeter of arc sodium pole lamps carved a clean rectangle in the dark. The station seemed closed, but I needed fuel and coasted to a stop. The building's facade was down-lit like an Edward Hopper painting, an illuminated oasis in the night. Under the eaves of the peaked roof, moths bounced off a high tin-shaded pendant lamp shining on a red five-pointed Texaco star. There was no one

THE LAST ROAD TRIP • 151

to be seen. To one side stood a long-empty, old-timey pump that looked like a miniature lighthouse, a glass prism atop a tall crimson cylinder. To the other side stood an Indian in full headdress, paint flaking from his stern countenance, one hand clutching a bundle of cigars to his chest, the other raised palm forward. Under the empty gaze of this wooden sentinel, I pumped a few gallons from one of two modern dispensers with pay-at-the-pump technology and swiped my credit card. As I drove away, I glanced over my shoulder at him, half expecting a wave or wink or nod, but he stared ahead, unblinking.

The driving was happily boring, mostly, the monotony periodically punctuated by heart-revving adrenaline spikes. I was driving along a two-lane desert highway in West Texas one afternoon, for example, when another driver impatiently passed me on the left, as drivers often did, pushing his Ford Explorer to eighty miles per hour before whipping it back into our shared lane. As he did, he smashed into a buzzard feasting on some roadkill in the middle of the highway ahead. The bird was killed instantly, momentarily frozen in a Cézanne leitmotif, all hard angles and impossible lines, before tumbling beneath the vehicle, body and wings broken and bent. As I swerved to avoid hitting it again, adding insult to mortal injury, I noticed with even more horror that it was not a buzzard but rather a bald eagle.

Across the nation I saw a lot of roadkill in the Southwest: squirrels and cats and dogs and raccoons and deer and pigs and snakes, plastered and pancaked, bodies littering the asphalt. In the frequent and devastating highway encounters between machines and animals, Mother Nature always lost. They were one-mile-per-hour creatures living in a seventy-mile-per-hour world.

There was something weirdly appropriate about the bloodiness of American roadways: apt reminders of the extreme violence to which Americans have long, tangled, blood-stained cords of connection. US history is so violent that we periodize it and remember it in terms of its violence, whether the colonial period, or the Civil War, or the pre- and postwar periods. The United States was settled by colonizers who wrested the land from native peoples and built an economy reliant on a system of unfree labor whose slaves were freed through a civil war whose casualties rivaled the worst conflicts of nineteenth-century Europe. Roads such as Military Trail were cut into the lower peninsula of Florida to allow the US

Army to wage war against the Seminole Indians hiding in the Everglades; even today, Military Trail remains a vital thoroughfare through Palm Beach County. The social violence of American history is rivaled only by the environmental war lustily waged against plants and animals. Millions of animals—birds, reptiles, mammals, and amphibians—are killed every year by vehicles traveling on America's roads. For example, partially as a result of roadkill, the population of one endangered cat—the ocelot— was reduced to double digits, according to the Federal Highway Administration; but habitat loss and habitat fragmentation caused by roads also did their part to reduce this population. Wide-ranging large carnivores, such as grizzly bears and panthers, and slow-moving animals, such as salamanders and turtles, are particularly vulnerable to becoming roadkill. In these ways, American highways are literal and metaphorical connectors to a chaotic, violent past. If Americans are mindful of these connectors, then perhaps highways can become part of the process of unifying and healing, part of the memory work needed to reconcile that violent past.

There were other adventures going back: dipping up to Roswell, New Mexico, with its UFOs and little green men; dipping down to Tombstone, Arizona, where cowboy-looking fellers openly carried six-guns on their hips. Outside of Las Cruces I picked up a hitchhiker, a woman traveling with her two large dogs. She stood on the side of road, looking calmly into oncoming traffic, gazing through the cars and drivers without making eye contact. Breaking all of my own rules regarding hitchhikers and smelly animals in the van, I pulled over. It was the dogs, really, who spoke to her need, wordlessly indicating that she imminently needed to get the hell away from wherever she was leaving. She tossed a couple of duffel bags into the floorboards, where the dogs quietly lay down. They all seemed tired. We rode together for hours, talking a little without sharing much. I learned virtually nothing about her—she didn't offer and I didn't ask—but I felt sure I had done the right thing by stopping to offer a ride. That evening I stopped at a pet-friendly motor lodge and paid for two rooms. The next morning we parted ways somewhere near the Colorado River, which divides Arizona from California. She was the first and last hitchhiker I ever picked up. I skittered across the hardpan of the Mojave, a cookie sheet buckling and popping in the oven heat.

I'm not recounting much about my return trip here because, even though I didn't realize it at the time, the trip was already over. It may have ended in Georgia, or it may have ended somewhere along the way back. I'm not exactly sure. But when the trip no longer took me, it was deader than disco and there was no resuscitating it. I was no longer *vacillando*: I was driving to get back to Berkeley. My research was fresh; I was anxious to start writing the dissertation. I missed my life in the Bay Area, and I rushed to return, sticking close to the interstate. The concession of searching for local flavor wore thin, and I sought out chains and franchises as known quantities, familiar and predictable, once eating at Taco Bell four times in one day—and I liked it. I was done with the trip, but it was done with me first, and the Bus galloped home like it knew the way.

Before the trip ended, however, something occurred to me on the ride westward, the proper American direction for expansion and discovery. It was an epiphany. I'm not the first to note how travel makes one aware of other places and peoples and cultures. It's kind of the whole point. What I hadn't realized is how moving from place to place can erase the self, a characteristic that travel shares with historical inquiry.

Everything that exists in the present comes out of the past, and no matter how novel it might seem, it carries a fragment of the past with it. By studying the stories and remnants of those who came before us, we can learn how they lived and how they dealt with problems they faced in everyday life. We incorporate their experiences into our own. In doing so, we access a collective memory: inherited wisdom passed on generationally that enriches and betters our own lives.

I didn't realize it when I started the trip, but travel works the same way, kind of like the storekeeper had suggested on the Crow Reservation. Traveling and studying history both leave a mark, embossing the self in whorls of texture like a fingerprint. For me, what had begun as a solipsistic quest to answer "who am I?" was replaced by the surreal epiphany that out there on the road there was no me. The traveling self is a new self, an absorptive self. Bathed in American idioms and stereotypes, travelers become part of everywhere they've been and all they've touched and seen, and all of it becomes a part of them.

The traveler, a zephyr moving through time and space across the great plains of American history, becomes the Taino fisherman paddling his dugout, and the Spanish conquistador, armored and encumbered. The traveler becomes the Puritan, pious and intolerant. The midwife cutting herbs with her athame. The Angolan field hand watering crops with sweat and blood. The Founder, elitist and egalitarian, aristocratic and democratic, conservative and liberal, unbigoted and racist. The Framer, wigged and wise, breeched and bespectacled. The stevedore, unloading cotton from steamboats with longshoreman's hooks. The Five Nations of the Iroquois: the Mohawk, Oneida, Onondaga, Cayuga, and Seneca. The Irish laborer laying Union Pacific rails westward from Omaha toward the Chinese laborer laying Central Pacific rails eastward from Sacramento. The Mexican vaquero galloping across Tejas. The unvanquished Seminole. The lettered and the uneducated, the refined and the roughhewn, the perfumed and the unwashed. The plantation owner and the abolitionist. The free and the enslaved.

The traveler becomes larger than life. Francis Drake and Squanto and Sacajawea and Blackbeard and Stagolee and Davy Crockett and Harriet Tubman and Geronimo and Billy the Kid. Pocahantas paddling, Betsy Ross sewing, Paul Bunyan chopping, Daniel Boone wrassling, John Henry hammering, Casey Jones chugga chugging. Crow and Wolf and Raven. The trickster. Brer Rabbit.

The traveler becomes the cornucopia of plenty and the cash crops of nothing you can eat. The hemp and cochineal and indigo and tobacco and cotton. The chickee and wigwam and longhouse and teepee and sharecropper's cabin and Philadelphia row house and Georgian mansion. The blunderbuss and smoothbore musket and Kentucky rifle and breechloader. The Sharps and Winchester and Colt. The Peacemaker. The tinkerer and inventor and entrepreneur. Whitney and Carver and Edison and Ford. The Wright Brothers. Kittyhawk and Menlo Park and Silicon Valley. The *Spirit of St. Louis* and *Saturn V. Falcon Heavy.*

The traveler becomes all of these things and more because the American road is the great connector. One from many. *E pluribus unum.*

Some years later, in the early 2000s, I was flying cross-country from Denver to Pittsburgh and looking down at what have since been dubbed the "flyover states." Frazzled from the heightened, post-9/11 security procedures—the strips and frisks and pats and sniffs—I settled into my seat and looked out the window. Wide swaths of farmland and nothingness peeped up through holes in the cloud floor below. I thought of the pretty women on the Weather Channel, waving their hands over the middle of the nation, describing big patterns and movements. I leaned over my knapsack, tucked under the seat in front of me, and dug out my tattered old copy of *Travels with Charley*. I finished reading it at thrity-five thousand feet on a jetliner cruising over the country, where it dawned on me that Steinbeck had not only written the Great American Road Novel, masquerading as creative nonfiction, but also undertaken what could be called the Last American Road Trip.

Charley's traveling companion bemoans the laxity, the softness, and the sterility he finds in 1962. Steinbeck paradoxically marvels at "the fantastic hugeness and energy of production," and decries the "frantic growth" and suburban sprawl. He ruminates on antiques in New England, lobster in Maine, barbecues in Texas, retirees in Florida, and racial prejudice in the South. He considers interstates and migrant labor and hunting and truck stops and mobile homes and redwood trees. Confirming Thomas Wolfe's suspicion that you can't go home again, Steinbeck returns to Monterey, California, only to find strangers. He attempts to distill it all into a single lesson, What I Learned in Driving across the United States:

> For all of our enormous geographic range, for all of our sectionalism, for all of our interwoven breeds drawn from every part of the ethnic world, we are a nation, a new breed. Americans are much more American than they are Northerners, Southerners, Westerners, or Easterners. And descendants of English, Irish, Italian, Jewish, German, Polish are essentially American. This is not patriotic whoopde-do; it is carefully observed fact. California Chinese, Boston Irish, Wisconsin German, yes, and Alabama Negroes have more in common than they have apart.

Congealing very quickly, in less than two hundred years and mostly in the last fifty, "American identity is an exact and provable thing."

Steinbeck recounts the moment his journey ended, even though he was still rolling along, "near Abingdon, in the dogleg of Virginia, at four o'clock of a windy afternoon, without warning or goodbye or kiss my foot." From that moment on he was simply going through the motions, seeing the journey through to its conclusion without the spirit of exploration or joy of discovery. "The road became an endless stone ribbon, the hills obstructions, the trees green blurs, the people simply moving figures with heads but no faces," he confesses. "All the food along the way tasted like soup, even the soup." I knew what he meant. Like Steinbeck, my own journey ended before I was through taking it. *Travels with Charley* ends on a very postmodern note. Forbidden from taking the Holland Tunnel into New York because of his camper's butane cannisters, he takes the ferry from Hoboken into the city, only to become disoriented. He pulls over, laughing hysterically, lost in Manhattan in his own backyard.

Even though some of the great American travel writing was done in the 1970s and 1980s, one could argue that everything since *Travels with Charley* has been derivative, variations on a formulaic theme: Joe or Jane American is restless, yearning, damaged in some way. They take to the road in hopes of healing and renewal. Finding solace in the expansiveness and natural beauty and courtesy of strangers, they remember that America is pretty terrific, returning home refreshed, reknitted, and reacquainted with the nation's grandeur.

But what really had Joe and Jane discovered? That America is big and diverse and difficult to sum up in a single book? Didn't we already know these things? The road trip motif was now rather fraught, a bit hackneyed and predictable. It is so difficult to describe big patterns and movements with anything other than a sweep of the hand. Steinbeck sensed it, saw it. His United States, at the height of its economic power and military strength in 1962, was already making its wide turn, the optimism that buoyed its institutions infinitesimally and imperceptibly waning, its sense of exceptionalism losing air, a Mylar balloon stuck in high branches.

Had I discovered anything different in my own travels? No, not really—unless one counts the revelation that coconut cream pie tastes pretty much the same all over. Nothing that hadn't already been said, nothing that *would* be said in the quarter-century interim between my trip and the publication of this book. What could I really see or know? Not much, certainly not without talking to folks more than I had done, not without engaging in what Kris Lackey has called "deep travel." I had skimmed along the surface of places like a stone skipped across a pond. I breezed right past families and feuds and customs and conflicts and convictions and dreams and loves and hatreds and the knots that bound all of these things together in place-bound communities. I was just passing through. My personal journey was hardly unique. Like other road writers, I discovered that I wasn't nearly as damaged as I thought I had been, nor was my nation.

THE LAST ROAD TRIP · 157

I discovered, like them, that it was a pretty fascinating place. But I was merely following in someone else's tire tracks. It was Steinbeck who had undertaken the Last Road Trip, not them and certainly not me.

Has everything since been imitative and unoriginal? Time honored and predictable, the genre has been deconstructed and analyzed by experts such as Lackey, who has expertly dissected its conventions, made plain in *Road Frames*:

> Nonfiction highway books often cultivate the illusion of intimacy, variously couched as "listening to America," "traveling the backroads," or "feeling the pulse of America," while denying the countervailing influences of regional stereotyping, historical nostalgia, superficial impressionism, and the simple quest for novelty. If the peregrine writer does not question the artificial nature of road perception, including the influence of convention and prejudice, what's usually left is an ersatz Transcendentalism: a vague wish to "change myself or rather to find out something I didn't yet know about myself," a paean to freedom, a pastoral epiphany.

Guilty as charged. In trying to recapitulate my own journey, I was perhaps unavoidably using the same themes and tropes as other travel writers had done before. It was as if all of us were racing up and down the same old road. Readers, for their part, expect certain leitmotifs: the crisis, the journey, the discovery, the healing, the homecoming. Enlightened and humbled, the knight errant circles back, the prodigal son returns. Nothing new here, it's all been said before.

This reading of the post-Steinbeck travel lit landscape is, of course, filtered through a generational ennui—a post-1960s, postindustrial, post-rock-and-roll, Gen-X melancholy—that is more than a little unfair to all of those who have described America since him. Perhaps these motifs recur because of the grains of truth at their core. After my own road trip, I came to love American travel lit—nostalgic, purposefully simple, full of adventure and wonder—devouring as much of it as I could, up to and including newer books such as Donald Miller's *Through Painted Deserts*, John Francis's *Planetwalker*, and Carrie Brownstein's road memoir, *Hunger Makes Me a Modern Girl*. There's something comforting in the fact that these authors—a prodigal son in a VW Bus looking for God, a wandering

African American environmentalist pledged to a vow of silence, a riot gr-rrl raging across the underground feminist punk scene—and many others, so different from one another, reach the same place of gratitude and appreciation. Perhaps that's the beauty of the road trip, that each generation can rediscover America on their own terms, even as they find certain aspects of it unchanged and unchanging. New-to-me is still new. We all discover America in a myriad of ways: in our hometowns, on the open road, in our great novels and our great founding documents, in our firsthand experiences, in our minds and imaginations. We discover it over and over again, remembering the hope, glorious and wretched like an old love affair. It is why we continue to quibble and argue and sometimes fight over the meaning of it all. America the Mighty. America the Terrible. America the Beautiful.

We discover this place in our shared histories, which, like our road trip stories and travel narratives, tend to accentuate highlights while glossing over lowlights. Told and retold, polished to a high sheen in the retelling, these stories sometimes obscure the contradictions and incongruities—how, for example, we have fought wars not only against totalitarianism but also against nature, not only for freedom and democracy but also for territory and oil. We have stamped out not only vicious tyrants but also the Native peoples who first inhabited this land (or tried to stamp them out, at least). For every *Spirit of St. Louis* there is an Exxon *Valdez*; for every Normandy, a My Lai. Its trials and scares and scandals and impeachments and "-isms" and pogroms and massacres and invasions lend credence to Ezra Pound's post–World War I assessment of the United States as "an old bitch, gone in the teeth," a "botched civilization." Fact and fiction blend into national origin myths that fold in on themselves, reconstituting and reappearing as settler-colonial narratives of conquest, displacement, dispossession, and genocide.

Herein lies a Catch-22. The nation's tales of repression cannot be repressed—but neither can its promise, the scaffolding of a democratic republic under construction. Its dual strengths are its ideas and its people, yoked together in what Michael Walzer calls "a political nation of cultural nationalities." In 1908, Israel Zangwill had used the term "melting pot" to describe the way people from different places blended here into something new and uniquely American. No hyphenated Americans here, only a nonethnic, mixed breed of egalitarians, entrepreneurs, and individualists united in their desire to create better lives for themselves. Horace Kallen, one of Zangwill's early critics, advanced the ideal that cultural diversity and national pride were compatible with each other and that ethnic and racial diversity strengthened this country rather than weakening it; he coined the term *cultural pluralism* to describe this phenomenon. For Kallen, Zangwill's melting pot suggested a soupy blandness, less than the homogeneous sum of its heterogeneous parts. Perhaps we're more of a chunky stew, partially blended with ingredients still retaining identifiable traits—others have similarly called the United States a salad bar—but these food analogies never worked for Kallen. In his 1915 essay "Democracy versus the Melting Pot," he likens the United States to a symphony orchestra, in which each nationality and ethnic group contributes its "own specific timbre and tonality" to create "a multiplicity in a unity, an orchestration of mankind." As Americans have wrestled with the ongoing dilemma embodied in *E pluribus unum*, the notion of a great symphony in which all groups blend together harmoniously offers one way to balance the pride individuals find in ethnic identity with the need for national unity.

There is no formula for how to harmonize and achieve that balance, and some still fret over who belongs here and who doesn't. "America was created by seventeenth- and eighteenth-century settlers who were overwhelmingly white, British, and Protestant," wrote Harvard political scientist Samuel P. Huntington in 2004, amid an influx of Hispanic immigrants. "Their values, institutions, and culture provided the foundation for and shaped the development of the United States in the following centuries." He's right, of course—and also dead wrong. He might have written, "From the start America was a multicultural venture of French, Dutch, Portuguese, African, and Spanish peoples in the fifteenth and sixteenth centuries, all predating the British who came in the seventeenth century," and he would have been just as correct. My travels had taught me something that Huntington may not have appreciated about the vastness and variety of these United States, but this diversity was early apparent to those who chose to see it. In 1643, a French Jesuit missionary visiting New Amsterdam reported hearing eighteen different languages spoken in that small but thriving seaport. New Amsterdam became New York in 1664, and the colonies became more British, but it's there, in this origins paradox, that many of America's contradictions are sewn up: America, the

British nation of non-British peoples; America, the free nation built with slave labor; America, the collective built on individualism. One could take an even longer view, noting that this larval nation, still in its developmental stages, was not "founded" past tense so much as it is being founded, less became than still becoming. Clearly there's a lot of work left to be done to make this nation live up to its lofty ideals.

There is yet another metaphor that captures this process of becoming, one aptly coined by a New Yorker. Pete Hamill, the eldest of seven children of Irish Catholic immigrants from Belfast, came of age in 1950s New York, where he became a renowned journalist, not only serving as editor of the *New York Post* but also winning a Grammy for penning the liner notes for Bob Dylan's 1975 album *Blood on the Tracks*. In a 2004 essay, Hamill used the word "alloy"—a combination of metals, each with its own qualities, heated and shaped into something harder and tougher—to describe post-9/11 New York and, by extension, America too. The language, the music, the food, the culture, the people themselves—they are forged in a crucible and come out stronger and better as a result.

Like the American people, my Bus was alloy too, and like them it was tough and hard, nothing flowery about it. There was some plastic, rubber, and fabric, sure, but her body, chassis, frame, steering, suspension, and wheels were all made from durable, flexible steel, an alloy of iron that bends instead of breaking on impact. When my vehicle was made in 1972, German steel manufacturing was at its peak, with production concentrated in the Ruhr region, one of the world's leading manufacturers of steel; since then, a number of plants have closed, just as they did here in the United States. A fine example of West German engineering, the Bus never failed to crank, never let me down. Never sputtered, never broke down. As reliable as sunrise, it was very un-VW-Bus-like in that regard. That I spent so much time exploring America in a German-made auto (with Nazi origins, no less!) was something I never stopped to contemplate.

I could have kept going, kept bussing—looking for America, growing my beard, dipping into the woods and cities for hikes and urban sojourns in equal measure, Thoreau-ing my life away. Part of me really wanted to stay on the road, and part of me has always been trying to get back to it, but I didn't go that route. Instead, I returned to Berkeley, cut my hair, threw out my old tour shirts, and finished my dissertation. I exchanged postcards with my surrogate road parents, Jean and Tom. I avoided Flagyl—though I wonder now if I had really been sick with giardia. Maybe it was an intestinal bug, something I'd eaten or drunk, but deep down I doubted, suspecting it was something in my head that wasn't digesting rather than something in my belly. Maybe I had fallen victim to my own anxieties, neurotic twitterings temporarily quelled on the road. Why did I feel out of sorts? I don't know—will probably never know—but I think that back home in Dalton, in mid-road trip, I was again afraid. Afraid of failure. Afraid of disappointing my parents and grandmother and professors and friends. Afraid of botching my own American Dream. Afraid of life and its many tingles. Graduate school taught me many things, but it also bequeathed neuroses, ones that overthinking and hyperintrospection honed to a razor edge. As Mark Twain once quipped, "I've been through some terrible things in my life, some of which actually happened."

My confidence had been carried off by the hairy monsters of my mind. And so I added a few more lessons to my TripTik, lessons harder to effect than to say aloud or jot down. *Lesson #11: Have grace for yourself. No one is perfect. Lesson #12: Feel the fear and do it anyway. Lesson #13: Don't borrow trouble.* I hoped that saying these affirmations aloud would help to actualize them, speaking truth to power.

Later—much later—I learned a term for my particular condition. Imposter syndrome is the feeling of inadequacy and unpreparedness one can feel when assuming others are more prepared or qualified for the same venture—that feeling of "I really shouldn't be doing X because I'm not good enough (or smart or strong or pretty or whatever enough)," that feeling of being a poser. How could I be a professor like Martin or Litwack or Takaki or any of the other brilliant minds who had taught me? Those titans who mentored me were intellectual giants. No one would mistake me, while clever enough and smart enough, with being a genius, the kind of person I imagined a professor to be.

Only recently did I learn another possibility regarding my affliction, more akin to the vapors than any somatic ailment. E. H. Van Deusen, an "alienist" (psychiatrist) at an asylum in Kalamazoo, coined the term *neurasthenia* in 1869 to describe the condition of farm wives made sick by isolation, but George Miller Beard, a neurologist in New York, borrowed the term to describe the grab bag of psychopathological symptoms—fatigue, anxiety, headache, heart palpitations, fainting, neuralgia, "hysteria," dyspepsia, depression—that he saw among the harried society women and overworked businessmen he treated. Largely forgotten today, it became a major diagnosis in Western medicine in the late nineteenth and early twentieth centuries. In Britain and across the British Empire, neurasthenia was explained as an exhaustion of the nervous system. What Freud interpreted as a function of sexual repression, Beard recognized as a side effect of urbanization, the new industrial order, and life in modern civilization: a bourgeois condition increasingly common among the middle and upper classes, working in sedentary occupations. Writers such as Marcel Proust, Virginia Woolf, and Charlotte Perkins Gilman, who famously wrote about it in "The Yellow Wallpaper" (1892), were susceptible. Doctors commonly prescribed "rest cures" at hospitals, sanatoriums, or resorts, though electrotherapy was not off limits for stubborn cases.

Americans were said to be particularly prone to "nervosism," as neurasthenia was also called, and it was an American who gave the condition yet another name. William James, a neurasthenic himself, termed it *Americanitis*. The nickname stuck. Theodore Roosevelt and Jane Addams were diagnosed with it; Theodore Dreiser fretted about it. Rexall first marketed its Americanitis Elixir—a patent medicine, a nerve tonic like Hires or Dr. Pepper or Coca-Cola—in 1903. Could it be that America's famous work ethic, its nose-to-the-grindstone go-getterism, was a form of mental illness? Was it toxic, killing us by hurry-and-worry degrees? If so, Rexall's Americanitis Elixir offered a chuggable cure-all.

In 1998, Greil Marcus, a journalist and music critic, came across an old poster for this magic potion, "a brown bottle promising an unspoiled land, a loving community and eternal life . . . the proclamation of a would-be national icon." Marcus found the poster in a dim corner of Gail's Oldies and Goodies, an "Old Fashioned Café and Ice Cream Parlour," on Main Street in St. Helena, California, in the heart of the Napa Valley wine country. He described this nostalgic advertisement for Americanitis Elixir in the *New York Times*:

> At the top, in the background, there's a spectacular mountain range, the Rockies crowned with a steeple-like peak and covered with snow down to their lowest foothills, which suddenly turn green and smooth, a sylvan glade. Emerging from a line of great oaks at the base of the hills is a long parade of men, women, boys and girls, all crossing a huge meadow and gathering at "The Fountain of Perpetual Youth."

Fig. 10: "The dose maketh the poison." Elixirs and tonics at the Old Drug Store, St. Augustine, Florida, circa 2023. Photo by author.

The fountain is made by an enormous bottle of Americanitis Elixir: "One of the Famous Rexall Remedies of Which There Is One for Each Ailment," "Especially Recommended for Nervous Disorders, Exhaustion, and All Troubles Arising from Americanitis." Emitting a white spray that forms a canopy of medicine and fills the fountain's pool, the bottle is as ugly as it is imposing; three winged fairies drape themselves around its side. On the ground, led by a boy or a midget dressed as a bellboy, throngs of excited children and calm, satisfied adults raise cups high, less to drink than to toast.

The picture all but screams with self-confidence, optimism and joy, with a celebration of the American small-town utopia generalized into its natural setting. Here people gather to be cured of some vague malaise, some not-quite-diagnosable condition, but it's plain that the setting is itself a cure.

It was the last line of Marcus's description of the Americanitis Elixir poster than made it all click for me, the reigning answer to the question of why so many Americans have taken to the open road to cure what ails them. *The setting is itself a cure.* It was so obvious. The cure for America is America. It was Paracelsus who noted that all things are poison and "only the dose makes a thing not a poison."

Teddy Roosevelt understood as much, finding his own cure for Americanitis. TR saw twentieth-century modernization—with its labor-saving automation, its office jobs, and its promise of ease and comfort—as a recipe for dandifying softness. He worried about the implications for America, which might lose its manly edge in world affairs. Roosevelt famously counseled strenuous living as the remedy for modern sissification, and the American West was his cure-all tonic. Better even than the kettlebells and calisthenics and gymnastics he used to strengthen his physique, being out there—*at* the frontier, *in* the West, *on* the trail—could fix Americans, particularly American men. With enough hiking and hunting and killing, with enough riding and roping and cowboying, American men could regain the manhood that modern living was siphoning away. The key was to put oneself *out there* where the action was in his view.

If I had contracted some sort of malingering, anachronistic case of Americanitis, then taking to the road seemed to quell it enough for me to keep functioning. I worked hard to finish grad school. My girlfriend got a great job opportunity and moved to Boston. We broke up. I got my degree, and I got a job as an American studies professor at a state university in South Florida. After taking it from the eleven-thousand-foot Beartooth Highway—US Route 212, America's "most scenic highway" along the Montana-Wyoming border—to the frying pan of Death Valley below sea level, I sold the Bus to a couple of hippies in Oakland for the same amount I paid for it (I figured the air-cooled engine wouldn't last in the heat and humidity of Palm Beach County). I got a cat, bought a condo, wrote a book, got tenure, got married, started a family, and bought a house. I helped to

THE LAST ROAD TRIP · 165

build a college, wrote some more books, and taught what I knew to students who wrote down what I said in spiral-bound notebooks.

My life since the trip has been less itinerant but no less exciting. In fact, I've found it to be more adventurous than I could have imagined, the best of life's passages so far. Being a husband and a father are their own adventures, full of daily challenges and joys. My wife, Melanie, loves the outdoors, loves to travel and camp. She keeps me active, gets me out of my own head. When my daughter, Lilli, was born, Melanie compared becoming a parent to discovering a new color, seeing it for the first time, and that description aptly sums up my life with the two of them. Because of Melanie we move and see and do, living big full lives. But there is a comfort in coming, going, and being home, where I love to be with them. As Gabel and Hahn point out in *Anthem*, rootedness is savored when preceded by exploration.

Today I remember only bits and pieces of the trip, which lives on in remarkably few photos, shadows and smudged light. The story I tell about it is mimesis, a reproduction of the real. I wonder how much of it I've misremembered and made up over the years. It is a trace, a residue. In this sense my own meanderings followed our collective national journey. Remembering a past that never existed, we yearn to be free of a history we cannot and will not remember, chained in false remembrances, imprisoned by counterfeit memories. We turn to history less for guidance and reckoning than for consolation and reassurance. Often we mess it up, though sometimes we get it right. Remember the kid who took Larry Walters's chair as he was led away for questioning by the police? His name was Jerry Fleck, and he kept the chair. Thirty years later, he donated it to the National Air and Space Museum. It's now on display at the Steven F. Udvar-Hazy Center, the Smithsonian annex at Dulles International Airport.

These days there are a lot of people out there, adrift on America's roadways. Some are simply vacationing, others are *vacillando*; some have chosen to be out there and some haven't. Van life is a phenomenon. It is also a cottage industry. The nomad movement has many guides and gurus, people who make YouTube videos and Instagram posts and websites providing boundless information about life in a camper van or RV, tutorials that teach others how to eat and bathe and keep from getting harassed if parked too long in the same place—that teach, in short, how to exist in sixty square feet or less, living transiently in a sedentary society.

Some of these souls have freed themselves in true 1960s fashion from the consumerist cycle of earning and spending. Some experienced a setback: an illness or divorce or bankruptcy that forced a life on the road. Some foresee no future: no meaningful vocation, no permanent home, no place to make a bed and dream their dream. And some are playing at the road until they sink roots—trustafarians with $100,000 4x4 Mercedes Sprinter vans. There are Boomers and Gen Xers and Millennials and Gen Zers. Some are retired, and some haven't yet started working. Whether old or young, despairing or joyful, whether they wound up there intentionally or not, they convince themselves that they are better off living in a vehicle without rent payments, that they're free of certain values and pressures and expectations, and that in transience they may find meaning and purpose and peace.

We all reinvent ourselves and are sometimes reinvented through no conscious effort of our own. My own latest iteration is young old man, a grizzled white guy looking past fifty, another of life's passages. I'm told that as we reach middle age we settle, becoming wiser, more assured, and less flappable, but I haven't found it to be so. At the end of the day, I'm still insecure, still afraid of failure and disappointing others as much if not more than disappointing myself. I'm neurotic, filled with self-doubt, but I've realized that most other folks are too and that questioning one's innate abilities is part of the human condition. I remind myself that fear is normal, even healthy, and that the important thing is not to deny fear but to feel it and plow ahead anyway. If anything, I have only upgraded my armor.

Sometime around 2017, I was cleaning out the cluttered garage of our house in Jupiter Farms, Florida. Piles of junk towered above, listing to one side, threatening to bury me like a hoarder entombed in his own filth. In a fit of pique, I threw out a lot of old boxes, including one that I'd been carting around with me for the past two decades. Never in those twenty years had I opened it to look at the contents. While it seemed important somehow, the box remained unopened after it was first taped up, schlepped from place to place: a weighty brick that accompanied me on moves between towns, a relic from a previous life. Clearly, it wasn't something I needed; but, when the idea to write this book became more insistent during the COVID-19 pandemic, I ran to the garage and vainly searched for the box of travel journals, maps, and AAA TripTiks from the trip that I had thrown out a few years earlier. I so wish that I had kept it.

THE LAST ROAD TRIP • 167

Memories of my vagabonding comfort the middle-aged me. If I were to do it all over again, I would've talked to more people along the way. Conversations were few and far between; I was moving across America in solitude. I would've taken more photographs. I would have visited Mt. Rushmore. I would have stopped at a Wisconsin supper club. Many of them have shuttered. Krok's, Candlelite, Casino Town House, and Pyramid of the Nile are all gone, a dying breed. Younger Wisconsinites prefer chain restaurants.

I wouldn't have fled the rest stop. I would have ventured across the northern border into Canada and also across the southern border into Mexico. I would've spent some time in San Antonio, where I would've eaten some good Tex-Mex and seen the Alamo. I would've visited the Grand Canyon, which I still haven't seen. I wouldn't have rushed back to California, and I wouldn't have rocketed past Joshua Tree. I would have slept in the desert in a sleeping bag without a tent under the Milky Way.

But mostly I would have just kept the Bus.

Acknowledgments

I am indebted to my friends in California—Greg Delaune, Billy Rhyne, J. P. Daughton, Karyn Panitch, and others—who supportively turned me loose on the nation's highways but also made me want to return after my adventure. Frank Hoppe, Mike Baughan, and Lizzie Baughan predate my California days as friends, but our friendships deepened and strengthened on the West Coast, and they were coconspirators on the trip. Special thanks to Jennifer Milne Tallagnon, who approved my meanderings or at least tolerated them. I'm not sure why she blessed my trip, but I'm so grateful that she did.

I am indebted to friends along the way who smoothed my path with hot showers, warm beds, cool beverages, and good food. Sheila Blackford and Doug Bloor in Seattle, Chris and Julie Stallman in Minneapolis, and friends of friends in Missoula and Ann Arbor all made the journey easier. While I lost touch with them many, many years ago, I also owe thanks to Jean Lawhead of Pentwater, Michigan, and her partner, Tom, who showed kindness to a scraggly graduate student on the high seas of Lake Michigan. I hope my painting job was passable.

Friends on the East Coast visited me in California when they were able, extended their friendship across the continent, and helped me find my way back home. I'm thinking particularly of Todd Flournoy, Lara Smith, Mike Armstrong, Ted Hogshead, and Ben Temples, but other friends manned the lighthouse too. Y'all know who you are.

Many of my professors at the University of California have passed on, but I am no less indebted to Leon Litwack, Ron Takaki, and Jim Kettner, among others. Waldo Martin continued (and continues) to mentor me long after I left Berkeley. He is the epitome of the professor I would like to be. The late Bill McFeely set me on the path to Berkeley from Athens, Georgia, and I will always be amazed at his faith in my potential.

In 2008, I went to an event at Florida Atlantic University where the featured speaker was Robert Pyle. He had just written his award-winning *Sky Time in Gray's River: Living for Keeps in a Forgotten Place* (2007), but he was in South Florida to talk about his expertise, butterflies, as a guest of our resident lepidopterist, Alana Edwards. It turns out that the American lepidoptery community is small and tightly knit. Everyone else there was talking butterflies, but when I sidled up to Bob with my dog-eared copy of *Where Bigfoot Walks*, his eyes bugged out of his head. What was *I* doing *here* in *South Florida* with *that* book, he asked. He was truly tickled. He then penned the best book inscription I've ever read. He drew two enormous feet treading across the title page, where he wrote: "This is for Chris, with real delight in meeting and seeing this here in Florida—may the Big Galoot continue to keep you good company, and the grace of gentle giants go with you." I treasure that book and appreciate how Bob demonstrated how to write academic prose lightly, beautifully, and unexpectedly.

I am indebted to my friends, colleagues, and students at FAU who've listened to me yammer on about puttering around in my old van. The librarians at the John D. Macarthur Campus and in Interlibrary Loan at the main campus in Boca Raton earned their pay in running down books and finding needed info.

Much appreciation to the University of Alabama Press editors and staff, especially Kristen Hop, who took a quick interest in this manuscript and worked with me to make it much better. UAP said yes to an unusual sort of book, and I couldn't be more thankful. I was fortunate to benefit from some excellent professional guidance, including some anonymous readers to whom I owe a hearty "thank you"; you know who you are, even if I don't. I've gotten tremendous help from colleagues in US history, American studies, and American literature, especially Steve Estes, Tom Hallock, and Julie Buckner Armstrong. Editor extraordinaire Eli Bortz and Sonia Dickey at the University of New Mexico Press supported this manuscript in its earliest iterations and gave invaluable guidance to improve it and help it find the right home.

Many thanks to my parents, Dan and Jean Strain, who filled my metaphorical and literal gas tank on the trip. They have never wavered in their support of my academic and personal endeavors, and the trip was both.

Uncle Ed—Edgar S. Barry Jr.—got me started in Roseville, California; I continue to appreciate his love, support, and interest in my scholarship and writing. My in-laws, the Haskells and Cerchios, have been terrific boosters and cheerleaders. Finally, the biggest thank you of all to my fellow explorers, my daughter, Lilli, and my wife, Melanie, to whom this book is dedicated. Writing a book can take a great toll on those around the author, and my family, both near and far, have been astonishingly supportive throughout the whole process.

Due to spatial constraints, there are a number of family members, friends, acquaintances, colleagues, and coworkers who are not mentioned here by name. It is not deliberate omission but the tyranny of the typeset. Please know that I love you, appreciate you, and extend heartfelt thanks to you too.

Appendix

Lesson #1: Think about where you're headed.

Lesson #2: Leave a trail of breadcrumbs.

Lesson #3: Hug a tree. Protect your mother.

Lesson #4: Keep your eyes on the road and your windscreen clean.

Lesson #5: The American road trip is a white man's prerogative.

Lesson #6: Like Huckleberry Finn, many Americans appreciate the option to "light out."

Lesson #7: Life is temporal. Be grateful for it.

Lesson #8: Test your brakes before you need 'em.

Lesson #9: It's okay to be slightly shattered.

Lesson #10: Always have an extra blanket.

Lesson #11: Have grace for yourself. No one is perfect.

Lesson #12: Feel the fear and do it anyway.

Lesson #13: Don't borrow trouble.

Notes

Introduction

[xi] **In the 1930s and 1940s:** For more on the history of the Road to Nowhere, see "Great Smoky Mountains National Park, the Road to Nowhere," Swain County Chamber of Commerce; and "The Road to Nowhere," Atlas Obscura, June 29, 2016.

[xiv] **To answer this question:** Franklin, quoted in Karen Liu, "Expanding World Views through Traveling," *Childhood Education* 85, no. 1 (2008): 32-A(2).

Chapter 1

[7] **Mark Twain did it twice:** Mark Twain, *Roughing It*, repr. ed. (New York: Penguin Classics, 1982); and Mark Twain, *Life on the Mississippi*, repr. ed. (New York: Signet, 2009).

[7] **Two years after:** Charles Siringo, *A Texas Cowboy, or Fifteen Years on the Hurricane Deck of a Spanish Pony*, repr. ed. (New York: Penguin, 2000).

[7] **In 1920:** F. Scott Fitzgerald, *The Cruise of the Rolling Junk*, repr. ed. (London: Hesperus Press, 2011).

[7] **It was during the mid-twentieth century:** Jack Kerouac, *On the Road*, repr. ed. (New York: Penguin, 1976).

[8] **Five years after Kerouac:** John Steinbeck, *Travels with Charley: In Search of America* (New York: Penguin, 1962), 5.

[8] **In the mid to late 1960s:** Tom Wolfe, *The Electric Kool-Aid Acid Test* (New York: Farrar Straus Giroux, 1968).

[9] **The 1970s brought a trio:** Hunter S. Thompson, *Fear and Loathing in Las Vegas: A Savage Journey to the Heart of the American Dream* (New York: Popular Library, 1971); Robert Pirsig, *Zen and the Art of Motorcycle Maintenance* (New York: William Morrow, 1974); Peter Jenkins, *A Walk across America* (New York: Harper Collins, 1979).

[9]   **When William Least Heat-Moon:** William Least Heat-Moon, *Blue Highways*, repr. ed. (Boston: Back Bay Books, 1999).

[10]   **With the exception:** John Howard Griffin, *Black Like Me* (New York: Houghton Mifflin, 1961); Eddy L. Harris, *Mississippi Solo* (Guilford, CT: Nick Lyons, 1988).

[10]   **A year after Harris:** Bill Bryson, *The Lost Continent: Travels in Small-Town America* (New York: Harper Perennial, 1989).

[10]   **Since then other writers:** Cheryl Strayed, *Wild: From Lost to Found on the Pacific Crest Trail* (New York: Vintage, 2013); Shainee Gabel and Kristin Hahn, *Anthem: An American Road Story* (New York: Avon, 1997); Donald Miller, *Through Painted Deserts: Light, God, and Beauty on the Open Road* (Nashville, TN: Nelson Books, 2008); and John Francis, *Planetwalker* (Washington, DC: National Geographic Books, 2008).

Chapter 2

[12]   **One can imagine:** For more on the Chinese in California, see Paul Yee, *Tales from Gold Mountain: Stories of the Chinese in the New World* (New York: Simon and Schuster, 1990).

[13]   **As John Steinbeck wrote:** Steinbeck, *Travels with Charley*, 198.

[13]   **To the east lies Sacramento:** For more on the history of Roseville, see "History of Roseville," City of Roseville, California.

[14]   **I had tools:** There are two literary John Muirs, one who wrote in the late nineteenth and early twentieth centuries, and one who wrote in the latter part of the twentieth century. The first John Muir was a famous naturalist whose writings include *The Mountains of California* (New York: Century, 1894), *Our National Parks* (Boston: Houghton Mifflin, 1901), *My First Summer in the Sierra* (Boston: Houghton Mifflin, 1911), and *A Thousand Mile Walk to the Gulf*, repr. ed. (Boston: Houghton Mifflin, 1981), among others. The second John Muir wrote a well-known repair manual, *How to Keep Your Volkswagen Alive: A Manual of Step-by-Step Procedures for the Compleat Idiot* (Santa Fe, NM: John Muir Publications, 1976), as well as *The Velvet Monkeywrench* (Santa Fe, NM: John Muir Publications, 1973), both available in reprint by Avalon Publishing Group.

[15]   **Klamath legend tells:** Patrick T. Pringle, *Roadside Geology of Mount St. Helens National Volcanic Monument and Vicinity*, Washington Department of Natural Resources, Division of Geology and Earth Resources Information, Circular 88, 1993, rev. ed. 2002.

[15]   **Non-Indian legends abound here:** John Muir's "Snow-Storm on Mount

Shasta" first appeared in *Harper's New Monthly Magazine* 55 no. 328 (September 1877): 521–30. The Sierra Club has reprinted it: John Muir, "Snow-Storm on Mount Shasta," Sierra Club, John Muir Exhibit.

[15] **A focus of New Age spirituality:** Jeremy M. Tuggle, "The Mt. Shasta Lemurians: Origin of a Legend," *Record Searchlight*, July 28, 2016. The *Record Searchlight* is the newspaper of record in Redding, California.

[15] **At Ashland:** For more on Ashland and the Ashland Springs Hotel, see "Ashland's Golden Spike," National Park Service, August 10, 2020.

[16] **Each winter deep snow:** See "Deep Water in a Sleeping Volcano," Crater Lake National Park, National Park Service, December 19, 2023; and "Crater Lake," US Geological Survey.

[16] ***Lesson #1:*** The enumerated "life lessons" throughout are collected in the appendix.

[19] **The psychology of places:** Algernon Blackwood, "The Willows," Blackwood Stories, 1907.

[20] **There in a pile of books:** Robert Michael Pyle, *Where Bigfoot Walks: Crossing the Dark Divide* (New York: Mariner Books, 1995).

[21] **How our hearts:** Pyle, *Where Bigfoot Walks*, 8.

[21] **I wanted to get inside:** Pyle, *Where Bigfoot Walks*, 17, 132, 149.

[21] **Pyle ponders the future:** Pyle, *Where Bigfoot Walks*, 65, 80, 83.

[23] **In the middle of the night:** Jack Kerouac, *The Dharma Bums*, repr. ed. (New York: Penguin: 1976), 234, 236.

[23] **No man should go:** Jack Kerouac, *Lonesome Traveler* (New York: McGraw Hill, 1960).

[23] **Toward the end:** David Quammen, quoted in Pyle, *Where Bigfoot Walks*, 222.

[24] **The love of learning:** Henry Wadsworth Longfellow, "Morituri Salutamus," *The Masque of Pandora and Other Poems* (London: George Routledge and Sons, 1875), 94.

Chapter 3

[26] **Battle not with monsters:** Friedrich Nietzsche, *Beyond Good and Evil*, trans. Helen Zimmern (New York: Modern Library Publishers, 1917), chap. 4 (146).

[26] **Great joy in camp:** William Clark, "November 7, 1805," Journals of the Lewis and Clark Expedition.

[28] **Tocqueville wrote:** Alexis de Tocqueville, *Democracy in America*, trans. by George Lawrence (New York: Anchor Books, 1969), 554.

[29] **Writing at the advent:** James Truslow Adams, *The Epic of America* (Boston: Little, Brown, 1931), 404, 411–12.

NOTES · **177**

[32] **Ships at a distance:** Zora Neale Hurston, *Their Eyes Were Watching God*, repr. ed. (New York: Harper Perennial, 1990), 1.

[34] **Having just left:** See Carl Sagan, *The Demon-Haunted World: Science as a Candle in the Dark* (New York: Random House, 1995); and F. W. Holiday, *The Gobin Universe* (London: Xanadu, 1986).

[35] **I pondered weather balloons:** Information about "Lawnchair Larry" Walters can be gleaned from a variety of sources, including the fact-checking site Snopes. One key source is George Plimpton, "The Man in the Flying Lawn Chair," *New Yorker*, June 1, 1998.

[38] **The higher I went:** Plimpton, "Man in the Flying Lawn Chair."

[42] **Contrary to popular opinion:** Nancy Gupton, "Benjamin Franklin and the Kite Experiment," Franklin Institute, June 12, 2017; and Benjamin Franklin, "The Kite Experiment, 19 October 1752," National Archives Founders Online.

[42] **Larry Walters was similarly lucky:** Gupton, "Benjamin Franklin and the Kite Experiment"; Myrna Oliver, "Larry Walters Soared to Fame on a Lawn Chair," *Los Angeles Times*, November 24, 1993.

[44] **From John Henry to Captain Marvel:** "Getting Fired: The Secret to Being Rich and Famous," *Sydney Morning Herald*, April 20, 2012. The *Sydney Morning Herald* is a daily tabloid newspaper in Australia.

[44] **As WWII pilot:** Peter Armenti, "John Gillespie Magee's 'High Flight,'" *From the Catbird Seat* (blog), Poetry at Library of Congress, *Library of Congress Blogs*, accessed October 13, 2023.

[44] **Indeed his exploits:** For more on the heirs of Walters, see Mark Karpel, "The Drifters," *Smithsonian Magazine*, August 2010; and Russ Neumeier, "Cluster Ballooning: More Than Urban-Legend, Darwin-Award Fodder," *Wired*, August 14, 2008.

Chapter 4

[50] **When I heard:** Walt Whitman, "When I Heard the Learn'd Astronomer," *Leaves of Grass* (New York: W. E. Chapin, 1867), 214. Whitman published the first edition of *Leaves of Grass* in 1855. He produced varied editions of the work ending with the ninth (or "deathbed") edition in 1891–92.

[51] **All is not as it seems:** For more on Richard Butler and the Christian Identity movement, see George Michael, ed., *Extremism in America* (Gainesville: University Press of Florida, 2013); and the PBS documentary *Extremism in America*, part 1, "The Order," April 19, 2022, PBS, WNET Group.

[52] **For more on Ruby Ridge,** see Adam Augustyn, "Ruby Ridge,"

Britannica, January 25, 2024; and Jess Walter, *Ruby Ridge: The Truth and Tragedy of the Randy Weaver Family*, updated and rev. ed. (New York: Harper Perennial, 2002),

[53] Chad Sokol, "North Idaho College Foundation Plans to Sell Former Site of Aryan Nations Compound," *Spokesman-Review* April 18, 2019. The *Spokesman-Review* is the newspaper of record in Spokane, Washington.

[54] **As Rafia Zakaria has noted:** Rafia Zakaria, "Traveling While White: Peering into the Solipsistic Worlds of Travel Influencers," *Baffler*, January 20, 2023.

[55] **In a 1962** *American Quarterly* **article:** George Wilson Pierson, "The M-Factor in American History," *American Quarterly* 14, no. 2 (1962): 275–89. *American Quarterly* is the official publication of the American Studies Association.

[56] **The U. S. Census Bureau:** For data on US residential mobility, see "Migration/Geographic Mobility," US Census Bureau; and "Survey of Income and Program Participation (SIPP)," US Census Bureau, November 15, 2023.

[59] **Rapidly outgrowing their own:** William Kittredge and Annick Smith, *The Last Best Place: A Montana Anthology* (Seattle: University of Washington Press, 1990).

[61] **Glacier had come:** "Crown of the Continent," Glacier National Park, National Park Service, November 22, 2023; and "Glacier National Park," National Park Foundation, April 21, 2023.

[61] **A contiguous high-country wonderland:** Joe Yogerst, "Everything to Know about Glacier National Park," *National Geographic*, August 16, 2019.

[63] **The plan for the first thoroughfare:** "Going-to-the-Sun Road," Glacier National Park, National Park Service, April 21, 2023.

Chapter 5

[69] **As Thoreau explained:** Henry David Thoreau's *Walden* (1854) is available in many different editions, including the Modern Library Edition first published in September 1937 (and renewed by Random House in 1965). See Thoreau, *Walden* (New York: Modern Library, 1937), 81–82.

[70] **Sometimes I rambled to pine groves:** Thoreau, *Walden*, 181.

[70] **When I first paddled a boat:** Thoreau, *Walden*, 173–174.

[71] **The mass of men lead lives:** Thoreau, *Walden*, 7.

[71] **to find out and pursue his own way:** Thoreau, *Walden*, 64.

[72] **If a man has faith:** Thoreau, *Walden*, 64.

[73] **Space west of the line:** Heat-Moon, *Blue Highways*, 132.

[74] **Talk to the car:** Muir, *How to Keep Your Volkswagen Alive*, 3.

[74] **When you strip a thread:** Muir, *How to Keep Your Volkswagen Alive*, 6.

[74] **If I get hung up:** Muir, *How to Keep Your Volkswagen Alive*, 6.

[74] **When you get interested:** Muir, *How to Keep Your Volkswagen Alive*, 83.

[76] **to see if in that strange perception:** Pirsig, *Zen and the Art*, 25.

[76] **You're completely in contact:** Pirsig, *Zen and the Art*, 4.

[76] **Coming or going:** Muir, *Velvet Monkeywrench*, 5.

[76] **This book presents a way:** Muir, *Velvet Monkeywrench*, 5.

[76] **We need a leaderless:** Muir, *Velvet Monkeywrench*, 5.

[77] **The kind of changes:** Muir, *Velvet Monkeywrench*, 9.

[77] **the science of finding out:** Muir, *Velvet Monkeywrench*, 24.

[77] **The major problem:** Muir, *Velvet Monkeywrench*, 27.

[77] **When I speak about** *Them*: Muir, *Velvet Monkeywrench*, 6.

[77] **timebinding:** Muir, *Velvet Monkeywrench*, 11.

[78] **Better written and organized:** For more on the first John Muir (the naturalist), see "John Muir: A Brief Biography," Sierra Club, John Muir Exhibit; and Donald Worster, *A Passion for Nature: The Life of John Muir* (New York: Oxford University Press, 2008); and Muir, *Thousand Mile Walk to the Gulf*.

[79] **The tendency nowadays:** John Muir, *Our National Parks*, chap. 1–2.

[80] **Exploring south of Missoula:** For more on Big Hole, see "Bearing Witness," Big Hole National Battlefield, Montana, National Park Service, December 18, 2023.

[82] **Ghost towns come:** For more on ghost towns, see Christopher Strain, "Ghost Towns, Vanishing Florida, and the Geography of Memory," *Journal of Florida Studies* 1, no. 2 (Spring 2013).

[84] For more on Bannack, see "Bannack State Park," Montana Fish, Wildlife & Parks.

Chapter 6

[86] **Yosemite Valley, to me:** Ansel Adams, *The Portfolios of Ansel Adams* (Boston: New York Graphic Society, 1977), 38.

[86] **It is by far:** "Letter from John Muir to Jeanne C. Carr, July 26, 1868," University of the Pacific Digital Archives, John Muir Correspondence.

[86] **You will find yourself:** Muir, *Our National Parks*.

[87] **magnificent to behold but:** David Quammen, "The Paradox of the Park," *National Geographic* 229 no. 5 (May 2016): 54+.

[87] **Accidents abound:** Lee Whittlesey, *Death in Yellowstone: Accidents and Foolhardiness in the First National Park*, repr. ed. (Lanham, Maryland: Roberts Rinehart Publishers, 2014).

[88] **The destruction wrought by:** Quammen, "Paradox of the Park."

[91] **the great brown father:** Kerouac, *On the Road*, 141.

[91] **There was a mystic wraith:** Kerouac, *On the Road*, 147.

[92] **I thought all the wilderness:** Kerouac, *On the Road*, 105.

[92] **that little sumpin:** Kerouac, *On the Road*, 10

[92] **two mindless cads:** Kerouac, *On the Road*, 111.

[93] **wishing I were a Negro:** Kerouac, *On the Road*, 180

[93] **They thought I was a Mexican:** Kerouac, *On the Road*, 97.

[93] **I preferred reading:** Kerouac, *On the Road*, 102.

[94] **final development:** Kerouac, *On the Road*, 188.

[94] **the HOLY GOOF:** Kerouac, *On the Road*, 195.

[95] **Three Stooges adventures:** Kerouac, *Dharma Bums*, 41.

[95] **The first sip is joy:** Kerouac, *Dharma Bums*, 67.

[95] **I looked up and saw Japhy:** Kerouac, *Dharma Bums*, 85–86

[96] **great rucksack revolution:** Kerouac, *Dharma Bums*, 97, 98.

[96] **I wanted to get me:** Kerouac, *Dharma Bums*, 105–6.

[97] **Orientalism:** Edward Said, *Orientalism* (New York: Vintage, 1978).

[97] **A parallel can be seen:** For more on wabi-sabi, see Leonard Koren, *Wabi-Sabi for Artists, Designers, Poets, and Philosophers* (Point Reyes, CA: Imperfect Publishing, 2008); and Lingbing Meng, "A Cross-Cultural Comparative Study of the Characteristics of Wang Wei's '"Zen-Style Poetry': A Reading of Wang Wei against Matsuo Bashō and Martin Heidegger's Poems," *Theoretical Studies in Literature and Art* 42, no. 2: 194–204. For more on kintsugi, see "The Beauty of Broken Objects," Smithsonian, August 7, 2020.

[98] **I later learned that:** Jen Carlson, "Here's the Handwritten Ultimatum Jack Kerouac Sent Publisher of *On the Road*," *Gothamist*, March 8, 2013.

Chapter 7

[100] **The words to "America the Beautiful":** "History Resources: 'America the Beautiful,' 1893," Gilder Lehrman Institute of American History.

[101] **demands but little of him:** St. Jean de Crèvecœur, *Letters from an American Farmer*, repr. ed. (New York: Oxford University Press, 1997), 23, 44.

[102] **enjoy explaining almost every act:** Tocqueville, *Democracy in America*, 527.

[102] **taste for physical pleasures:** Tocqueville, *Democracy in America*, 536.

[102] **To clear, cultivate, and transform:** Tocqueville, *Democracy in America*, 621, 639.

[103] **Sometimes he [the American]:** Tocqueville, *Democracy in America*, 541.

[103] **He celebrated individualism:** Tocqueville, *Democracy in America*, 237, 527.

[106] **The first national monument:** "Many People, Many Stories, One Place," Devils Tower National Park, National Park Service, March 29, 2023; and "Devil's Tower National Monument," US Geological Survey.

[108] **In the northern Hills:** "Deadwood: Topics in Chronicling America," Library of Congress Research Guides.

[109] **Thinking about Native Americans:** Heat-Moon, *Blue Highways*, 5, 9, 16, 26.

[110] **wholly Anglo point of view:** "William Least Heat-Moon," Encyclopedia. com.

[110] **Maybe a tonic of curiosity:** Heat-Moon, *Blue Highways*, 17, 28.

[111] **Originally called Hay Camp:** "The Story of Rapid City," BH Visitor, January 5, 2017.

[112] **In the United States:** Gertrude Stein, *The Geographical History of America* (New York: Vintage, 1973), 11.

[113] **291 Miles to Wall Drug:** Ted Hustead, "History of Wall Drug," Wall Drug.com; and "Wall Drug," University of South Dakota LibGuide, August 11, 2023.

[113] **A cup of ice water:** For more on the Badlands, see "Land of Stone and Light," Badlands National Park, National Park Service, December 8, 2020.

[113] **The Bad Lands grade:** Theodore Roosevelt, quoted in "Geologic Formations," Theodore Roosevelt National Park, National Park Service, April 10, 2015.

[114] **They deserve this name:** Steinbeck, *Travels with Charley*, 154.

[114] **Unlike its natural history:** "American Originals," National Archives and Records Administration, March 1996; and "Western Frontier History," Black Hills National Forest, US Forest Service.

[117] For more on Pine Ridge, see "Pine Ridge Agency," US Department of the Interior Indian Affairs; and "American Community Survey 5-Year Estimates: Pine Ridge," US Census Bureau; and "Pine Ridge Agency," Indian Archives Project, South Dakota State Historical Society.

Chapter 8

[118] **We were somewhere around Barstow:** Thompson, *Fear and Loathing in Las Vegas*, 3, 12, 18, 67–68.

[119] **The real-life inspiration:** See Oscar Zeta Acosta, *The Autobiography of a Brown Buffalo* (New York: Random House, 1972); and Acosta, *Revolt of the Cockroach People* (New York: Knopf, 1973).

[120] **In the walking I discover:** Francis, *Planetwalker*, 38,

[120] **the ethical justification of my choices:** Francis, *Planetwalker*, 9.

[120] **Arnold Van Gennep:** Francis, *Planetwalker*, 8–9.

[125] **the great Mississippi:** Mark Twain, "Old Times on the Mississippi (Part 1)," *Atlantic*, January 1875; and Charles Dickens, *American Notes for General Circulation* (London: Chapman and Hall, 1850), 118. This edition of *American Notes* may be viewed as a series of scanned images available at the Library of Congress website.

[126] Ron Faiola has written a number of books about Wisconsin supper clubs, including *The Wisconsin Supper Clubs Story: An Illustrated History with Relish* (Evanston, IL: Agate Midway, 2021).

[126] **the SS Badger:** For more on the *Badger*, see "Badger," Lake Michigan Carferry, an Interlake Maritime Services Company.

[127] **this monster land:** Steinbeck, *Travels with Charley*, 5–6.

[128] **I saw in their eyes:** Steinbeck, *Travels with Charley*, 10.

[128] **Nearly every American hungers:** Steinbeck, *Travels with Charley*, 3, 10.

[128] **the steady rooted ones:** Steinbeck, *Travels with Charley*, 103.

Chapter 9

[136] **the first suburban development:** For more on Levittown, see Dolores Hayden, *Redesigning the American Dream: Gender, Housing, and Family Life* (New York: W. W. Norton, 1984); and Craig Whitaker, *Architecture and the American Dream* (New York: Clarkson Potter, 1996).

[137] **Many American towns:** Whitaker, *Architecture and the American Dream*, xi.

[137] **New Urbanist designers:** For more on New Urbanism and American sprawl, see Peter Calthorpe, *The New Urbanism: Toward an Architecture of Community* (New York: McGraw Hill, 1993); and Howard Kunstler, *The Geography of Nowhere: The Rise and Decline of America's Man-Made Landscape* (New York: Free Press, 1994); and Andres Duany, Elizabeth Plater-Zyberk, and Jeff Speck, *Suburban Nation: The Rise of Sprawl and the Decline of the American Dream* (New York: Macmillan, 2000).

[138] **The American has not root:** Michel Chevalier, *Society, Manners, and Politics in the United States, Being a Series of Letters on North America* (Boston: Weeks, Jordan, 1839), 286. This book may be viewed as a series of scanned images available at the Library of Congress website.

[138] **our excessive mobility:** Pierson, "M-Factor in American History," 276, 283, 284, 288.

[138] **Come on! Get going!:** Pierson, "M-Factor in American History," 288.

[139] **seasonal migrations:** See William Cronon, *Changes in the Land: Indians, Colonists, and the Ecology of New England* (New York: Hill and Wang, 1983).

[140] **travel for Black folks:** For travel and Jim Crow segregation, see Victor Hugo Green, *The Negro Motorist Green Book*, 1940, repr. ed. (Camarillo, CA: About Comics, 2016), The *Green Book* is available as facsimile in various reprints. See also Gary Totten, *African American Travel Narratives from Abroad: Mobility and Cultural Work in the Age of Jim Crow* (Amherst: University of Massachusetts Press, 2015).

[140] **vagrancy laws:** For a brief synopsis of vagrancy laws and Black Codes, see Nancy Bercaw, "Black Codes," Mississippi Encyclopedia, April 13, 2018.

[141] **the chain gang:** See Alex Lichtenstein, "Good Roads and Chain Gangs in the Progressive South: 'The Negro Convict Is a Slave,'" *Journal of Southern History* 59, no. 1 (February 1993): 85–110.

[141] **good roads movement:** For more on the "good roads movement," see "Better Roads," Smithsonian National Museum of American History.

[141] **Susan Roberson notes:** Susan Roberson, *Women, America, and Movement: Narratives of Relocation* (Columbia: University of Missouri Press, 1998), 8.

[141] **there have always been women:** Marilyn C. Wesley, *Secret Journeys: The Trope of Women's Travel in American Literature* (Albany: State University of New York Press, 1999), ix, 130.

[142] **a time capsule road movie:** Gabel and Hahn, *Anthem*, 3.

[144] **or are you *friends*?:** Gabel and Hahn, *Anthem*, 193.

[144] **Kris kept her eyes:** Gabel and Hahn, *Anthem*, 45.

[144] **One thing I knew:** Gabel and Hahn, *Anthem*, 83.

[144] **an ugly, unfeminist longing:** Gabel and Hahn, *Anthem*, 58.

[144] **From Governor Ann Richards:** Gabel and Hahn, *Anthem*, 52.

[144] **a sense of community:** Gabel and Hahn, *Anthem*, 199–200.

[145] **In *Road Frames*:** For an excellent analysis of US travel literature, see Kris Lackey, *RoadFrames: The American Highway Narrative* (Lincoln: University of Nebraska Press, 1998).

[145] **highway consciousness:** Lackey, *RoadFrames*, 7.

[145] **road phenomenology:** Lackey, *RoadFrames*, 7.

[145] **when the center becomes decentered:** Roberson, *Women, America, and Movement*, 9.

[146] **Once you have traveled:** Pat Conroy, *The Prince of Tides* (Boston: Houghton Mifflin, 1986), 127.

Chapter 10

[150] **as beautiful and elusive:** H. G. Bissinger, *Friday Night Lights: A Town, a Team, and a Dream*, paperback ed. (New York: Harper Perennial, 1991), 264.

[153] **roadkill:** "Public Roads—March/April 2000," US Department of Transportation, Federal Highway Administration, March/April 2000.

[156] **the fantastic hugeness and energy of production: Steinbeck,** *Travels with Charley*, **108.**

[156] **For all out enormous geographic range:** Steinbeck, *Travels with Charley*, 210.

[156] **near Abingdon:** Steinbeck, *Travels with Charley*, 274–275.

[157] **deep travel:** Lackey, *RoadFrames*, 30.

[158] **Nonfiction highway books:** Lackey, *RoadFrames*, 16–17.

[159] **a riot grrrl:** For more, see Miller, *Through Painted Deserts*; Francis, *Planetwalker*, and Carrie Brownstein, *Hunger Makes Me a Modern Girl: A Memoir*, repr. ed. (New York: Riverhead Books, 2016). In *Through Painted Deserts*, Donald Miller takes his own cross-country journey in a VW Bus with his friend Paul.

[159] **a political nation of cultural nationalities:** Michael Walzer, *What It Means to be an American: Essays on the American Experience* (Venice: Marsilio Publishers, 1992), 9.

[160] **own specific timbre and tonality:** Horace Kallen, "Democracy versus the Melting Pot: A Study of American Nationality," in *Theories of Ethnicity: A Classical Reader*, ed. Werner Sollors, (New York: New York University Press, 1996), 92.

[160] **America was created by:** Samuel P. Huntington, "The Hispanic Challenge," *Foreign Policy* 141 (March–April 2004): 30.

[161] **Pete Hamill,** "The Alloy of New York," in *Reinventing the Melting Pot: The New Immigrants and What It Means to Be American*, ed. Tamar Jacoby (New York: Basic Books, 2004), 168.

[162] **coined the term neurasthenia:** For more on neurasthenia and Americanitis, see F. G. Gosling, *Before Freud: Neurasthenia and the American Medical Community, 1870-1910* (Urbana: University of Illinois Press, 1987); David G. Schuster, *Neurasthenic Nation: America's Search for Health, Comfort, and Happiness, 1869-1920* (New Brunswick, NJ: Rutgers University Press, 2011); and Greg Daugherty, "The Brief History of 'Americanitis,'" *Smithsonian Magazine*, March 25, 2015.

[163] **Americanitis Elixir:** Greil Marcus, "One Step Back: Where Are the Elixirs of Yesteryear When We Hurt?" *New York Times*, January 26, 1998, sec. 1, p. 2

[166] **His name was Jerry Fleck:** Rebecca Maksel, "How the Balloon-Borne 'Flying Lawn Chair' Got into the Smithsonian," *Smithsonian Magazine*, September 2019.

[166] **rootedness is savored when preceded by exploration:** Gabel and Hahn, *Anthem*, 159.

Works Cited

Acosta, Oscar Zeta. *The Autobiography of a Brown Buffalo*. New York: Random House, 1972.

———. *Revolt of the Cockroach People*. New York: Knopf, 1973.

Adams, Ansel. *The Portfolios of Ansel Adams*. Boston: New York Graphic Society, 1977.

Adams, James Truslow. *The Epic of America*. Boston: Little, Brown, 1931.

"American Community Survey 5-Year Estimates: Pine Ridge." US Census Bureau.

"American Originals." National Archives and Records Administration, March 1996.

Armenti, Peter. "John Gillespie Magee's 'High Flight.'" *From the Catbird Seat* (blog), Poetry at the Library of Congress, *Library of Congress Blogs*, September 3, 2023.

"Ashland's Golden Spike." National Park Service, August 10, 2020.

Augustyn, Adam. "Ruby Ridge." Britannica, January 25, 2024.

"Bannack State Park." Montana Fish, Wildlife & Parks.

"Bearing Witness." Big Hole National Battlefield, Montana. National Park Service, December 18, 2023.

"Beauty of Broken Objects, The." Smithsonian, August 7, 2020.

Bercaw, Nancy. "Black Codes." Mississippi Encyclopedia, April 13, 2018.

"Better Roads," Smithsonian National Museum of American History.

Bissinger, H. G. *Friday Night Lights: A Town, a Team, and a Dream*. Paperback ed. New York: Harper Perennial, 1991.

Blackwood, Algernon. "The Willows." Blackwood Stories, 1907.

Brownstein, Carrie. *Hunger Makes Me a Modern Girl: A Memoir*. Repr. ed. New York: Riverhead Books, 2016.

Bryson, Bill. *The Lost Continent: Travels in Small-Town America*. New York: Harper Perennial, 1989.

Calthorpe, Peter. *The New Urbanism: Toward an Architecture of Community*. New York: McGraw Hill, 1993.

Carlson, Jen. "Here's the Handwritten Ultimatum Jack Kerouac Sent Publisher of *On the Road.*" *Gothamist*, March 8, 2013.

Chevalier, Michel. *Society, Manners, and Politics in the United States, Being a Series of Letters on North America.* Boston: Weeks, Jordan, 1839.

Clark, William. "November 7, 1805." Journals of the Lewis and Clark Expedition.

Conroy, Pat. *The Prince of Tides.* Boston: Houghton Mifflin, 1986.

"Crater Lake." US Geological Survey.

de Crèvecœur, St. Jean. *Letters from an American Farmer.* Repr. ed. New York: Oxford University Press, 1997.

Cronon, William. *Changes in the Land: Indians, Colonists, and the Ecology of New England.* New York: Hill and Wang, 1983.

"Crown of the Continent." Glacier National Park, National Park Service, November 22, 2023.

Daugherty, Greg. "The Brief History of 'Americanitis.'" *Smithsonian Magazine*, March 25, 2015.

"Deadwood: Topics in Chronicling America." Library of Congress Research Guides.

"Deep Water in a Sleeping Volcano." Crater Lake National Park, National Park Service, December 19, 2023.

"Devil's Tower National Monument." US Geological Survey.

Dickens, Charles. *American Notes for General Circulation.* London: Chapman and Hall, 1850.

Duany, Andres, Elizabeth Plater-Zyberk, and Jeff Speck. *Suburban Nation: The Rise of Sprawl and the Decline of the American Dream.* New York: Macmillan, 2000.

Extremism in America. Part 1, "The Order." April 19, 2022, WNET Group (website).

Faiola, Ron. *The Wisconsin Supper Clubs Story: An Illustrated History with Relish.* Evanston, IL: Agate Midway, 2021.

Fitzgerald, F. Scott. *The Cruise of the Rolling Junk.* Repr. ed. London: Hesperus Press, 2011.

Francis, John. *Planetwalker.* Washington, DC: National Geographic Books, 2008.

Franklin, Benjamin. "The Kite Experiment, 19 October 1752." National Archives Founders Online.

Gabel, Shainee, and Kristin Hahn. *Anthem: An American Road Story.* New York: Avon, 1997.

"Geologic Formations." Theodore Roosevelt National Park, National Park Service, April 10, 2015.

"Getting Fired: The Secret to Being Rich and Famous." *Sydney Morning Herald*, April 20, 2012.

"Glacier National Park." National Park Foundation, April 21, 2023.

"Going-to-the-Sun Road." Glacier National Park, National Park Service, April 21, 2023.

Gosling, F. G. *Before Freud: Neurasthenia and the American Medical Community, 1870–1910*. Urbana: University of Illinois Press, 1987.

"Great Smoky Mountains National Park, the Road to Nowhere." Swain County Chamber of Commerce.

Green, Victor Hugo. *The Negro Motorist Green Book*. 1940. Repr. ed. Camarillo, CA: About Comics, 2016.

Griffin, John Howard. *Black Like Me*. New York: Houghton Mifflin, 1961.

Gupton, Nancy. "Benjamin Franklin and the Kite Experiment." Franklin Institute, June 12, 2017.

Hamill, Pete. "The Alloy of New York." In *Reinventing the Melting Pot: The New Immigrants and What It Means to Be American*, edited by Tamar Jacoby, 167–79. New York: Basic Books, 2004.

Harris, Eddy L. *Mississippi Solo*. Guilford, CT: Nick Lyons, 1988.

Hayden, Dolores. *Redesigning the American Dream: Gender, Housing, and Family Life*. New York: W. W. Norton, 1984.

Heat-Moon, William Least. *Blue Highways*. Repr. ed. Boston: Back Bay Books, 1999.

"History of Roseville." City of Roseville, California.

Holiday, F. W. *The Gobin Universe*. London: Xanadu, 1986.

Huntington, Samuel P. "The Hispanic Challenge." *Foreign Policy* 141 (March–April 2004): 30.

Hurston, Zora Neale. *Their Eyes Were Watching God*. Repr. ed. New York: Harper Perennial, 1990.

Jenkins, Peter. *A Walk across America*. New York: Harper Collins, 1979.

"John Muir: A Brief Biography." Sierra Club, the John Muir Exhibit.

Kallen, Horace. "Democracy versus the Melting Pot: A Study of American Nationality." In *Theories of Ethnicity: A Classical Reader*, edited by Werner Sollors, 67–92. New York: New York University Press, 1996.

Karpel, Mark. "The Drifters." *Smithsonian Magazine*, August 2010.

Kerouac, Jack. *The Dharma Bums*. Repr. ed. New York: Penguin: 1976.

———. *Lonesome Traveler*. New York: McGraw Hill, 1960.

———. *On the Road*. Repr. ed. New York: Penguin, 1976.

"Kite Experiment." Benjamin Franklin Historical Society.

Kittredge, William, and Annick Smith. *The Last Best Place: A Montana Anthology*. Seattle: University of Washington Press, 1990.

Koren, Leonard. *Wabi-Sabi for Artists, Designers, Poets, and Philosophers*. Point Reyes, CA: Imperfect Publishing, 2008.

Kunstler, Howard. *The Geography of Nowhere: The Rise and Decline of America's Man-Made Landscape*. New York: Free Press, 1994.

Lackey, Kris. *RoadFrames: The American Highway Narrative*. Lincoln: University of Nebraska Press, 1998.

"Land of Stone and Light." Badlands National Park, National Park Service, December 8, 2020.

"Letter from John Muir to Jeanne Carr. July 26, 1868." University of the Pacific Digital Archives, John Muir Correspondence.

Lichtenstein, Alex. "Good Roads and Chain Gangs in the Progressive South: 'The Negro Convict Is a Slave.'" *Journal of Southern History* 59, no. 1 (February 1993): 85–110.

Liu, Karen. "Expanding World Views through Traveling." *Childhood Education* 85, no. 1 (2008): 32-A(2).

Longfellow, Henry Wadsworth. *The Masque of Pandora and Other Poems.* London: George Routledge and Sons, 1875.

Maksel, Rebecca. "How the Balloon-Borne 'Flying Lawn Chair' Got into the Smithsonian." *Smithsonian Magazine*, September 2019.

"Many People, Many Stories, One Place." Devils Tower National Monument, National Park Service, March 29, 2023.

Marcus, Greil. "One Step Back: Where Are the Elixirs of Yesteryear When We Hurt?" *New York Times*, January 26, 1998, sec. A, p. 2.

Meng, Lingbing. "A Cross-Cultural Comparative Study of the Characteristics of Wang Wei's 'Zen-Style Poetry': A Reading of Wang Wei against Matsuo Bashō and Martin Heidegger's Poems," *Theoretical Studies in Literature and Art* 42, no. 2: 194–204.

Michael, George, ed. *Extremism in America.* Gainesville: University Press of Florida, 2013.

"Migration/Geographic Mobility." US Census Bureau.

Miller, Donald. *Through Painted Deserts: Light, God, and Beauty on the Open Road.* Nashville, TN: Nelson Books, 2008.

Muir, John. *The Mountains of California.* New York: Century, 1894.

———. *My First Summer in the Sierra.* Boston: Houghton Mifflin, 1911.

———. *Our National Parks.* Boston: Houghton Mifflin, 1901.

———. "Snow-Storm on Mount Shasta." *Harper's New Monthly Magazine* 55, no. 328 (September 1877): 521–30.

———. *A Thousand Mile Walk to the Gulf.* Repr. ed. Boston: Houghton Mifflin, 1981.

Muir, John. *How to Keep Your Volkswagen Alive: A Manual of Step-by-Step Procedures for the Compleat Idiot.* Santa Fe, NM: John Muir Publications, 1976.

———. *The Velvet Monkeywrench.* Santa Fe, NM: John Muir Publications, 1973.

Neumeier, Russ. "Cluster Ballooning: More Than Urban-Legend, Darwin-Award Fodder." *Wired*, August 14, 2008.

Nietzsche, Friedrich. *Beyond Good and Evil.* Translated by Helen Zimmern. New York: Modern Library Publishers, 1917.

Oliver, Myrna. "Larry Walters Soared to Fame on a Lawn Chair." *Los Angeles Times*, November 24, 1993.

Pierson, George Wilson. "The M-Factor in American History." *American Quarterly* 14, no. 2 (1962): 275–89.

"Pine Ridge Agency." Indian Archives Project. South Dakota State Historical Society.

"Pine Ridge Agency." US Department of the Interior Indian Affairs.

Pirsig, Robert. *Zen and the Art of Motorcycle Maintenance*. New York: William Morrow, 1974.

Plimpton, George. "The Man in the Flying Lawn Chair." *New Yorker*, June 1, 1998.

Pringle, Patrick. *Roadside Geology of Mount St. Helens National Volcanic Monument and Vicinity*. Washington Department of Natural Resources, Division of Geology and Earth Resources Information. Circular 88, 1993, rev. ed., 2002.

"Public Roads—March/April 2000." US Department of Transportation, Federal Highway Administration, March/April 2000.

Pyle, Robert Michael. *Where Bigfoot Walks: Crossing the Dark Divide*. New York: Mariner Books, 1995.

Quammen, David. "The Paradox of the Park." *National Geographic* 229, no. 5 (May 2016): 54+.

"Road to Nowhere, The." Atlas Obscura, June 29, 2016.

Roberson, Susan. *Women, America, and Movement: Narratives of Relocation*. Columbia: University of Missouri Press, 1998.

Sagan, Carl. *The Demon-Haunted World: Science as a Candle in the Dark*. New York: Random House, 1995.

Said, Edward. *Orientalism*. New York, Vintage, 1978.

Schuster, David G. *Neurasthenic Nation: America's Search for Health, Comfort, and Happiness, 1869–1920*. New Brunswick, NJ: Rutgers University Press, 2011.

Siringo, Charles. *A Texas Cowboy, or Fifteen Years on the Hurricane Deck of a Spanish Pony*. Repr. ed. New York: Penguin, 2000.

Sokol, Chad. "North Idaho College Foundation Plans to Sell Former Site of Aryan Nations Compound." *Spokesman-Review*, April 18, 2019.

Stein, Gertrude. *The Geographical History of America*. New York: Vintage, 1973.

Steinbeck, John. *Travels with Charley: In Search of America*. New York: Penguin, 1962.

"Story of Rapid City, The." BH Visitor, January 5, 2017.

Strain, Christopher B. "Ghost Towns, Vanishing Florida, and the Geography of Memory." *Journal of Florida Studies* 1, no. 2 (spring 2013).

Strayed, Cheryl. *Wild: From Lost to Found on the Pacific Crest Trail*. New York: Vintage, 2013.

"Survey of Income and Program Participation (SIPP)." US Census Bureau, November 15, 2023.

Thompson, Hunter S. *Fear and Loathing in Las Vegas: A Savage Journey to the Heart of the American Dream*. New York: Popular Library, 1971.

Thoreau, Henry David. *Walden*. New York: Modern Library, 1937.

Tocqueville, Alexis de. *Democracy in America*. Translated by George Lawrence. New York: Anchor Books, 1969.

Totten, Gary. *African American Travel Narratives from Abroad: Mobility and Cultural Work in the Age of Jim Crow*. Amherst: University of Massachusetts Press, 2015.

Tuggle, Jeremy M. "The Mt. Shasta Lemurians: Origin of a Legend," *Record Searchlight*, July 28, 2016.

Twain, Mark. *Life on the Mississippi*. Repr. ed. New York: Signet, 2009.

———. "Old Times on the Mississippi (Part 1)." *Atlantic*, January 1875.

———. *Roughing It*. Repr. ed. New York: Penguin Classics, 1982.

"Wall Drug." University of South Dakota LibGuide, August 11, 2023.

Wall Drug Store. "Wall Drug Store: Celebrating 90 Years." April 8, 2021.

Walter, Jess. *Ruby Ridge: The Truth and Tragedy of the Randy Weaver Family*. Updated and rev. ed. New York: Harper Perennial, 2002.

Walzer, Michael. *What It Means to Be an American: Essays on the American Experience*. Venice: Marsilio Publishers, 1992.

Wesley, Marilyn. *Secret Journeys: The Trope of Women's Travel in American Literature*. Albany: State University of New York Press, 1999.

"Western Frontier History." Black Hills National Forest, US Forest Service.

Whitaker, Craig. *Architecture and the American Dream*. New York: Clarkson Potter, 1996.

Whitman, Walt. *Leaves of Grass*. New York: W. E. Chapin, 1867.

Whittlesey, Lee. *Death in Yellowstone: Accidents and Foolhardiness in the First National Park*. Repr. ed. Lanham, MD: Roberts Rinehart Publishers, 2014.

"William Least Heat-Moon." Encyclopedia.com.

Wolfe, Tom. *The Electric Kool-Aid Acid Test*. New York: Farrar Straus Giroux, 1968.

Worster, Donald. *A Passion for Nature: The Life of John Muir*. New York: Oxford University Press, 2008.

Yee, Paul. *Tales from Gold Mountain: Stories of the Chinese in the New World*. New York: Simon and Schuster, 1990.

Yogerst, Joe. "Everything to Know about Glacier National Park." *National Geographic*, August 16, 2019.

Zakaria, Rafia. "Traveling While White: Peering into the Solipsistic Worlds of Travel Influencers." *Baffler*, January 20, 2023.

Index

Page numbers in italics refer to figures.

AAA TripTiks, 6, 162, 187
Acosta, Oscar Zeta, 119, 182, 187
Adams, Ansel, 86, 180, 187
Adams, James Truslow, 29–30, 177, 187. See also *Epic of America*
African Americans. *See* mobility: African Americans and
American Dream, the: 9, 22, 27–31, 36, 45, 56, 68, 71, 93, 101–4, 118, 123, 136–37, 142, 150, 162, 183; excess and 29, 90–91, 93–94, 118–19; housing and, 136–137. *See also* Americanism; Americanness; individualism; work
American exceptionalism, 119, 157
American Indian Movement (AIM), 116, 117
Americanism, definition of, 124, 138. *See also* American Dream; Americanness; equality; individualism; patriotism; race and racism
Americanitis, 162–*164*, 165. *See also* neurasthenia
Americanness, xiii–xiv, 36, 100–104, 118–119, 122–23, 124, 154–55, 156–161, 165, 166. *See also* American Dream; American exceptionalism; Americanism; equality; individualism; landscape, the American; patriotism; pluralism; race and racism; space, open; West, the American
Americans, Native, 10, 15, 29, 50, 53–54, 61–63, 64, 68, 69, 80–*81*, 88, 92, 104–*6*, 107, 109, 111, 113–117, 125, 139, 152, 153, 155, 176, 182, 184, 188, 191; forced migrations of, 53–54, 116–17, 139. *See also individual Native American nations*
"America the Beautiful," 100–101
Anthem, 10, 141–44, 145, 166, 176, 184, 186. *See also* Gabel, Shainee, and Kristin Hahn
Apache Indians, 117
Aryan Nations, 51–53
Aschwanden, Peter, 74

Badger, SS, 126–27, 130. *See also* Lake Michigan
Badlands National Park, 113–115, 182, 190
barbecue, 54, 126, 147, 156

Bay Area, 6, 13, 33, 47, 54, 117, 154. *See also* Berkeley; Oakland

bears, grizzly, 58, 65–66, 67, 68, 88, 89, 120, 153

Beat poetry and Beat poets, 8, 90–97. *See also* Kerouac, Jack

Berkeley (California), xiii, 1–6, 13, 26, 33, 57, 74, 95, 151, 154, 161, 169, 170

Bigfoot, 18, 20–23, 26, 74, 78, 170. *See also* Pyle, Robert Michael; *Where Bigfoot Walks*

Big Hole National Battlefield, 80–*81*, 82, 105, 106, 180, 187

bighorn sheep, 64, 68, 88

Black Americans. *See* mobility: African Americans and

Blackfeet Indians, 61, 68, 105

Black Hills, 108, 111, 114–15, 182, 192

Black Like Me, 10, 176, 189

Blackwood, Algernon, 19, 177, 187

Blue Highways, 9, 109–111, 176, 179, 182, 189. *See also* Heat-Moon, William Least

Boone, Daniel, 35, 60, 92, 155

Brownstein, Carrie, 158, 185, 187

Bryson, Bill, 10, 138, 176, 187. See also *Lost Continent, The*

buffalo, 61, 80, 84, 85, 99, 113, 117, 139

bumper stickers, 121–24

Bus, "the," 4, 5, 6, 13–14, 16, 24, 25, 33–34, 46, 47–49, 64–65, 66, 90, 109, 121, 124, 126, 129, 131, 133, 151, 154, 161, 165, 168; camping in, 13–14, 16–19, 25, 47–49, 65–66, 73, 90, 104–5, 129, 132–34, 137–38; driving in, 5, 15, 16, 32–33, 61, 63–65, 88–*89*. *See also* Volkswagens/VWs

Butler, Richard, 51, 52

California, xiii, 1–6, 8, 12–15, 25, 35–41, 45, 57, 58, 59, 75, 79, 91, 97, 111, 136, 150, 151, 153, 156, 163, 168, 169. *See also* Bay Area; Berkeley; Mount Shasta; Oakland; Roseville; San Francisco; Sierra Nevada Mountains

Calthorpe, Peter, 137, 183

Canary, Calamity Jane, 108

Cascade Mountains, 14, 15, *17*, 20, 23, 34, 57, 64, 133, 138

chain restaurants, 6, 54, 146, 154, 168

Cherokee Indians, 62–63, 117, 139

Civil War, the, 7, 78, 80, 82, 140, 152

coconut cream pie, 54, 57, 67, 104, 135, 147, 157

Crater Lake, 15–16

Creek Indians, 63

Crevecœur, St. Jean de, 101–102

Crockett, Davy, 35, 56, 60, 155

Crow Indians, 88, 104–105, 112, 133, 154

Cruise of the Rolling Junk, The, 7, 121, 175, 188

Custer, George Armstrong, 114, 105–106, 109

Dakota Indians, 125

Deadwood (South Dakota), 108, 114–15, 182, 188

Democracy in America, 28, 102, 177, 181, 182, 192. *See also* Tocqueville, Alexis de

Devils Tower National Monument, 106–7, 182, 190

Dharma Bums, The, 23, 94–96, 177, 181, 189. *See also* Kerouac, Jack

diners, 54–55, 57, 109, 126, 146–47

Earhart, Amelia, 43, 44, 56

Electric Kool Aid Acid Test, The, 8, 175, 192. *See also* Wolfe, Tom elk, 88, 89–90

Emerson, Ralph Waldo, 49, 69, 91

environmentalism, 21–23, 69–72, 77, 78–80, 96, 139. *See also* Americanness; Muir, John (naturalist); Thoreau, Henry David; wilderness

equality, 27, 29, 101–104, 134–35, 159–61

Fear and Loathing in Las Vegas, 9, 118–19, 175, 182, 192. *See also* Thompson, Hunter S.

Fitzgerald, F. Scott, 7, 150, 175, 188. See also *Cruise of the Rolling Junk, The*

Fitzgerald, Zelda, 7

Flathead Indian Reservation, 61. *See also* Kootenai Indians, Salish Indians

Fontana Lake, xi–xii

Founding Fathers, 29, 30, 42, 92, 135, 144, 155. *See also names of individuals*

Francis, John, 10, 119–121, 158–59, 176, 183, 185, 188. See also *Planetwalker*

Franklin, Benjamin, 42, 92, 101, 178, 188, 189

Gabel, Shainee, and Kristin Hahn, 10, 141–44, 145, 166, 176, 184, 186. See also *Anthem*

Georgia, 1, 2, 6, 14, 33, 34, 59, 63, 72, 78, 110, 117, 126, 139, 141, 148, 149–50, 154, 170

Ghost Dance, the, 115

ghost towns, 82–84, 180, 191

Glacier National Park, 61, 63–68, 86, 179, 188, 192; Going-to-the-Sun Road, 63–65, 86; Logan Pass, 63, 65, 67–68

Green, Victor Hugo, 140, 184, 189. See also *Green Book, The Negro Motorist*

Green Book, The Negro Motorist, 140, 184, 189. *See also* Green, Victor Hugo

Griffin, John Howard, 10, 176, 189. See also *Black Like Me*

Hamill, Pete, 161, 185, 189

Harris, Eddy L., 10, 140, 176, 189. See also *Mississippi Solo*

hauntings, 81–82, 91–92

Hayden, Delores, 136–37, 183

Heat-Moon, William Least, 9, 10, 73, 109–11, 117, 140, 146, 176, 179, 182, 189, 192. See also *Blue Highways*

Hickok, Wild Bill, 108

How to Keep Your Volkswagen Alive, 14, 73–75, 76, 176, 180, 190. *See also* Muir, John (mechanic)

Hurston, Zora Neale, 32, 178, 189. See also *Their Eyes Were Watching God*

Idaho, 14, 50–54, 57–58, 120, 179; Couer d'Alene, 50, 51, 53, 54; Hayden Lake, 51–53; Ruby Ridge, 52

Indians. See Americans, Native.

individualism, 28, 30, 69, 71–72, 101, 102–4, 124, 137, 144–45, 161, 182

Iroquois Indians, 155

Jackson, Andrew, 28, 29, 30, 139

Jefferson, Thomas, 30, 109, 144

Jenkins, Peter, 9, 120, 138, 175, 189. See also *Walk Across America, A*

Joseph, Chief, 54, 80

Kentucky, 14, 78, 147, 148

Kerouac, Jack, 8, 22–23, 53, 90–99, 119, 175, 177, 181, 188. See also *Dharma Bums, The*; *On the Road*

INDEX · **195**

Kesey, Ken, 8. *See also* Merry
Pranksters
King, Martin Luther King, Jr., 6, 56,
149
kintsugi, 97, 181
Klamath Indians, 15, 176
Kootenai Indians, 50, 61. *See also* Flat-
head Indian Reservation

Lackey, Kris, 145, 157, 158, 184, 185,
189. See also *Road Frames*
Lake Michigan, 126–27
landscape, the American: fauna of,
21–23, 25, 60, 61, 64, 65–66, 69, 70,
84–90, 108, 113–14, 138, 148, 152–
53, 180, 187; flora of, 16, 21–23, 50,
64, 68, 70–71, 79, 80, 89, 108, 148;
maps and, 19–20, 82, 167; place
names of, 15, 58, 59, 62, 64, 92,
107,115. *See also* West, the American
lessons, xiii, 16, 18, 22, 24, 46, 53, 55,
66, 89, 99, 138, 156, 162. *See also
the appendix to this volume*
Lincoln, Abraham, 81, 109
Lindbergh, Charles, 36, 43
Little Bighorn Battlefield National
Monument: 105–*106*, 109
Lost Continent, The, 10, 121, 176, 187.
See also Bryson, Bill

Merry Pranksters, 8. *See also* Kesey,
Ken
M-Factor, 55–57, 179, 183, 184, 191.
See also mobility; Pierson, George
Wilson
Michigan, 14, 85, 125, 126–*130*, 131–
133, 169, 183
Midwest, the, 135–36
Miller, Donald, 10, 158–59, 176, 185,
190

Minnesota, 140, 141, 184, 187
Mississippi, 140, 141, 184, 187
Mississippi River, 7, 10, 29, 91, 120,
125, 175, 176, 183, 189, 192
Mississippi Solo, 10, 121, 176, 189. *See
also* Harris, Eddy L.
mobility, 128, 138–41, 144–46, 154–55,
165–68; African Americans and, 10,
15, 119–20, 140–41, 184, 187, 192;
forced, 53–54, 116–17, 139; gender and, 53–54, 141–44; race and,
53–54; women and, 53–54, 141–45,
153, 184, 191, 192. *See also* M-Factor;
road trips
Montana, vii, 14, 50, 51, 52, 53, 57–90,
91, 101, 120, 165, 179, 180, 187, 189;
Bannack, 82–84; Missoula, 59–61;
Nevada City, 82–84; St. Ignatius,
61–62
Mormons, 53–54
Mount Rushmore, 108–109
Mount Shasta, 15, 78, 176–77, 190, 192
Muir, John (mechanic), 14, 73–75,
76–78, 124, 176, 180, 190. See also
*How to Keep Your Volkswagen
Alive*; *Velvet Monkeywrench, The*
Muir, John (naturalist), 15, 22, 78–80,
86, 95, 176–77, 180, 189, 190, 192

National Geographic, 9, 61, 87, 121,
176, 179, 180, 188
Native Americans. *See* Americans,
Native
Navajo Indians, 117
neurasthenia, 162–63. *See also*
Americanitis
New Jersey, 100, 120, 126
Nez Perce Indians, 50, 53–54, 80
North Carolina, xi–xiii, 54, 110. *See also*
Road to Nowhere

Oakland (California), 4, 13, 165
Ohio, 14, 133–38, 146–47, 150
On the Road, 7–8, 90–99, 119, 175, 188.
  See also Kerouac, Jack
Order, The, 51
Oregon, 6, 14, 15–20, 25, 57, 133
Osage Indians, 110
"out there," 11, 23, 25, 45, 50, 55, 93,
  112, 117, 128, 138, 141, 144–46, 154–
  55, 165, 166

Paiute Indians, 115, 117
patriotism, 100–101, 103, 108, 138, 141,
  156
Pennsylvania, 20, 42, 91–92, 119
Phaedrus, 26, 75–76. See also *Zen and
  the Art of Motorcycle Maintenance*
Pierson, George Wilson, 55–57, 179,
  183, 184, 191
Pine Ridge Indian Reservation, 115–
  117, 182, 187, 191
Pirsig, Robert, 9, 75–76, 175, 180, 191.
  See also *Zen and the Art of Motorcycle Maintenance*
Planetwalker, 120–121, 158, 176, 183,
  185, 188. *See also* Francis, John
pluralism, 155, 160–61
Pyle, Robert Michael, 21–24, 170, 177,
  191. *See also* Bigfoot; *Where Bigfoot
  Walks*

Quammen, David, 23–24, 87, 88, 177,
  180, 181, 191

race and racism, 29, 31, 51–53, 59, 93,
  106, 110, 111, 122–23, 139–41, 151,
  156, 159–61
Road Frames, 145, 158, 184, 185, 189.
  See also Lackey, Kris
Road to Nowhere, the, xi–xiii

roadkill, 152–53
road trips, xiv, 6–11, 110–12, 120–21,
  166–68; dangers of, 132–33, 139–
  41, 143–44
Rock City, ix, *148*
Roosevelt, Theodore, 60, 79, 107, 109,
  113, 163, 165, 182, 188
Roseville (California), 13, 171, 176, 189

Sacagawea, 117, 155
Sagan, Carl, 34
Said, Edward, 96–97, 181
Salish Indians, 61, 62. *See also* Flat-
  head Indian Reservation
San Francisco, 12–13, 15, 25, 78, 79, 96,
  117, 119
Seminole Indians, 63, 153, 155
Shoshone Indians, 88
Sierra Nevada Mountains, 12, 78, 95, 96
Sinclair, Upton, 94
Sioux Indians, 105–106, 107, 110, 113,
  114, 115–16. *See also* Ghost Dance,
  the
Siringo, Charles, 7, 175, 191. See also
  Texas Cowboy, A
Sitting Bull, 105, 109, 115
South Dakota, 14, 91, 108–17, 182;
  Rapid City, 109, 111–112. *See also*
  Mount Rushmore; Wall Drug Store
space, open, 23, 68, 69, 73, 83, 92, 112,
  135, 137, 141, 148, 154, 179. *See also*
  landscape, the American; "Weather
  Channelification of America"
Spirit of St. Louis, 43, 155, 159. *See also*
  Lindbergh, Charles
stargazing, 72–73, 137–38
Steinbeck, John, 8, 13, 53, 114, 127–
  28, 138, 156–57, 158, 175, 176, 182,
  183, 185, 191. See also *Travels with
  Charley*

Strayed, Cheryl, 10, 176, 191
supper clubs, 125–26, 168, 183, 188. *See also* Wisconsin

Tennessee, xi, 14, 34, 117, 147, *148*
Texas, 150–51
Texas Cowboy, A, 7, 175, 191. *See also* Siringo, Charles
Their Eyes Were Watching God, 32, 178, 189. *See also* Hurston, Zora Neale
Thompson, Hunter S., 9, 118–19, 142, 144, 175, 182, 192. See also *Fear and Loathing in Las Vegas*
Thoreau, Henry David, 49–50, 69–72,73, 78, 82, 91, 96, 161, 179
Thoreau-ing, 72, 161
Through Painted Deserts, 10, 158–159, 176, 185, 190. *See also* Miller, Donald
Tocqueville, Alexis de, 28, 102–4, 177, 181–82. See also *Democracy in America*
transcendentalism, 49, 71, 91, 96, 145, 158. *See also* Emerson, Ralph Waldo; Thoreau, Henry David
travel, 154–55. *See also* mobility
Travels with Charley, 8, 114, 127–28, 131, 156–57, 175, 176, 182, 183, 185, 191. *See also* Steinbeck, John
Twain, Mark, 7, 91, 125, 138, 146, 162, 175, 183, 192

United States Forest Service (USFS), 22, 41, 65, 182, 192
Ute Indians, 117

van life, 166–67
Velvet Monkeywrench, The, 76–78. *See also* Muir, John (mechanic)

Volkswagens/VWs, 4, *5*, 6, 15, 32–34, 46, 47–49, 59, 64–66, 68, 73–75, 76, 98, 104–5, 122, 147, 149, 151, 158, 161, 176, 180, 185, 190; Fahrvergnügen, 34; repair, 5, 33, 73–75. *See also* Bus, "the"

wabi sabi, 97–98, 181, 189
Walden, 69–71, 96, 179, 192. *See also* Thoreau, Henry David
Walk Across America, A, 9, 120, 138, 175, 189
Wall Drug Store, 112–13
Walters, Larry, 35–45, 47, 166
Washington (state), 6, 14, 20, 26, 31–32, 34, 46, 50, 51, 57
Washington, D.C., 81, 82
Washington, George, 92, 109
"Weather Channelification of America," the, 112, 155–56, 157. *See also* space, open
Weaver, Randy, 52
West, the American, 68, 73, 82, 88
Where Bigfoot Walks, 21–24, 170, 177, 191. *See also* Pyle, Robert Michael
Whitaker, Craig, 137, 183
Whitman, Walt, 50, 91, 92, 95, 109, 129, 178, 192
wilderness, vii, xiv, 20–23, 61, 69, 70, 78–79, 86–88, 91–92, 96, 115, 181. *See also* environmentalism; Muir, John (naturalist); Thoreau, Henry David
wildlife. *See* bears, grizzly; bighorn sheep; elk; environmentalism; landscape, the American: fauna of; roadkill; wilderness
Winnebago Indians, 117
Wisconsin, 14, 78, 117, 125–26, 156, 168. *See also* supper clubs

Wolfe, Thomas, 136

Wolfe, Tom, 8, 156, 175, 192. See also *Electric Kool Aid Acid Test, The*

women and travel. *See* mobility, women and

work, 27–31, 101–104, 163, 165. *See also* American Dream, the

Wounded Knee, 105, 115, 116

Wright, Orville and Wilbur, 41, 43, 80–81, 155

Yeager, Chuck, 41, 43

Yellowstone National Park, vii, ix, 50, 66, 84–90, 98, 100–101, 180, 192

Yosemite National Park, 79–80, 86, 180

Zen and the Art of Motorcycle Maintenance, 9, 75–76, 175, 180, 191

Zuni Indians, 117